SUSTAINABILITY AND SPORT

EDITORS:
JILL SAVERY & KEITH GILBERT

SUSTAINABILITY AND SPORT

EDITORS:
JILL SAVERY & KEITH GILBERT

Common Ground

First published in Champaign, Illinois in 2011
by Common Ground Publishing LLC
at the series imprint Sport and Society

Cover Photo: *Ironman Triathlon* by Wayne Levin

Library of Congress Cataloging-in-Publication Data

Sustainability and Sport / editors, Jill Savery & Keith Gilbert.

   p. cm.

Includes bibliographical references and index.
ISBN 978-1-86335-912-2 (pbk. : alk. paper) -- ISBN 978-1-86335-913-9 (pdf : alk. paper)
1. Sports--Social aspects. 2. Sports--Environmental aspects. I. Savery, Jill. II. Gilbert, Keith,
1950-

GV706.5.S96 2011
306.483--dc22

2011007342

Cover image *Ironman Triathlon* Wayne Levin

This book is dedicated to Julius de Heer, a pioneer
in the sustainability and sport movement.

Table of Contents

Contributor Biographies

Robert Accarino

Robert A. Accarino, J.D., is a Director for Abbott Laboratories, located outside Chicago (USA) with responsibilities for global energy strategy. He was seconded to the Chicago 2016 bid team from August 2006 through October 2009, where he led the team that created the Chicago 2016 Blue Green Games environmental plan. He earned his Juris Doctor from the University of Akron in 1988 and his Bachelor of Science in Chemical Engineering/Engineering and Public Policy from Carnegie Mellon University in 1977. Mr. Accarino has worked on environmental sustainability projects throughout the world for more than 30 years.

Graham Barnfield

Graham Barnfield, PhD, is Programme Leader in Journalism at the University of East London. He earned his Doctor of Philosophy degree and Bachelor of Arts from Sheffield Hallam and Sussex Universities respectively. A Fellow of the Wolfsonian-FIU and a domain editor of *Reconstruction: Studies in Contemporary Culture,* he spent a year working on the public relations accounts of both the Aspire Academy and Dubai Sports City.

Denis Bochatay

Denis Bochatay graduated with a joint degree in geography and environmental protection. In 2005 he joined J. de Heer Consulting, where he was active in several projects in sustainable sport development, including the Rugby World Cup in France 2007, the Asian Winter Games in Almaty 2011, and the bid of Annecy for the 2018 Winter Olympic Games. He has produced several case studies about the Olympic Games, evaluating several Olympic Games from Mexico in 1972 to Beijing in 2008, highlighting the social, economic and environmental legacies. In early 2011 he joined Quantis International in Lausanne, Switzerland, where he specializes in developing strategic concepts for sustainable sport events and infrastructure, and quantifying environmental impacts through the life cycle assessment methodology.

Deborah Carlson

Deborah Carlson is Staff Counsel, Green Communities and Climate Change Projects, for West Coast Environmental Law in Vancouver, Canada. She previously worked at the David Suzuki Foundation, developing strategies and promoting best practices for businesses and other organizations (including for the Vancouver 2010 Organising Committee for the

Olympic and Paralympic Winter Games) to manage and reduce their climate impacts. From 1997 – 2005 she practiced litigation in Vancouver, and Geneva, Switzerland. She is co-author of several publications, including: *Meeting the Challenge: A Carbon Neutral 2010 Winter Games Discussion Paper* (2007), *Purchasing Carbon Offsets: A Guide for Canadian Consumers, Businesses and other Organizations* (2009), and *Doing Business in a New Climate: A Guide to Measuring, Reducing and Offsetting Greenhouse Gas Emissions* (2010).

David Chernushenko

David Chernushenko is a Canadian sustainability consultant, professional speaker and film-maker. He served on the International Olympic Committee's Sport and Environment Commission from 1998 – 2004. He recently served as Vice Chair of Canada's prestigious National Round Table on the Environment and the Economy, and his films *Be the Change* (2008) and *Powerful: Energy for Everyone* (2010) offer a vision of a positive future for all. David is a "green building" professional accredited in the LEED (Leadership in Energy and Environmental Design) certification program. As owner of the consulting firm Green & Gold Inc. since 1998, David has advised public, private, and non-profit organizations on adopting more sustainable and socially responsible practices. David has written several books on sustainable management practices, including *Sustainable Sport Management* (UNEP, 2001) and *Greening Our Games: Running Sports Events & Facilities that Won't Cost the Earth* (Centurion,1994), and the electronic publication *Greening Campuses and their Communities* (IISD/ACCC/UNEP, 1996). In 2001, he co-founded Clean Air Champions, a national charity that engages athletes in raising awareness about air pollution, climate change and the benefits of physical activity.

Lamartine DaCosta

Dr. Lamartine DaCosta, PhD, is Professor of Knowledge Management in the University Gama Filho – Rio de Janeiro, Brazil, for PhD and Masters in Physical Education. He also supervises research lines on Olympic Studies, Sport Management and Environment and Sport at Gama Filho and University of East London, UK, as a Visiting Professor. DaCosta earned his Doctoral degree at Gama Filho in Philosophy (1989) and at State University of Rio de Janeiro in Sport Management (1988), developing an international reputation later as a IOC Research Council member (2001 – 2008) a WADA member (1999 – 2008) and as a Regional Coordinator for Latin America in ICSSPE (to date). Extensively published in several languages and themes, he has been an innovative researcher in Environment and Sport starting his works in the early 1960s.

Julius de Heer (in memory, 2010)

Julius de Heer, PhD, was the Founder and Director of J. de Heer Consulting, in Lausanne, Switzerland. Dr. de Heer was a pioneer in sustainable sport development, implementing green concepts in sport organisations and events, and eco-designing sport facilities. In 1994, he drafted the first "Green Book" of an Olympic candidature for the Sion 2002 Olympic Games bid. He then worked with many Olympic Games Bid Organizations (Sion 2006, Paris 2012, Almaty 2014, Tokyo 2016, and Geneva 2018) and event organizations (Ecosport Award of SwissOlympic, Asian Winter Games in Almaty 2011, and the World Cup of Rugby 2007 in France). Dr. de Heer also served as an expert advisor for the International Olympic Committee.

Matt Dolf

Matt Dolf was recently the Assistant Director and Research & Projects Manager at the International Academy of Sports Science and Technology (AISTS) based in Lausanne, Switzerland. Matt led research work at the AISTS in the fields of Event Management and Sustainability in Sport. He is a co-author of the AISTS/VANOC Sustainable Sport and Event Toolkit (SSET) designed for sport events and organisations and managed the AISTS SSET Centre. He also has extensive experience working with and advising sport organisations and events on sustainable development. Matt comes from a background as a tennis athlete, event manager, professional tennis coach, international tennis official, and was formerly the director of high performance for Tennis British Columbia. Matt completed his undergraduate degree in sport and leisure administration at the University of Victoria, Canada and his Masters of Advanced Studies in Sports Administration and Technology at the AISTS, and is currently pursuing a joint Doctorate at the University of British Columbia and the Ecole Polytechnique Fédérale de Lausanne. He firmly believes that sport is a tremendous vehicle for positive change in society and that we have a fundamental responsibility to improve our environmental and social practices.

Ann Duffy

Ann is an international advisor and speaker on sustainability and social responsibility, and President of the Ann Duffy Group. As an advisor to the mega sport event sector, the Olympic Movement and sponsors, Ann conducts consultations, workshops, and public speaking engagements. She was the media spokesperson and architect of Vancouver 2010's corporate-wide Sustainability Management and Reporting System, an Olympic Movement first. Under her leadership, teams and initiatives were created to establish the Games' first sustainable reporting, sourcing and innovation recognition programs. On a national level, Ann chaired the development of Canada's first sustainable event management standard, CSA Z2010. She advises Sochi

2014, the next Winter Olympic and Paralympic Games host on its sustainability and legacy strategy, engagement and management system project. Previously Ann served as Vice President, Sustainable Development for CH2M HILL Canada where she established the firm's sustainable enterprise solutions consulting practice and managed corporate accountability program. She has also worked for the World Wildlife Fund (WWF) International in Switzerland on multi-regional education and communication programs. Ann is a technical member of the Canadian Standards Association Steering Committee for Business, Management and Sustainability; chair of the 2010 Sustainable Event Management Standard Technical Committee; member of the GRI Events Sector Supplement Technical Team and Canadian mirror committee for ISO 120121 Sustainable Event Management Standard. She is the International Director for Clean Air Champions and has served on several boards including The Natural Step Canada and the International Centre for Sustainable Cities. She holds a Master of Communications Studies, University of Calgary and a Bachelor of Arts (Honours) in Human Geography and Environmental Studies, University of Guelph.

Dan Epstein

Dan Epstein, BSc MSc Oxon, is the Director of Sustainability for the Useful Simple Trust, where he is working with a number of clients in Brazil, Russia, Australia and UK about how to embed sustainable development into sporting events and major regeneration projects. Before then Dan was the Head of Sustainable Development and Regeneration for the Olympic Delivery Authority (ODA) for four years, where he was responsible for developing and delivering a comprehensive sustainability program for the London 2012 Olympic and Paralympic Games, which aspires to be the greenest Olympic Games ever. Dan managed a team which set targets, provided technical support, and assured all the major construction projects on the Olympic Park, including major venues, highway, bridge, utility and landscape construction, with a total value of £9 billion. Dan has spent 30 years working in sustainable development, international construction, infrastructure, regeneration, urban development and housing projects. Dan has worked both in policy and strategy and in developing and implementing sustainable development objectives and standards. Throughout his career he has pushed boundaries and promoted innovation on major projects.

Vincent Gaillard

Vincent Gaillard is a sports and sustainability expert specializing in global events and Corporate Sustainability Management. He has worked in the strategic planning and operational delivery of Olympic Games and FIFA World Cup™ projects for The Coca-Cola Company since 1998. Recently, he led the planning and implementation of a ground-breaking "Green Games" platform at the Beijing 2008 Olympic Games, which was awarded the first "Green Medal" by the non-governmental organisation Greenpeace. He is steering an ambitious sustainability effort for the London 2012 Olympic Games, which is set to become the most far-reaching activation for Coca-Cola to date. In July 2011, Vincent will take on a new role as Director General of SportAccord, the umbrella organisation for both Olympic and non-Olympic sports, based in Lausanne, Switzerland. In parallel to his work, Vincent collaborates on a variety of related sustainability projects and is completing a Master's of Science in Corporate Environmental Management at the Centre for Environmental Strategy of the University of Surrey.

Keith Gilbert

Dr. Keith Gilbert is a full Professor in the School of Health & Bioscience at the University of East London. He researches in the area of sport sociology and disability of sport and has a strong interest in qualitative, interpretive and narrative research methodologies. He has numerous publications and has edited several books in the broad areas of sport, sociology, cultural studies and disability which include the following: *The Paralympics: Empowerment or Sideshow; Sexuality, Sport and the Culture of Risk; Extending the Boundaries: Theoretical Frameworks for Research in Sports Management; Some like It Hot: The Beach as Cultural Dimension; Life on the Margins: Implications for Health Research; Reconstructing Lives: The Problem of Retirement from Elite Sport*; and, *Striving for Balance: Modernity and Elite Sport from an Islamic Perspective*. Along with the above, Dr. Gilbert has written over 55 published research articles and is currently on the publications board of the International Council of Sport Science and Physical Education (ICSSPE). Professor Gilbert is editor of the International Journal of Sport and Society and he has two book series: one in the area of Disability and Sport and the other in the broad area of Sport and Society.

Alex Goldenberg

Alex Goldenberg is the Coordinator for the International Motorcycling Federation's (FIM) International Environment Commission, FIM Alternative Energy Working Group and the FIM Trial Commission. He started working for the FIM in 2004 and has represented the FIM at various conferences and forums on Sport and the Environment. He earned his Federal Certificate of Capacity from the Ecole de Commerce André Chavannes in Geneva, Switzerland. He is involved in several projects linked with alternative energy, and has also worked closely with the FIM International Environmental Commission to develop the FIM Environmental Policy. He leads on all issues at the FIM related to environment and alternative energy. He has written several articles on the FIM's environmental actions and initiatives.

Kirsten Henson

Kirsten Henson is the Director of KLH Sustainability, and formally Senior Sustainability Advisor for the Olympic Delivery Authority's Delivery Partner for the London 2012 Olympic and Paralympic Games. She earned her Master of Engineering degree from Cambridge University, and later returned to complete a Master of Philosophy degree in Engineering for Sustainable Development. Kirsten is a new and ambitious face on the sustainability circuit. Highly regarded by the client, designers and contractors on the London 2012 Olympic Park as an innovative thinker with an ability to deliver, she is taking her engagement methods and technical solutions to the wider world through her own business, KLH Sustainability. She is a member of the Technical Board for the Royal Institute of Chartered Surveyors new Ska Rating sustainable fit-out assessment methodology (2009).

Neil Herrington

Neil Herrington is a Principal Lecturer at the University of East London, and has been with UEL since 2001. Previously, he worked as a high school teacher for 15 years. Neil's role at UEL includes working in initial teacher education and carrying out research in the areas of education for sustainable development and Place Based Education. He is currently researching the educational legacy of sporting mega events. Neil is on the management board of EcoActive, an environmental education charity and on the steering group of the London Regional Centre for Expertise in Education for Sustainable Development.

Paul Lingl

Paul Lingl has been with the climate change program of the David Suzuki Foundation in Vancouver, Canada since 2001. He has authored or co-authored a number of publications, including *Doing Business in a New Climate: A Guide to Measuring, Reducing and Offsetting Greenhouse Gas Emissions* (2010), a how-to guide for businesses that wish to reduce their climate impact, as well as *Meeting the Challenge: A Carbon Neutral 2010 Winter Games Discussion Paper* (2007), a report commissioned by the Vancouver 2010 Organizing Committee for the Olympic and Paralympic Winter Games that offered recommendations for making the event carbon neutral. Before joining the David Suzuki Foundation, Paul worked for some of Canada's leading green businesses. He has also been actively involved with several environmental organizations since the late 1980s, both as a volunteer and board member. In 1992, he attended the United Nations Earth Summit in Rio de Janeiro, where the Framework Convention on Climate Change was signed.

Iain MacRury

Dr. Iain MacRury is Associate Dean, Humanities and Social Sciences and Reader in Cultural Sociology at University of East London. He is the Director of the London East Research Institute. He is co-editor of *Olympic Cities: 2012 and the Remaking of London* (Ashgate 2009) and has published research on the legacy of hosting the Olympic Games in a number of academic journals and for commissioning public bodies (London Assembly, DCMS and Dept. Communities and Local Government and OECD). He is author and editor of a number of books including *Advertising* (Routledge 2009) and *The Advertising Handbook* (Routledge 2009).

Shaun McCarthy

Shaun McCarthy is a leading advocate of sustainable business. He has over 20 years of senior management experience with large companies, mainly Shell and BAA. During his time with BAA (a leading airport operator), Shaun developed pioneering strategies for carbon management, sustainable construction and procurement. He also developed programmes in the mid-1990s to increase business participation by small, local and ethnic minority businesses. His current work includes:

- Chair of the Commission for a Sustainable London 2012 – a ground breaking independent body which monitors and assures the sustainability of the London 2012 Olympic and Paralympic Games, reporting to the London 2012 Olympic Board and the public;
- Director of Action Sustainability, a social enterprise with a mission to inspire sustainable procurement;
- Environmental Advisor for Transport for London – expert advisor to the non-executive Health, Safety and Environment board;
- Senior Advisor to the Institute for Sustainability – a research based charity for sustainable solutions; and,
- Commissioner for the London Sustainable Development Commission – a strategic advisory body to the Mayor of London.

Tony Majakas

Tony Majakas is the Vice President for Health and Green Business Development globally for Technogym, and is the London 2012 UK Project Director for the implementation of Technogym's programme as the Official Supplier of the London 2012 Olympic and Paralympic Games. Tony started Technogym UK, the first branch of the company outside of Italy, seventeen years ago and has had roles in the Technogym Headquarters in Italy, primarily working on the Business to Business segment. Tony has been involved in sport, education and wellness for over 30 years. He is a graduate of Leeds University and a postgraduate of Loughborough University.

Maxine Newlands

Maxine Newlands is a Senior Lecturer in Journalism and convener of the Sports Journalism (UG) and Sports Media (PG) degrees in the School of Humanities and Social Science at the University of East London (London, England). Maxine is a former media practitioner. She has years of experience as a senior producer and sports journalist for a national sports radio station. Maxine combines her research and passion in environmentalism with her experience of sports media to explore the emerging fields around the environmental impacts of sporting events. Maxine is also a Research Fellow at the London East Research Institute (LERI).

Beth Nicholls

Beth Nicholls is the Director of Responsible Sport*, a boutique consultancy specialising in major event legacy planning, socially responsible sport sponsorship activation and sustainable event solutions. She was the Head of Legacy Development for England's bid to host the FIFA World Cup™ in 2018. Beth was instrumental in the design and development of *International Inspiration*, the international social legacy programme of the London 2012 Olympic Games and Paralympic Games. She is a member of the London 2012 Social Legacy Board, on the Advisory Panel for Beyond Sport and on the Steering Committee for the Sport Industry Awards. Beth worked for UNICEF for several years, leading on a number of major sports partnerships, working with some of the world's top sporting personalities and helping develop the organisation's global sport strategy. Beth gained her BA degree from the University of Durham and her MA degree from the University of Bath. She speaks fluent Japanese and has acted as athlete liaison for Team GB and Team Japan at numerous major international sports events, including the Olympic Winter Games, the IAAF World Athletics Championships, World Games, FIFA Confederations Cup and the FINA World Swimming Championships.

   * Responsible Sport is a trading name of Miyako Consulting Ltd

Theodore Oben

Theodore Oben has worked for the United Nations Environment Programme (UNEP) since 1993. He is currently the Chief of the Outreach Unit of UNEP, and is directly responsible for coordinating activities on children and youth and sport and the environment. Since joining UNEP, he has initiated and coordinated several processes and organized numerous global conferences to engage children and youth and sport stakeholders in sustainable development issues. He has coordinated UNEP's work with sport organizations, notably the International Olympic Committee, and with organizers of major sport events including the Olympic Games in Torino (2006), Beijing (2008), Vancouver (2010), London (2012) and Sochi (2014) and FIFA

World Cup™ in Germany (2006) and South Africa (2010). He has also coordinated the development of several publications for children and youth and sport and the environment, including environmental assessments of the Beijing Olympic Games and the 2010 World Exposition in Shanghai. He holds a Master of Science Degree in Management and Organizational Development. He is a national of Cameroon and is passionate about the environment. He also loves and engages in sports and plays football and tennis.

Athanasios Pappous

Athanasios (Sakis) Pappous is a Senior Lecturer at the Centre for Sports Studies and course director of Sport and Exercise Management at the University of Kent. His research interests include sport for sustainable development, the social and psychological aspects of physical activity and health, sports media and issues of disability, active living and health promotion. In 2004, he was employed as a Supervisor for the Organizing Committee of the Athens 2004 Olympic and Paralympic Games in Greece. Dr. Pappous' extensive international experience includes lecturing and researching in four European countries: Greece, Spain, France and currently in UK. His commitment to academia has been combined with sporting excellence through his elite athletic career in fencing.

Fiona Pelham

Fiona Pelham is the Managing Director of Sustainable Events Ltd, a company focused on supporting the event industry with the implementation and measurement of sustainability. She was the Environmental Technical Advisor for England's FIFA World Cup™ 2018 bid, and is providing consultancy support for the Global Reporting Initiative's Event Organizer's Sector Supplement. Fiona has chaired ISO 20121 since 2007 (when it existed as BS8901). Her experience in the event industry includes five years of managing Organise This, an event management company focused on delivering events in a sustainable way, and the creation of Event Sustainability, an online measurement framework. She is also the President of the UK and Ireland Chapter of Meeting Professionals International. Fiona has developed an international reputation for engaging the event industry with sustainability issues, and in 2005 set up the not-for-profit education provider Positive Impact.

Matthew Philpott

Matthew Philpott is the Programme Lead for the European Healthy Stadia Network, coordinated by UK cardiovascular health charity Heart of Mersey. Heart of Mersey aims to add value to regional initiatives and programmes by working at local, regional, national and European levels to prevent CVD in the regional population, and also works to alleviate the health inequalities associated with CVD through integrated, evidence-based interventions. Matthew is responsible for the strategic direction of the European Healthy Stadia Network, and plays a development role in increasing the membership of sports stadia and country focal points within the Network. He also liaises directly with the Network's current funding body, the World Heart Federation. With MA and PhD degrees in Social Sciences from the University of Warwick, UK, and an initial background in academic research, Matthew now has over nine years of experience in marketing-communications and project management in both the private and public sectors. He lives in Liverpool and has a keen interest in playing and watching many sports, in particular cricket, football and rugby union.

Arianne Carvalhedo Reis

Arianne Carvalhedo Reis, PhD, is a postdoctoral researcher with the School of Tourism and Hospitality Management, Southern Cross University, Australia. Originally from Brazil, Dr. Reis has a combined Bachelor's and Teaching degree in Physical Education and a Master's degree with a focus on Sport Tourism from Gama Filho University, Brazil. She has recently completed her PhD in Tourism at University of Otago, New Zealand. Her experience in the field of Sport Tourism includes both practical and academic involvement, having worked for governmental and private institutions in Brazil, and lectured and researched in this area in Brazil, New Zealand and Australia.

Sue Riddlestone

Sue Riddlestone is Chief Executive and co-founder of BioRegional Development Group, an award-winning organisation which develops real-life solutions for sustainability. She is a member of the Mayor's London Sustainable Development Commission. In March 2009, Sue won the prestigious Skoll Award for Social Entrepreneurship with BioRegional co-founder and husband Pooran Desai. Sue co-founded the One Planet Living concept – a global initiative which aims to show through real life examples of communities and organisations that sustainability is attractive and affordable all around the world. As part of this, Sue and her team are working with local partners to introduce sustainable communities around the world, from China to the United States, and also with companies and local authorities to enable one planet living in their operations and for their customers, clients and residents. Sue has also pioneered projects on sustainable paper production. She is the co-author of *BioRegional Solutions* (2002), co-author of the London 2012 bid sustainability strategy *Towards a One Planet Olympics* (2005), and as a member of the UK Government-appointed Eco-towns Challenge Panel is the lead author of *What makes an eco-town?* (2008).

Jill Savery

Jill Savery is a sustainability advisor with a particular emphasis on the intersection of sport and sustainability. Her professional experience includes supporting organizations such as: the London 2012 Organizing Committee for the Olympic Games and Paralympic Games, the Chicago 2016 Olympic and Paralympic Games bid team, the America's Cup Event Authority, the England 2018 FIFA World Cup™ bid team, and several municipalities in the United States. From 2008 to 2011, she led the London 2012 sustainability work program of a London-based NGO. Jill serves as a co-opted expert to the Commission for a Sustainable London 2012, and as a member of the Beyond Sport Advisory Panel. She has held Board positions for the United States Olympic Committee, United States Synchronized Swimming, International Children's Games, and Northern California Olympians. Her educational background includes a Master's Degree in Environmental Management from Yale University, and a Bachelor's Degree from the University of California at Berkeley. In 1996, Jill won an Olympic gold medal in synchronized swimming, and was later inducted into the International Swimming Hall of Fame.

Russell Seymour

Russell Seymour is the Sustainability Manager for Marylebone Cricket Club. MCC is a Members Club that owns and runs Lord's Cricket Ground in St John's Wood, London, which is the largest and busiest cricket Ground in England. Russell reports on sustainability performance and interacts with all departments to develop and implement sustainability strategies that affect the management and operation of the Ground, including Test, One-Day International and Domestic cricket matches. Russell's background is in environmental sciences and biodiversity management with postgraduate degrees from the University of London and the University of Kent. He has an interest in most sports and has been actively involved in British American football as a player, coach and manager for over twenty years.

David Stubbs

David Stubbs is the Head of Sustainability for the London 2012 Organising Committee of the Olympic Games and Paralympic Games – a role he has held since joining the London 2012 bid team in November 2003. In this role he is responsible for developing and coordinating the sustainability programme for the London 2012 Games. He is an internationally renowned specialist in the field of sport and environment. During the 1990s he was Director of the European Golf Association Ecology Unit and he established the first pan-European environmental management programme for golf courses. In 1998 he began advising the British Olympic Association on environmental matters, and in 2000 he worked with the Environment Team at the Sydney Olympic Games. David's career started in the field of conservation biology. He is a full member of the Institute of Ecology and Environmental Management and is a Chartered Environmentalist.

Katherine Symonds

Katherine Symonds is Head of Sustainable Olympic Games for Coca-Cola Great Britain's London 2012 team, with responsibility for delivering a range of ambitious community and environment programmes at the Olympic Games. Prior to joining Coca-Cola in early 2009, she was Climate Change Manager for Tesco, where she helped found the Sustainable Consumption Institute at the University of Manchester, launched carbon labeling on products and initiated a national climate change education campaign for all store staff.

Joseph Weiler

Joseph Weiler is Professor at the University of British Columbia (UBC) Faculty of Law in Vancouver. He earned his BA with Honors at the University of Toronto in 1969, his LLB at Osgoode Hall Law School, York University in 1972, and his LLM at the University of California, Berkeley School of Law in 1974. He joined the Faculty of Law at UBC in 1974, first as Assistant Professor and then as Associate Professor. He became a Full Professor in 1987. He has taught courses on criminal law, criminal procedure, constitutional law, and the law of cyberspace, and currently teaches courses on labor law and policy, sports law, media and entertainment law, and the law of the Olympic Games. Professor Weiler is the author, co-author and editor of numerous publications, including books and journal articles, in all of the areas that he has taught over the years at UBC. Professor Weiler was called to the Bar in British Columbia in 1973 and has acted as counsel in numerous cases at all judicial levels, including the provincial and county courts, the Supreme of British Columbia, the BC Court of Appeal and the Supreme Court of Canada. Professor Weiler has also had a long career in the field of alternative dispute resolution, and he has acted as a mediator and arbitrator in over 400 disputes, and was the Commissioner of the Vancouver Port Container Traffic Inquiry in 1986-88. He was elected a member of the National Academy of Arbitrators in 1984 and he served as counsel to the Vancouver Canucks Hockey Club from 1990 to 1995.

Patrick Weiler

Patrick Weiler is a student in the Faculty of Law of the University of British Columbia, and will graduate with a Juris Doctor (J.D.) degree in 2012 with a specialization in environment and natural resources law. Patrick was Co-Chair of the UBC Students Environmental Law Group in 2010 – 2011, and was the recipient of the prestigious Andrew R. Thompson Award to support his work during the spring and summer of 2011 with an international environmental NGO in the area of natural resources governance and sustainable development. Patrick obtained BA in History at McGill University in 2008. Beginning in 2006, Patrick was part of the UBC Olympic Studies Research Team that prepared reports on various sustainability issues regarding sport mega events for the Vancouver 2010 Organizing Committee for the Olympic Winter Games (VANOC). From the summer of 2010 to the spring of 2011, Patrick served as the lead research associate and co-author for a series of 10 legacy reports on the Social, Environmental and Economic Impacts of the Vancouver 2010 Olympic Winter Games.

Andrew Winston

Andrew Winston is a globally recognized expert on how businesses can profit from environmental thinking. He has advised some of the world's leading companies, including Bank of America, Bayer, Boeing, HP, Kimberly-Clark, and Pepsi. Andrew is the author of two best selling books on environmental strategy: *Green to Gold* (2006, co-author) and *Green Recovery* (2009). His earlier career included corporate strategy at Boston Consulting Group and management positions in marketing and business development at Time Warner and MTV. Andrew received his BA in Economics from Princeton University, an MBA from Columbia University, and a Masters of Environmental Management from Yale University.

Part I
Conceptualizing Sustainability and Sport

Chapter 1
Sustainability and Sport

Jill Savery and Keith Gilbert

Introduction

This book represents one of the very first of its kind, and we hope it will be an important addition to the literature to support practical strategies and theoretical positions regarding sustainability and sport into the future. It can be used as a guide for good practice within the sports industry, as well as a guide for undergraduate and postgraduate students of sustainability and sport around the world. Throughout the process of compiling this book, we have been supported admirably by our academic peers and work colleagues, many of whom we class as friends. They have intrigued us by offering a myriad of ideas, innovations and perspectives to support our themes, without which this book would not have been possible. These individuals continue to play key roles in the expansion of sustainable solutions by practicing and theorizing about sport and sustainability. The book includes perspectives from event managers, athletes, sport event sponsors, academics, sport organizations, NGOs and others working in this emerging discipline that have come together in this text to share their ideas and views on sustainability and sport. As such, contributors have contemplated the most important aspects of their work and learning in order to contribute to the growing body of material available to practitioners and students. Although resources on sustainable sport events do exist, they explore primarily how to run a more sustainable event.

As authors we argue that the discoveries developed in this text may have important implications for the ways in which we conceptualize the relationships between sustainability and sport, and also issues of regeneration, and thereby provide modernization regarding the way such concepts can be researched and documented in the future.

This book is seminal in that it introduces new and important information regarding what constitutes sustainability and sport where currently there is little in the way of a synthesized collection of empirical accounts; such a collection of chapters has not been previously published. It also provides a mixture of theory and empirical research by various experts in order to build a comprehensive and grounded account of the challenges and opportunities of sustainable sport. We provide herein an innovative and informed look at the intricacies of sustainability and sport and major sport events, and review the idiosyncrasies, shortcomings and other interesting ideas which are required to be explored and researched further to provide researchers and the public with deeper insights into the world of sustainability and sport.

Sustainability and Sport

As mentioned previously, the development of this book is a premeditated attempt to uncover the varied and complex issues surrounding the notion of sustainability and sport. Furthermore, this book highlights the history, as well as the social, economic, and environmental imperatives, challenges and benefits of sustainability and sport.

Traditionally, sport can be viewed as the encouragement of human effort in harmony with the natural environment. After all, sport was developed in outdoor settings, by taking advantage of nature and available water, land and fresh air. Over time international elite sport has emerged along with its prerequisite sport development activities, major sports events and worldwide sponsor and media attention. With regard to environmental sustainability, the relationship between sport and the environment has been compromised by the dawn and subsequent rise of elite sport and contemporary major sporting events, as well as issues such as urbanization and associated pollution. It is clear that without a clean environment, athletic achievements are hampered. Athletes cannot perform to their best when the air they breathe is polluted, nor when contamination enters their training grounds. Health is of primary concern to most athletes. Athletes are now speaking out to protect the environment and are encouraging further requirements by major sport events and organizations to mitigate environmental impacts and provide sustainable solutions.

Modern sport events and their associated venues, whether natural or man-made, impose a significant impact on the environment. Even venues located in natural areas such as ski slopes and trails require alteration of the natural landscape. Athletes, coaches and officials travel to national and international competitions on planes, trains, buses and cars, all of which emit climate changing greenhouse gases. The sporting goods industry produces a plethora of sport products that require natural resources. Spectators travel to events and also purchase sporting goods and event merchandise, and athletes require sports equipment to compete. All of these activities have environmental consequences, including: the removal of natural vegetation; pollution of land, water and air; energy and water consumption; and waste production. Large sporting events such as the Tour de France, the FIFA World Cup™, and the Olympic Games have tremendous impacts on the environment. Building new and improved infrastructure and venues utilizes resources and raw materials. Additional capacity for energy and water must be developed. Hundreds of thousands of people must be moved into, around, and out of host cities, causing an increase in greenhouse gas emissions. Spectators, athletes and volunteers eat, drink, and consume, all of which result in the need for increased waste disposal facilities. The ecological footprint of sport and associated events to grown exponentially throughout the last century.

Sustainability, however, is a holistic concept with much more depth than just environmental considerations alone. In a broad sense, sustainability refers to a holistic perspective that harmonizes social, economic and environmental dimensions and systems, and balances opportunities and constraints. *Sustainability* has become a well-used term of late, and a multitude of definitions abound. In this text we attempt to develop a stronger definition of the notion of sustainability and sport which encapsulates the complexity of the issues.

Defining Sustainability

The World Commission on Environment and Development, a body derived from the United Nations, created a report entitled *Our Common Future*. It was submitted to the General Assembly of the United Nations in August of 1987 (The 42nd Session of the General Assembly of the United Nations, August 4, 1987). The report outlined global environmental concerns and related development challenges, and attempted to address these issues relative to necessary future actions to promote an improved quality of life while protecting the planet's ecosystems. The link between environment and development was emphasized repeatedly, noting the particular interrelation between poverty and the environment.

The report's introduction states: "the environment does not exist as a sphere separate from human actions, ambitions, and needs." The report called for the prevention of environmental degradation associated with development activities, versus the repair of the environment after these activities have occurred. Most importantly, the report became known for its definition of *sustainable development* and argues that:

"Humanity has the ability to make development sustainable to ensure that it meets the needs of the present without compromising the ability of future generations to meet their own needs. The concept of sustainable development does imply limits – not absolute limits but limitations imposed by the present state of technology and social organization on environmental resources and by the ability of the biosphere to absorb the effects of human activities."

Brundtland Report[1]

The report goes on to state that it will only be possible to meet these objectives if we take into account the long-term impacts of our resource use. *Sustainability* means consuming resources now at a rate that will allow similar yields in the future. Given the global environmental problems that plague the planet, such as deforestation, climate change, and contamination, we must foster "the common understanding and common spirit of responsibility" for our environment and with regard to the impacts of our actions.

Sustainability has since become a well-used term in various disciplines around the world. However, many definitions of sustainability exist and it is necessary to define *sustainability* in a relevant way to promote clarity.

The *Random House Webster's College Dictionary* defines *sustain* as follows: to keep up or keep going, as an action or process; maintain." Are we simply aiming to keep our human race going in some direction associated with our current state? Or do we seek more for future generations than maintaining the status quo? Rather, if our aim is to improve the human condition through time, might we choose to leave future generations with more opportunities, rather than just the same opportunities that we have now? We may not be able to alter the terminology we have grown accustomed to using, but our definition of *sustainability* can incorporate fostering a society that allows individuals the capability to enrich their lives well into the future.

A widely cited definition of *sustainability* is perhaps the most comprehensive: configuring civilization and human activity so that we are able to meet our needs and express our greatest potential in the present, while preserving biodiversity and natural ecosystems, and planning and acting for the ability to maintain these ideals indefinitely.[2] However, David Chernushenko, a widely recognized sustainability specialist, provides the following definition for consideration as applied to sport (see Chapter 2): "Sport is sustainable when it meets the needs of today's sporting community while contributing to the improvement of future sport opportunities for all and the improvement of the integrity of the natural and social environment on which it depends." We feel that the above definition by Chernushenko best fits the purposes of this book and that it is appropriate to consider this definition as paramount in the ensuing discussions and theoretical considerations.

---

1. Brundtland, G. (1987). (Eds.) Our Common Future: The World Commission on Environment and Development. Oxford: Oxford University Press. page 24.

2. WordIQ. Available at: http://www.wordiq.com/definition/Sustainability

Anthology

Sustainability and Sport provides an anthology of significant topics at the core of sustainability and sport research and practice. Of importance is that the chapters herein have been written by practitioners and academics and they are formulated into a serious analysis of the role of different aspects of sustainability within the confines of sport. This is achieved by developing some fundamental issues and discussions raised by the authors in their individual chapters. We have been very fortunate to gain the services and support of individuals who have had personal knowledge of sport and also the holistic concept of sustainability; this book details their thoughts, and as such, acts as a form of historical perspective of sustainability and sport. In this manner we have developed the area of sustainability research within not only the university context, but also to add to the literature so that managers, administrators, athletes, students and business people can better understand the notion of sustainability and sport and how they can participate in the growing and requisite movement. It is also hoped that the information in this book might be used to further develop sport event bidding documents, event management frameworks, sport legacy strategies, public awareness and other important projects which support the wider sports movement.

The chapters herein have been divided into five sections. Part I, simply titled *'Conceptualizing Sustainability and Sport,'* places the book firmly into a historical framework in order that some of the critical issues of sustainability in the sporting context can then be discussed. These first two chapters highlight the nature of *sustainability* and its relationship to sport. For example, Chapter 1 refers specifically to the relationship between sustainability and sport by providing a feasible working definition, and follows this with a breakdown of all the following chapters in the volume. Chapter 2 by David Chernushenko titled *'Promoting Sustainability in Sport and Through Sport: An Industry Veteran Looks Back, and Forward, and Issues a Challenge'* asks important questions of the reader: Where have we been in terms of sustainability in the sport context? Where are we now and where are we going in the future? He reviews the significance of sustainability for specific events, healthy conditions for athletes, sports clubs, and sporting goods industry and suggests the top priorities for sustainability in sport for the future by putting a series of challenges forward.

Part II titled *'Organizations and Tools Promoting Sustainability and Sport'* includes perspectives from organizations involved in promoting sustainability in sport, and reviews the tools available to support the development of sustainable sport events and programs. Chapter 3 titled *'Sport and the Environment: A UNEP Perspective'* by Theodore Oben is significant in reviewing the involvement of the United Nations Environment Program (UNEP) in fostering sustainable sport. He argues that major sport events should do more to promote environmental awareness, and that sport is a means to achieve a sustainable future. Matt Dolf's Chapter 4 titled *'SSETing Up Sport with Tools for Sustainability'* places the issues of sports events firmly on the sustainability agenda. He describes how the Sustainable Sport and Event Toolkit (SSET) evolved and discusses how it is being used as a practical tool to support International Sports Federations (IFs) and National Olympic Committees (NOCs). Finally, he argues that as sport develops, so does the need for guidance, standardization and tools to assist sports administrators and event managers in promoting sustainability. Chapter 5 titled '*Sustainable Event Management: The Journey to ISO 20121*' by Fiona Pelham reviews the development of the emerging International Organization for Standardization's (ISO) 20121 standard (Specifications for Sustainable Event Management Systems). She argues that there is considerable interest in sustainability from the events industry, and that major sports events can be a catalyst for change. Chapter 6 by Deborah Carlson and Paul Lingl titled '*Greening Sport and Inspiring Societal Change: An ENGO Perspective from the Vancouver 2010 Olympic and Paralympic Winter Games*' places sustainability and sport into the environmental frame of reference by discussing the role of the David Suzuki Foundation in the Vancouver 2010 Olympic and Paralympic Winter Games (2010 Games). They specifically highlight the relationships which they formed with athletes who supported their efforts leading up to the 2010 Games. Of particular interest is their perspective on winter sports and climate change. Finally, they provide recommendations for the International Olympic Committee and other sporting organizations. Chapter 7 by Sue Riddlestone informs us of the work being carried out by non-governmental organizations (NGOs) and how they can assist in the transformation of sustainability into the sporting arena. Her chapter titled '*One Planet 2012: How NGOs Can Help to Transform Sustainability in Sport*' considers the role of BioRegional Development Group in a large sport event setting, citing building energy use and zero carbon as two of the many important issues to consider when planning a major sport event. Finally, Riddlestone argues that NGOs can bring something extra to the table and to the sustainability and sport agenda. This is followed by insight from Matthew Philpott and Russell Seymour, whose Chapter 8 titled '*The European Healthy Stadia Network: Sports Stadia, Public Health and Sustainability*' provides a description of the concept of 'healthy stadia' and increasing public health through their development and environmental theory.

Part III is the largest section of the book, titled '*Sustainability and the Olympic Games and Paralympic Games*,' and is important because it delivers interesting ideas regarding introducing sustainability to mega events in the postmodern era. We knew this would take up a large section of the book as many of the current innovative ideas around sustainability and sport have been initiated at the Olympic and Paralympic Games. What we did not expect was the range of ideas from the group charged with this task. For example, Chapter 9 from Athanasios Pappous titled '*Do the Olympic Games Lead to a Sustainable Increase in Grassroots Sport Participation? A Secondary Analysis of Athens 2004*' sets the scene for the section by reviewing empirical evidence of grassroots sport participation in Greece before and after the 2004 Olympic and Paralympic Games. He poses the question: Does hosting of

sport mega events such as the Games contribute to sustainable economic and social development, making them worthwhile governmental investments? His work stems from the promise of the London 2012 Olympic and
Paralympic Games (2012 Games) organizers that increased sport participation will result from hosting the 2012 Games. He uses the Eurobarometer survey method established by the European Union as evidence to show a
lack of a long term sport participation legacy occurring in Greece as a result
of hosting the 2004 Games. Ann Duffy's Chapter 10 titled *Vancouver 2010:
Raising the Bar for Sustainable Olympic and Paralympic Winter Games'* describes
how the 2010 Games organizers prioritized and defined sustainability related to hosting these mega events. She outlines the organizing committee's
priorities, performance goals and achievements in embedding sustainability across the program of work for all stages of the event. Throughout her
chapter she refers to the ideas of accountability, environmental stewardship and impact reduction. Her final section passes on ideas specifically related to the aboriginal community, social responsibility, collaboration and
participation. Duffy argues that all the above issues relate to sport for sustainable living. Joseph Weiler and Patrick Weiler in Chapter 11 titled *Vancouver Green Capital: Branding the Host City of the Olympic Games'* also tackle
some vexing questions regarding sustainability and the 2010 Games. Interestingly, they take a close look at the green credentials of the city of Vancouver by referring to issues of community planning, the 2010 Games venues and infrastructure, as well as partnerships fostered between government
and the business community. The outcome of this in depth discussion re-
volves around the positive initiatives created by the community and government in Vancouver leading up to and during the 2010 Games that justify it being classed as a 'green capital'. Finally, they argue that Vancouver
Green Capital is an important and current example of how an Olympic and
Paralympic Games host city translates the sustainability elements of hosting a mega event into its post-Games industrial strategy. David Stubbs in
Chapter 12 discusses *The Olympic Movement as a Leader in Sustainability.'* He
argues that the Olympic and Paralympic Games provide a "unique platform
for making sustainability relevant." He begins with a brief discussion of the
origins of the modern Olympic Movement, and his views on what is meant
by *sustainability* in this context. While acknowledging that mega events are
inherently unsustainable endeavors, the Games can have an important impact on a society, and event partners can step up to the plate and provide
leadership and focus around the area of sustainability and sport. He then
goes on to review unique strategies underway for embedding sustainability into the event management activities associated with hosting the 2012
Games.

   Dan Epstein in Chapter 13 titled *The London 2012 Olympic and Paralympic
Games: A Framework for Sustainable Development and Regeneration for Sport'* reviews the Olympic Delivery Authority's (ODA) Sustainable Development
Strategy. He highlights the processes and tools developed by the ODA in
order to build sustainable venues and infrastructure for the 2012 Games.

He strongly suggests that the ODA is setting new and exacting standards for sustainable development, and highlights the regeneration taking place in East London in the Olympic Park, which will serve as a lasting legacy for sport and the community. Chapter 14 by Shaun McCarthy titled *'Sustainable Olympics – Assuring a Legacy: the Commission for a Sustainable London 2012'* describes the purpose and chronological establishment of the Commission for a Sustainable London 2012 (CSL). He highlights CSL's sustainability assurance framework, and reviews the results of CSL's work to date. Importantly, he provides practical advice for the development of a well-functioning Commission based on lessons learned. Iain MacRury in the following Chapter 15 provides a comparative analysis of the sustainability aspects of the Athletes Villages for the 2010 Games and London 2012 Games. In *'A Tale of Two Villages: London, Vancouver and Sustainability'* he compares the Villages in terms of cost, financial planning, sustainable attributes, and legacies. In his final comments he suggests that the 2012 organizers learn lessons from the challenges faced by the Vancouver team, including providing a sustainable legacy for the local community. Maxine Newlands in Chapter 16 deconstructs the Team Green Britain concept. In *'Green Britannia: Deconstructing 'Team Green Britain' and the London 2012 Olympic and Paralympic Games'* she reviews London 2012's sustainability commitments, and media criticism of greenwashing related to the event. Newlands raises the question of whether the Games and the Olympic Movement contradict environmental values. Faced with international pressure, she argues that the International Olympic Committee was forced to consider how environmental protection and the Games should co-exist. She also discusses event sponsorship as it relates to sustainability, and in her final section argues that future organizing committees need to ensure their choice of sponsors can circumvent accusations of greenwashing.

Reis and DaCosta provide a synthesis of recent Olympic and Paralympic Games bids, comparing *Green Games* with *Sustainable Games*. In Chapter 17 titled *'Is the Booming Sustainability of the Olympic and Paralympic Games Here to Stay? Environment-Based Procedures Versus Dubious Legacy,'* they suggest that the International Olympic Committee's actions have served to slow the adoption of the holistic concept of sustainability by associating the Olympic Movement with the Environment. They argue that recent event bid teams and organizing committees have provided a new approach by embedding sustainability into their rhetoric and plans. They then look towards the future with their take on the environment, sustainability and the 2016 Olympic and Paralympic Games to be held in Rio de Janeiro. They argue that although the environment and sustainability are mentioned many times in the winning event bid document, there are indicators thus far that the terms have been utilized loosely and without any real meaning. In Chapter 18, Robert Accarino, who was a member of the Chicago 2016 Olympic and Paralympic Games bid team, reflects on the sustainable legacies which were prepared by the bidding city group. In *'Bidding Cities and Sustainable Legacies,'* he works his way through the bid timeline, the environmental and sustainable features of the 2016 Games bid, the International Olympic Committee and its relationship to sustainability, and most importantly the lessons learned. The Chicago 2016 Blue Green Games strategy is described in detail. Chapter 19 provides an inside perspective of Coca-Cola (the longest continuous partner of the Olympic Movement) and their aspirations around sustainability. Vincent Gaillard and Katherine Symonds review in *'Coca-Cola, Sustainability and the Olympic Games'* the company's sustainability vision and their view that sports events such as the Olympic Games provide the ideal opportunity to share this with consumers, customers, employees and stakeholders. They describe the influence of the 1992 Rio Earth Summit on the Olympic Movement and also the company's ensuing sustainability initiatives. Coca-Cola leveraged their Olympic Games sponsorship to showcase these initiatives at the 2000 Games in Sydney and every one held since. Their final section explains the importance of sustainability to the company, and highlight their achievements at the 2010 Games, and their ideas and preparations for the 2012 Games. Chapter 20 written by Tony Majakas provides a different perspective of sport and sustainability. In *'Sport and Wellness – A Lifetime Journey,'* he describes the approach of long-time Olympic partner Technogym in promoting *wellness*, which is an important component of sustainability. Majakas discusses the benefits of having "healthy people and therefore a healthy planet;" Technogym argues that sport can play an important role in helping tackle the epidemic of physical inactivity and contribute significantly to sustainable lifestyles. He describes the new Technogym Village concept which they have developed for their staff, local residents and institutions in Italy, including their guiding principles. He also reviews the Technogym Vision 2012, in support of the 2012 Games and aligned with regard to sustainability.

Part IV of this book called *'General Themes on Sustainability and Sport'* reviews several overarching concepts applying sustainability to sport more broadly. It is kicked off with Chapter 21 by Jill Savery titled *'Fostering Pro-Environmental Behavior Through Sport.'* She argues that sport events can serve as a catalyst to foster a shift towards more sustainable behavior, and that large sports events to date have been largely unsuccessful at engaging with constituents around sustainability and achieving change. Savery then provides a framework whereby a holistic event strategy can be developed to engage with target audiences, referencing theories of behavior change and social marketing. The following Chapter 22, *'The Polar Bear Rules: How International Sport Events Can Address Climate Change'* by Jules de Heer and Denis Bochatay focuses on the imperative of climate change mitigation at major sport events. They review the history of climate change activities at major sport events, beginning with the first major campaign at the 2000 Games. They compare the methodologies used by several major sport events to assess event greenhouse gas (GHG) emissions and compensation measures. They then outline seven clever Polar Bear Rules which they specifically suggest that all major sport and non-sport events utilize to reduce, mitigate and compensate for event GHG emissions. Chapter 23 written by Beth Nicholls takes us carefully through the process of sustainable social legacy planning for major sporting events. *'Using a Major Sports Event to Deliver a Sustainable Social Legacy of Lasting Positive Change'* provides a structure she has created for the development of a social event legacy, which takes into consideration the objectives of the Local Organizing Committee (LOC) and various stakeholders. She reviews the imperative to develop a social event legacy from the perspective of the event bid team, the LOC, the rights holder, government, sport federations, and local communities. Nicholls' tools are illustrated through a case study of the England 2018 FIFA World Cup™ bid. She argues throughout that it is possible to have a sustainability social legacy woven throughout a sport event bid and throughout the event timeline. Chapter 24 by Andrew Winston presents a review and comparison of sport and sustainable business. In *'Can Sports and the Sustainable Business Movement Learn from Each Other?'* Winston examines the issues which drive sustainable thinking in business and argues through the key steps in developing and executing a sustainable business strategy. He suggests that the sporting world can learn from businesses leaders, who are taking sustainability seriously and are realizing value from reducing their social and environmental impacts. He suggests priorities for developing a sustainability strategy, such as the need for sport businesses and events to understand their sustainability footprint, and creating standards for the supply chain and vendors. Throughout Winston provides examples from leading global businesses to support his ideas of "heretical innovation."

Chapter 25 by Kirsten Henson is titled *'The Sporting Stage: Delivering Sustainable Venues and Infrastructure.'* Henson outlines clear delivery mechanisms and processes to deliver sustainable event infrastructure and venues, based on her experience on the team building the sporting stage for the 2012 Games. She uses case studies from three major sport events, and focuses on delivering resource efficiency (or environmental sustainability). From setting a clear sustainability vision and targets, recommendations on structuring delivery teams to engaging contractors and the supply chain, her emphasis is on how to embed sustainability and achieve sustainable outcomes. She also argues that accountability and reporting are two vital aspects of the sustainability often ignored in the sporting context which should go hand in hand with venue infrastructure development. Alex Goldenberg's Chapter 26 titled *'Motorcycling and the Environment: An impossible Marriage?'* describes the evolution of sustainable practices by the IF for the sport of motorcycling. Goldenberg reviews the evolution of the FIM (International Motorcycling Federation) Environmental Commission and Environmental Code, and the co-operation between the FIM and UNEP. Recognizing the impact of the sport of motorcycling on the environment, the FIM has developed a series of environmental initiatives aimed at reducing this impact, and educating riders, event managers and national sports federations. The FIM now also promotes the use of alternative energy through electric motorcycling as a means to reduce the environmental impact. Chapter 27 by Graham Barnfield refers specifically to the development and promotion of major sport projects and mega events in the Arabian Gulf region, in particular the Aspire Zone in Qatar and Dubai Sports City in the United Arab Emirates. Titled '*2016, 2022, 2030 Go! Sustainability and Arabian Gulf Sporting Megaprojects,*' Barnfield begins by describing conventional views that sport development in a desert environment can be seen as "environmentally suspect." He reviews the environmental rhetoric surrounding the two aforementioned sport mega projects, and relates this to the wider transition taking place in national planning documents of these countries around sustainable development. He argues that accepting the idea of sport development in the area as unsustainable serves to inhibit wider opportunities, such as limiting the rights of local people to engage in sport and promote health through physical activity, and misses opportunities to develop sustainable technology like clean energy and irrigation systems.

The final chapter in the fourth section, Chapter 28, is written by Neil Herrington and is titled '*Sports, Social Capital and Public Space: Developing an Educational Legacy.*' He begins by arguing that we must foster environmental care by making sure our children interact with the environment, and how sporting mega events can achieve environmental awareness. Herrington takes us on a journey into the heart of a sustainable educational legacy from sports mega events, by drawing specifically on the example of the 2002 Commonwealth Games held in Manchester, UK. He presents research findings suggesting that the event resulted in positive educational outcomes. He then discusses how the regeneration of East London in preparation for the 2012 Games can learn from the experiences in Manchester, and result in educational legacies. He provides suggestions on how schools and educators can foster links between the local community and schools through sports facilities using mega events as an organizing principle to link people and programs.

The final section of the book, Part V, is titled '*Towards Sustainability and Sport,*' and delves into the lessons learned from the perspectives presented in the book. Chapter 29, '*A Metasynthesis of Sustainability and Sport,*' offers a way to better understand the notion of Sustainability and Sport by utilizing a metasynthesis approach to dissect the previous chapters and draw out the important perspectives of sustainability in the sport realm. Important philosophical questions are put forward regarding the relationship between sustainability and sport in the global context.

Indeed, the above five sections adequately reflect the areas of sustainability and sport which we felt required highlighting in the literature. This book has been edited in order to support students in higher education, and is also relevant for those for those working in the world of sport and those who wish to become involved in researching and working in this field. We also hope that the chapters herein will foster sustainability and sport, and that the text will support the development of further research by academics into sustainability. It is therefore anticipated that this anthology of chapters will provide the reader a discerning synopsis of the current thinking in the innovative discipline of sustainability and sport.

To summarize, this book examines the relationship between Sport and Sustainability. Principally, the volume is attempting to achieve something new and ground-breaking while opening up new areas of research. In achieving this we believe that we should and will continue to challenge convention and hopefully support and change perceptions and ultimately the sporting world for the better.

Chapter 2

Promoting Sustainability in Sport and Through Sport

An Industry Veteran Looks Back, and Forward, and Issues a Challenge

David Chernushenko

Introduction

In a perfect world, all athletes would train and compete in clean air and water, all stadiums would generate more energy than they consumed, all sporting goods would be produced without waste, pollution or greenhouse gas emissions, and all boys and girls would have safe, affordable and unrestricted opportunities to engage in sport and physical activity. Sure, this is a dream; but don't most great things in life begin with a dream?

My dream started in 1992, when I began to write and to speak about "sustainable sport". I was convinced that the world of sport could adopt better, more ecologically and socially sustainable practices, and could play a leadership role in promoting sustainable development around the globe. It was a big dream, but not, I was convinced, a hopeless one. In 1994 I published the first book in any language on sport and the environment. The book, *'Greening Our Games: Running Sports Events and Facilities that Won't Cost the Earth'* brought together three of my great passions: sport, healthy living and the environment. However, in 1994, only a few in the sporting world were connecting these three subjects. In the book I argued that sport could, and indeed should, be conducted in ways that do more good than harm, to the environment and to the athlete. I put forward that this was not only possible, but that it would be in the vested interest of sport and of society as a whole. Furthermore, I asserted that sport could be both exciting and indeed profitable. The invitation to write this chapter offered me an opportunity to reflect on where we have been, where we are now, and where we can and almost certainly must go both "in sport" and "through sport". This task is not easy, and maybe not especially useful, to make a broad assessment of such a diverse industry, covering a wide array of actors in diverse countries and communities. I will, therefore, limit myself to personal observations on some broad international trends and on some specific issues that deserve attention.

Where have we been?

Seven years later, when I published *Sustainable Sport Management* (UNEP, 2001), much had changed. Sport managers, governing bodies, sporting goods manufacturers, athletes, stadium architects and many others were deeply immersed in learning how to adopt the principles of sustainability into their respective fields. Not everyone was on the "green bandwagon", but many were, and most others had become aware that they had new and important responsibilities.

By 2001, we had seen a variety of initiatives taken at all levels, and in all sectors of the sports industry and community. The International Olympic Committee (IOC) was leading the charge to shift awareness and behaviour among Olympic Games host and candidate cities, as well as National Olympic Committees and International Sports Federations. This in turn was influencing hosts of the FIFA World Cup™ and championships in sports ranging from soccer, to triathlon to mountain biking. Other multi-sport event hosts (e.g., Commonwealth and Pan-American Games, and national youth games such as the Canada Games) had accepted the torch and were "going green" to some extent. Even some professional leagues or clubs were getting the green ball rolling (e.g., the Premier League and Bundesliga clubs and stadiums, NFL Super Bowl hosts cities).

Manufacturers had also begun to look seriously at their products and their manufacturing processes. Companies like Nike, Adidas, Patagonia and Mizuno had by 2001 implemented initiatives to address toxic materials, energy use, water pollution, waste and much more. There was every reason to believe that tighter regulations, consumer pressure and increasing costs of raw materials and waste disposal would push corporate commitment to sustainability ever wider and deeper.

Athletes were speaking out too. In Europe, Japan, South America and around the world, prominent athletes were stepping up to promote better practices and to draw attention to pressing environmental issues. In Canada, I co-founded Clean Air Champions with the support of two former national team athletes, to draw attention to air pollution, and to encourage young Canadians to "get active for cleaner air". We had no difficulty finding athletes who wished to join and support our work, and to take our message into schools and sport circles.

By 2002, the IOC and the United Nations Environment Programme (UNEP) had come together to organize four World Conferences on Sport and the Environment, as well as multiple regional seminars. Other groups had similarly hosted workshops and produced educational material. A wide array of educational and guidance material had become available, ranging from general and theoretical to practical and technical.

The architecture profession was also moving forward with sustainable sport facility design, often in close collaboration with developers and engineers. Stadiums and arenas were going up all over Europe, North America and Australia with a range of environmental features to save energy and water and to use better products and avoid more hazardous materials.

By the time Beijing won the right to host the 2008 Olympic and Paralympic Games, and Vancouver to host the 2010 Olympic and Paralympic Winter Games, the pursuit of sustainability in sport and through sport had moved into the mainstream. You could almost call it a movement.

Where are we now?

Now, as we have just passed another eight year marker, we can ask whether the movement has grown even further, consolidated its gains, or begun to slip. Is sustainable sport commonplace, or still relegated to a minority of committed leaders? Since many of the people involved in the sport and environment "movement" to date tell their stories and give their reflections in subsequent chapters of this book, I will offer a more sweeping analysis and attempt to provide context for what follows.

Greener Facilities

New buildings are subject to increasingly stringent standards and higher expectations in much of the industrialized world, and yet many uninspiring boxes are still being built to house sporting activity, with barely a nod given to environmental concerns and with little thought towards the rising costs of energy, growing scarcity of water and the rising urgency of cutting emissions of greenhouse gases. In the wealthy city of Ottawa, I have watched from my front window several new athletics buildings erected on a university campus. None of them will achieve a LEED (Leadership in Energy and Environmental Design) certification for green buildings, something that should be a bare minimum at a time when the price of oil recently hit record highs but is expected to climb again, water is becoming even more precious a commodity and climate change is upon us. I had expected better from the university. We should expect better in all new sports buildings.

Perhaps we should not be too surprised that smaller facility developers and owners are not at the forefront in sport facility construction. Whereas large clubs and host cities for major events can leverage access to significant financing for "showcase" facilities, city recreation departments and colleges must usually make do with a capital budget sufficient to build a cheap box. But is this impediment as real as it first appears, or is it time to question a key assumption about green building – that it is more expensive?

The simplest answer is yes, it is time to question that assumption/myth. Many highly innovative and efficient buildings are being constructed with no price premium for being green. At worst, they require a modest additional capital investment, but the payback period on this outlay is so significant and so secure, that it should be simple to finance. Clearly, the obstacle to building green lies more in the mind of the various players in the building industry: the project developer, the designer, the public or private lender. With oil prices once again on the rise despite the recession, with a cost now being attached to the emission of greenhouse gases in more and more states, with water becoming more scarce and expensive, with public expectations growing, and with regulations getting tighter, it is not naïve to expect that pressure will continue to grow and willingness to act will follow suit. There has always been a health and environmental argument for building more sustainably. Now there is a compelling business case to do so. Smart designers, builders and lenders "get it", but it is up to the client to ask for a green building, and to insist on the best, so as to protect themselves against a variety of risks from not doing so.

Events

When Lillehammer (1994) and Sydney (2000) hosted what have become known as the first "green" Olympic Games, it was big news. When subsequent sport event hosts followed suit, in the first few years of this century, it continued to be exciting, innovative and a reason for media coverage and public interest. Is it still? Somewhat. Should it be? No. How can a new idea be new for more than a decade without inviting cynicism about either the substance of the claims to be green, or the depth of the commitment?

When it comes to sustainable events, how far has the sport community come, and where does it go next? Like the stock market, there are ups and there are downs. One leap forward by a particular event host does not guarantee that every subsequent event will do better. Nowhere is this clearer than with the Olympic Games, where Sydney's achievements in 2000 have been matched by few subsequent hosts. At the bid stage to host the Olympic and Paralympic Games, the level of ambition and the detail of plans have risen steadily, but delivery has often fallen well short of stated intention. I see no excuse for this. Any event host, no matter the sport or the geo-political situation, has access to guidance materials, case studies and personal experience and expertise. Will they choose to make use of these?

It was and continues to be my dream that sometime soon nobody will bother to promise a sustainable event. No candidate city will expect to impress a selection committee, a sponsor or a local citizen by promising to be green, or to be the greenest ever. It will simply be expected. It will be common practice. A professional, well-managed event will be, by definition, as sustainable as possible under local circumstances.

Healthy Conditions for the Athlete

No athlete should be expected to or forced to train and compete in unhealthy conditions. This has been my personal conviction since 1992, when I listened to athletes recount their personal experiences of sailing and rowing through raw sewage, running in lung-burning smog, playing on skin-blistering fields, around the world. Our athletes are what sport is about. The health of our athletes, from the recreational youth right up to the elite professional, should be the top priority of the industry: governing bodies, event hosts, equipment manufacturers, coaches and parents. But it is not, despite the lip service paid.

No sport event should be awarded to a host that cannot guarantee healthy air (indoor and outdoor), water and food for training and competition. It is as simple as that. Any governing body, club, coach or parent that allows otherwise is guilty of negligence, and should be held liable for their decision. This has enormous implications, I realize, and that is precisely why I state it. If a city cannot guarantee clean air to its athletes, then it cannot guarantee healthy conditions for life to its citizens. Does this mean a polluted city should not host a sports event of any kind? Yes. If sport is so important, then clean up your air. Make it a priority. Make it the top priority. Make it a point of principle and a point of pride!

Imagine the positive headlines: "City X guarantees that by 2012 no citizen will be subjected to polluted air and all sports activity will take place in clean air!" It is a big task, but with more than 500,000 people dying prematurely from air pollution worldwide every year, what could be more important. Can any one city make such a guarantee? Not by itself. It will require the collaboration of neighboring cities, industry, all levels of government, and even neighboring countries. So, who can be first? higher, faster longer/stronger.

Sport Clubs

Sport clubs are beginning to step forward in a major way to adopt a sustainable sport management approach. Until now, the initiative of an individual club to build a more sustainable stadium, to participate in education programs on environmental or social issues, to partner with environmental groups, to showcase renewable energy, etc., has been done in isolation. Enormous potential exists for leagues and governing bodies to get involved in coordinating and promoting broader programmes that involve all clubs.

We are seeing the beginning of such an approach in soccer, in golf, in mountain biking, and now in professional football in North America (NFL and CFL). Clubs can show leadership on a range of issues, such as:

- Conserve energy and water in all facilities;
- Use renewable energy on-site or purchases by a green energy provider;
- Tackle climate change by purchasing off-sets/credits (verifiable and transparent);
- Launch transport initiatives to maximize the use of public transit;
- Boost waste reduction initiatives through food and merchandise practices;
- Engage in public education involving players in the community;
- Create partnerships with media outlets, including game-time broadcasts; and,
- Create partnerships with sporting goods suppliers.

Sporting Goods Manufacturers

Corporate social responsibility continues to grow as an expectation placed on all private sector actors in sport, but perhaps most on manufacturers. In most countries, public expectations are rising in parallel with the growth of new regulations and ever-tighter enforcement of existing regulations.

With strong leadership and recognition of the "sustainability imperative", a manufacturer will move beyond worrying about compliance. Instead, it will shift its focus to reducing and even eliminating those products and practices that are by necessity regulated. By re-examining material choices and production processes, it is impossible to "design out" many or all of the hazardous and risky practices in which a company may currently be engaged. Won't this take time and energy and money? Yes. So, start now. A healthy transition can begin today. Otherwise demonstrable negligence starts tomorrow.

Where next?

It is my view that the top priorities for the sports movement should be to focus on the following major environmental issues: climate change; energy security; water quality and availability, health of the athlete and community, and toxic materials and processes.

Conclusion

It is a time for leaders and a time for vision. We as a society and we in the sports industry have seen environmental challenges coming for decades, and have been told about the need to adopt more sustainable practices since at least 1994. The time has come for bold steps, not defensive actions and delay. People and organizations that choose to step up and promote sustainability as a priority in their lives and their public roles stand to reap multiple benefits. These may be commercial rewards. They may lead to a higher standing in the community. Above all, however, they will be personal. The sustainable sport leader will know that she is making a difference, that he is part of a solution, and that what they do in sport and through sport really does matter.

At this final juncture I would like to offer a definition of sustainability and sport:

Sport is sustainable when it meets the needs of today's sporting community while contributing to the improvement of future sport opportunities for all and the improvement of the integrity of the natural and social environment on which it depends.

Part II

Organizations and Tools Promoting Sustainability and Sport

Chapter 3
Sport and the Environment

A UNEP Perspective

Theodore Oben

Introduction

I work for the United Nations Environment Programme (UNEP) and am responsible for what I consider one of our most exciting programmes: Sport and the Environment. Sport thrills crowds and feeds the passions of billions sport enthusiasts worldwide. It creates people that we look up to as role models. Media attention around sport events is unparalled; athletes provide the media with stories of their successes and what drives them to their remarkable achievements.

Many people have never thought about the connection between sport and the environment. Even some of us in the environmental field have often questioned the rationale for putting so much emphasis on this issue. However, the connections are becoming clearer as we are beginning to appreciate sports beyond the events themselves. Below are some of my justifications.

First, like any other activity sport is affected by the quality of the environment. Try playing sports like outdoor running, football, or rugby near where people are burning garbage or in a polluted area. Many people in developing countries have had this experience. In developed countries researchers have been trying to understand links between high levels of air pollution (such as ozone) and asthma in children. Dr. Rob McConnell and colleagues from the University of California at Los Angeles undertook a study reported in 2002 in the British Medical Journal *The Lancelet*[1] which concluded that there might be a connection between exercise and asthma in children who engage in outdoor sports in areas with high levels of ozone. There was widespread media coverage leading up to the 2008 Olympic and Paralympic Games in Beijing about severe air pollution in the city, and Government undertook several major projects to reduce air pollution so that athletes could compete in a clean environment.

Second, sport affects the environment. Think about the massive construction needed for an Olympic and Paralympic Games (Games), a FIFA World Cup™ or any other major sport event. These events use huge amounts of energy, require major transport infrastructure, generate waste and also greenhouse gas emissions. Imagine how much waste 40,000 to 90,000 spectators leave behind after a match, and the systems required to take care of this waste. Think about all the chemicals and water required to keep a golf course. These are real environmental issues which demonstrate sport activities have an impact on the environment.

Third, sport organizations have been doing a lot to address their environmental impact. The organizers of the Games are taking the lead, and other event organizers are following the examples of Games host cities such as Torino, Vancouver, London and Sochi. Several sporting goods manufacturers are also championing the development of environmentally friendly products in the lifestyle industry. Sport is increasingly becoming part of the solution rather than part of the problem, even though a lot more needs to be done.

Fourth, sport presents a unique vehicle to promote environmental awareness and actions. People from virtually every country are passionate about one form of sport or another. Sport could, therefore, be an important tool to reach out to fans and the public to not only communicate environmental messages but to get people to adopt environmentally friendly behavior.

These are the issues that underpin UNEP's Sport and the Environment Programme. The UNEP strategy on Sport and the Environment focuses on three areas:

1.The Lancet, Volume 359, Issue 9304, Pages 386 - 391, 2 February 2002; Rob McConnell and colleagues. See also a critique of the proposed associations from Joel Schwartz in his article 'Breathe Easier on Asthma-Air Pollution Link' published by the National Center for Policy Analysis in March 2002: http://www.ncpa.org/pub/ba390

1. To promote the incorporation of the environment in sport;
2. To promote the development of environmentally friendly sport facilities and sporting goods;
3. To promote environmental awareness and action through sport.

UNEP and the Olympic Movement

UNEP has worked very closely with the International Olympic Committee (IOC) since 1994, when the IOC amended the Olympic Charter to recognize the Environment as the third dimension of Olympism. An IOC Sport and Environment Commission was established to advise the IOC Executive Board on the incorporation of the Environment in the activities of the Olympic Movement. An Agenda 21 for the Olympic Movement was developed by the IOC, and several guides on the environment and sustainability in the Olympic Games have been developed.

I am focusing on the Olympic Movement herein, as in my view it is the point of reference for greening sport events. The Winter Games in 1994 were the first Games to initiate an environmental programme. Since then the focus on the environment in Games planning has grown.

When the IOC and UNEP began their partnership in 1994, the issue of the environment was new to the sport world. Games organizers did not have the necessary expertise to help effectively incorporate environmental issues in their work and UNEP did not have internal experts on the subject of major sport events. It took some time for UNEP and Games organizers to build their capacity and begin working collaboratively.

The 2000 Games in Sydney became the first Games to integrate environmental management systems into the preparation and staging of the event. The greening efforts were also carried forward by the organizers of the 2004 Games in Athens. UNEP signed a Memorandum of Understanding (MoU) with the Athens Organizing Committee just two months before the event took place, which meant that there was very little UNEP could do to help the environmental efforts of the 2004 Games. UNEP felt that the environment was not given enough attention by the Organizing Committee. UNEP organized several roundtable consultations between NGOs and the Athens Organizing Committee, but was unable to get both sides to agree on the best way to approach the greening of the Games.

The 2006 Games in Torino marked a turning point for UNEP's relationship with Games organizers, and became the point of reference for UNEP. Environmental performance was an important issue to the 2006 Torino Organizing Committee for the Olympic and Paralympic Games (TOROC). TOROC's CEO was personally behind the environmental efforts which made it easier for their Environmental Managers to be able to push through their agenda within the entire TOROC operations. TOROC adopted the ISO 14001 standard for Environmental Management Systems and the European Union's Eco-Management and Audit Scheme (EMAS).

Their environmental efforts also received the backing of the local authorities within whose territories the Games were to take place. TOROC was the first Games Organizing Committee to subscribe to international environmental management systems and also the first global event to have initiated a comprehensive programme to address the impact of the Games on climate change. Standards such as green procurement were also adhered to.

UNEP worked very closely with the the 2008 Beijing Organising Committe for the Olympic and Paralympic Games (BOCOG). Specifically, UNEP helped in bridging the communications gap between environmental NGOs and BOCOG. UNEP also conducted two environmental assessments of these Games. The first assessment was published one year before the Games, while the second was conducted immediately after the Games.

The 2008 Games posed multiple challenges to BOCOG, the city of Beijing and the Government of China. Most notable was the poor air quality in the city. The city's transport system was also in serious need of an upgrade. While the environment was a major issue for the 2008 Games, it is my belief that BOCOG's Environmental Department was not given a high enough profile within the organizational structure. Unlike with TOROC, BOCOG's Environmental Department was not able to have any serious influence over the activities of other sectors of BOCOG. Issues such as environmental requirements for contractors and suppliers were voluntary and the Environmental Department did not have any way of ensuring that those requirements were followed. Despite these shortcomings, BOCOG made tremendous efforts on greening the Games. For example, the transport network was modernized with a highly functional and affordable metro, and efforts were made to change the energy mix from an over-dependency in coal to sources of renewable energy.

It can be argued that the 2008 Games have led to the institution of a comprehensive effort on cleaning up the air quality in Beijing. These measures are likely to inspire other cities in China to undertake similar activities. Already, we can see that a lot of the projects, particularly those related to transport, were replicated by the organizers of the World Exposition in Shanghai.

It can also be argued that the 2008 Games presented the strongest associations between sport and the environment. The concerns over air quality in Beijing generated extensive media and public attention about the impact of air pollution on the health of the athletes. In fact, several athletes contemplated whether to attend the 2008 Games because of poor conditions. In my view, this generated awareness about the linkages between sport and the environment.

UNEP also worked very closely with the 2010 Vancouver Organizing Committee for the Olympic and Paralympic Winter Games (VANOC). Based on the initial results from the 2010 Games, we can conclude that VANOC raised the bar on the integration of the environment in Winter Games. Vancouver had the most environmentally friendly venues ever; two of the venues achieved the highest Platinum level of certification under the US Green Building Council's Leadership in Energy and Environmental

Design (LEED) programme (achieved by very few buildings in North America), and several other venues achieved the second highest LEED Gold certification. The Athletes Village in downtown Vancouver, which achieved the LEED Platinum certification, reduces operational energy and water use by up to 50 per cent. Solar energy and waste-generated energy is used extensively. The 2010 Games led to a revamp of the public transport system in Vancouver. Venues were developed with a sustainable legacy use in mind. The communities therefore stand a chance to benefit from the 2010 Games, as these sport facilities are to serve the communities after the event.

The 2010 Games also inspired Vancouver and British Colombia's drive towards a low carbon society. UNEP and VANOC also engaged young people in British Colombia in 2008/2009 and young people in Canada in 2009/2010 in competitions to demonstrate ways of living sustainably.

UNEP started working with the Organizing Committee for the 2014 Olympic and Paralympic Winter Games (2014 Games) in 2008 and signed an MoU with the Sochi 2014 Organizing Committee (Sochi 2014) in 2009. The engagement involves supporting Sochi 2014's efforts to meet its environmental obligations. UNEP's engagement with Sochi 2014 also involves bridging the communications gap between the Sochi 2014, the various contractors and environmental NGOs. Based on the experience of UNEP in dealing with Games-related environmental issues, the Russian Government, Sochi 2014 and the IOC are relying on UNEP to provide extensive support to Sochi's effort to organize an environmentally friendly Games.

UNEP plans to continue engaging with Games Organizing Committees through MoUs, such as with the London Organizing Committee for the Olympic Games and Paralympic Games (LOCOG). Areas of engagement are determine on a case by case basis.

We can see from the above that the nature and scope of UNEP's support to organizers of the Games is growing. UNEP's engagement has changed over the years from promoting the integration of the greening concept within the IOC to fully engaging the Games Organizing Committees. UNEP is also becoming the point of reference for providing information on the extent to which Games meet their environmental objectives through an independent post-Games environmental assessment.

UNEP's work with other major sport events

Based on UNEP's experience in working with the IOC and the Games organizers, other sports organizations are becoming increasingly interested in working with UNEP. A few of these are explained below.

FIFA World Cup™

UNEP worked with the organizers of both the 2006 and 2010 FIFA World Cup™ events in Germany and South Africa respectively. The 2006 FIFA World Cup™ in Germany was the first FIFA World Cup™ to integrate a comprehensive programme on the environment, named the Green Goal. The organizers, with whom UNEP had signed an MoU, approached the event with a target of reducing the use of water, transport, energy and the generation of waste by 20 per cent. The organizers also committed to compensating for all greenhouse gas emissions that were generated within Germany as a result of the event. Several measures were undertaken to encourage fans to use public transport, such as free public transport for 24 hours on game day for match ticket holders in the city where the matches were taking place. The "Cup of the Cup" initiative reduced the amount of drinks cups used during matches. Spectators paid a deposit for a cup with every purchase of a drink, and would receive back the deposit when the cup was finally returned. In several stadiums, water saving devices were installed in washrooms and rainwater was collected for use inside the stadium and for green areas around the stadiums. One hundred thousand tonnes of greenhouse gas emissions were compensated through Gold Standard projects in India and South Africa[2].

Leading up to the 2010 FIFA World Cup™ in South Africa, UNEP worked with the Department of Environmental Affairs (DEA) and the Local Organizing Committee to provide support for the greening of the event. A partnership between UNEP, the DEA and the Global Environment Facility provided US$1,000,000 towards the installation of solar-powered street lamps, traffic lights and advertising boards in several of the venues. This support was also used to develop and distribute the "Green Passport", a UNEP handbook that provided tourists and spectators with tips on how to make their stay and touristic experience more environmentally friendly. UNEP is currently conducting an environmental assessment of the event to determine the impact of the greening efforts and to provide lessons learned.

International Sport Federations

UNEP has also signed agreements of cooperation with several international sport federations to support their environmental efforts, including the International Motorcycling Federation (FIM), the International Association of Athletics Federations (IAAF), and the International Powerboat Federation (UIM). In addition to FIM and UIM, UNEP is also working with the International Automobile Federation (FIA) and the International Air Sports Federation (FAI) to review efforts on alternative energy.

The Indian Premier League

UNEP worked with the Indian Premier League (IPL) on the greening of the IPL 2010 season and the use of IPL events to promote environmental awareness. A comprehensive review of the environmental footprint of the IPL was conducted for the IPL 2010 season: five of the 60 IPL matches were climate neutral, efforts were undertaken to promote the use of solar

---

2. Stahl, H., Hochfeld, C. & M. Schmied (2006). Green Goal Legacy Report. Can be viewed at: http://www.oeko.de/include/dok/225.php?id=292&dokid=292&anzeige=det&ITitel1=&IAutor1=&ISchlagw1=&sortieren=&suchbegriff=greeen%20goal&match=or&LAN=1 (accessed August 2010).

energy in the Mohali stadium and fans were engaged in the greening afforts of one of the franchises – the Royal Challengers of Bangalore – with fans encouraged to use public transport and the team engaging its players in tree planting efforts. Environmental 'tip of the days' were developed and read out at the start of each match, and environmental video messages were played during matches.

UNEP-Puma Play for Life Campaign

UNEP and Puma launched a campaign in 2010 to work with African football teams and individual athlete stars to promote the International Year of Biodiversity. The Campaign used international friendly matches and messages from football stars, including Samuel Eto'o and Emmanuel Eboue, to promote biodiversity conservation. A special football kit – the African Unity Kit – was developed to promote the year. Profit from the sale of the replica kit was used to support biodiversity conservation projects in Africa. Fans and the public voted online for the projects to receive the support.

Commonwealth Games

UNEP also partnered with the organizers of the 2010 Commonwealth Games in Delhi to foster environmental stewardship.

Conclusion

We can conclude that tremendous efforts are being made to integrate environmental issues in sports. Most sport organizations are making deliberate efforts to incorporate environmental issues into planning activities at their events. The IOC has played a pioneering role in the greening of sport events. Several others are following their example, from the organizers of the FIFA World Cup™ to the motorsports federations. However, efforts to integrate environmental issues and sport need to systematized. Mandatory requirements for environmental considerations should be adopted for all sport events. Follow-up on the implementation of these requirements should be incorporated in the regular assessments on whether the preparations are on track. Environmental Managers should be given enough power within the structure of the Organizing Committees with the involvement of the CEO to champion environmental leadership.

One area that has not been well explored is the use of the Games to promote environmental awareness. A few efforts were made in the 2006, 2008 and 2010 Games and the FIFA World Cup™ in South Africa, but these were not comprehensive enough. Sport reaches out to billions of people and can influence them to adopt more environmentally friendly attitutes. UNEP's experience is that Games organizers have not yet mastered spectator engagement through well-targeted environmental messaging or public campaigns that achieve measured behaviour change. UNEP will continue to work with major sport event organizers and sport federations to help them reduce their environmental impact, and hope that we can use sport as a means to communicate and achieve a sustainable future.

Chapter 4

SSETing Up Sport with Tools for Sustainability

Matt Dolf

The Uniqueness of Sport Events

As Kermit the Frog once famously said, "It's not easy being green". Sport organizations, and in particular sport events, are increasingly concerned with being more environmentally, socially and economically sustainable, but don't always know the best way to get started. What should they do first? What else is being done? How can they tackle the issues of sustainability with limited time, money and technical resources? How can they be sure that they are doing something beneficial and communicating this in a credible manner? This chapter will discuss how the Sustainable Sport and Event Toolkit (SSET) can be used by event organizers to guide them down the path of sustainability. Before going into SSET, it is useful to set the stage about how sustainability is relevant for sport and its stakeholders.

As with any industry, sport has a growing responsibility to manage its own social, economic and environmental impacts. In terms of environmental impacts, international sports events rely heavily on air travel, require significant venue construction and maintenance, and make heavy use of energy and water resources to cater to the needs of the large number of fans and participants. Some sports like mountain biking or rowing rely on nature to provide a venue, and therefore require careful course management to mitigate harmful impacts on local habitats and biodiversity. Sports such as these often already see the direct link between protecting natural environments and the longevity of the sport. Rowers do not want to fall out of their boat into polluted lakes, and skiers are already worried about their seasons getting shorter and shorter due to climate change and lack of snowpack.

For the most part, however, sports federations, athletes and event organisers still need to be convinced that their time and resources are well invested in the area of sustainability. While it may be difficult to make an argument based solely on short-term financial gains, there is significant potential from longer term investments, especially in soft benefits such as enhanced image and social integration.

Sport event organizers have a special opportunity to reach out to a wide audience and become a platform to get stakeholders (such as sponsors, host cities, sport governing bodies, athletes and spectators) to engage and effect change around sustainability. Indeed, Kofi Annan recently said: "Sport is a universal language... it engages and brings our world together in a way few, if any other activity, can manage". He also added "Maybe the most important aspect of our joint future is linked to the environment...It is extremely important that athletes, as role models, and sporting federations show proactiveness in caring about the environment".[1]

Sports events are an ideal focus for sustainable development efforts for a number of reasons: they have incredible reach and popularity; they tend to have an authentic image of being clean and ethical; they engage many stakeholders; they have a very clear scope; they are gaining in size and importance; they are open to innovation and change; and, they can inspire passion and emotion in others.

High visibility sporting events such as the Super Bowl or Tour de France provide an ideal communication platform for sustainability. Initiatives such as the Billy Jean King campaign take advantage of the US Open's millions of spectators and TV viewers by putting environmental messages from tennis athletes on the big screen during changeovers at the US Open. Smaller events such as marathons and community cycling events can also get tens of thousands of participants to engage in positive actions such as traveling by public transport versus the private car.

One of the challenges that sport event organisers face when tackling sustainability is that it is such a broad and transversal topic. On the social side we see issues ranging from education, to community integration, to issues of democracy and population health. On the economic side we deal with fair labor policies, good governance and corruption issues, to poverty eradication. Environmental issues range from global warming to resource conservation to protecting ecosystems. Many of these areas overlap; for example, poverty eradication may be as much a social issue as an economic

---

1.Address by Kofi Annan at the 2010 SportAccord Convention, Dubai: 29 April 2010.

one. Sustainability is not just limited to one department in any organization; it needs to be integrated into communication, logistics, accounting, and most importantly into the decision making process of an organization's leaders.

This complexity can be overwhelming and therefore external guidance and support relevant to sport is needed to help event organisers get started in simple and effective ways.

SSET

In 2008, the AISTS (International Academy of Sports Science and Technology) partnered with VANOC (Vancouver Organizing Committee for the 2010 Olympic and Paralympic Winter Games) to develop a new tool aimed at helping sport implement sustainable development. The aim of the tool that became known as SSET is to give sport organizations the knowledge and means to incorporate sustainability into their business practices, and in particular into their sport events.

SSET creates a common language and framework around sustainability in sport so organizers need not reinvent the wheel when taking on this seemingly broad and complex topic. It targets the stakeholders of sport events, in particular the organizers and governing bodies of sport that do not necessarily have the resources or expertise internally to integrate sustainability on their own. The design of SSET made ease of use a priority when guiding non-experts through the step-by-step process of creating a sustainability plan.

SSET was born out of a unique partnership between the AISTS and VANOC. For VANOC, this was an opportunity to leave a body of knowledge as a legacy in their effort to be the first sustainable Olympic and Paralympic Games, incorporating the social development dimension along with environmental and economic considerations. VANOC developed a comprehensive Sustainable Management and Reporting System, and was also the first Games to follow the Global Reporting Initiative (GRI) guidelines for reporting on sustainability. It was important to VANOC that SSET be an ongoing resource both for sport organizations in Canada, and internationally through its partnership with the AISTS.

AISTS chose to co-develop this tool as part of its mission of providing academic research, education and knowledge that benefits the management of international sport. AISTS had already done extensive work in the area of sport and sustainable development, in particular having created the Olympic Games Impact assessment framework (OGI) that the International Olympic Committee (IOC) requires all Olympic and Paralympic Games organizers to use as part of a seven year study of the impact of each Games. AISTS is a not-for-profit academic association based in Lausanne, Switzerland, and was founded by the IOC, the City of Lausanne, the Canton of Vaud, and five Swiss Academic Centers: IMD Business School, the Swiss

Federal Institute of Technology, the Swiss Graduate School of Public Administration, the University of Geneva and the University of Lausanne. AISTS also works with many of the almost 40 International Sport Organizations and countless other technology and research labs, businesses, NGOs and academic institutions that form a unique sport cluster in Switzerland.

While a number of standards and guidelines exist on the topic of sustainable development, including ISO 14001 on Environmental Management Systems and BS 8901 for Sustainable Event Management, no major standards exist for sport events; although the International Organization for Standardization (ISO) is in the process of creating a new ISO 20121 Sustainability in Event Management standard for sport in time for the London 2012 Olympic and Paralympic Games. There are two important documents in the sports world that focus solely on applying sustainable development to sport. In 1999, the Olympic Movement's Agenda 21 was adopted by the IOC. It is a comprehensive blueprint of action which states that it "... aims to encourage members of the Movement to play an active part in the sustainable development of our planet".[2] The other is a practical guide based on the Olympic Movement's Agenda 21 that was developed in 1997 and updated in 2005, entitled the *IOC Manual on Sport, Environment, and Sustainable Development*.

SSET goes a step further by integrating the concepts set out in these two documents with the management and sustainability practices recommended by the following standards and guidelines:

- ISO 14001-14006 on Environmental Management Systems – ISO sets 14001 as the standard for Environmental Management Systems that addresses policy, planning, implementation/operation, checking/corrective action, and management review.
- ISO 26000 on Social Responsibility – A new guidance standard that encourages a voluntary commitment to social responsibility and aims for common guidance on concepts, definitions and methods of evaluation.
- BSI 8900-8901 on Sustainable Event Management – Developed by the British Standards Institution (BSI), this standard provides requirements for planning and managing sustainable events of all sizes and types. BSI 8901 is also used by the London 2012 Olympic and Paralympic Games.
- CSA Z2010 on Sustainable Events – Another new standard by the Canadian Standards Association (CSA) that was put out for public review stage in early 2010. Z2010 sets out requirements and guidance for organizers of sustainable events and was based on the SSET framework.
- GRI G3 Sustainable Reporting Guidelines – GRI is a global, multi-stakeholder initiative that has developed a *Sustainability Reporting Framework*.

2.*Olympic Movement's Agenda 21: Sport for Sustainable Development*. International Olympic Committee, 1999, page 21.

For a non-expert in environmental or sustainable planning, these standards and guidelines can be daunting, and many of these do not make the step between guidance and application very clear. SSET addresses this challenge by not only incorporating essential guidance elements but also by providing practical how-to action items to implement. For example, under the general objective "Implement responsible energy management practices", users are then asked to undertake specific actions such as "install energy efficient lighting and temperature control systems" and "measure kilowatts of energy consumed". If an event organizer follows the action items in SSET, they will be well on their way to meeting ISO 14001 or GRI G3 certification requirements.

How does SSET work?

SSET asks the user to begin by creating a commitment statement and a strategy. Here you must set out your vision, identify key issues and stakeholders, define your scope, set out key measures and reporting parameters, allocate resources for implementation, identify the people responsible, and define vehicles for communication both internally and externally. The rest of the SSET toolkit is divided into sections that are most relevant for sport event organizers and correspond to their organizational responsibility charts and functional areas. These are:

- Site selection and construction
- Procurement and supply chain
- Transportation
- Accommodation
- Catering, food and beverage
- Marketing and communication
- Community involvement and accessibility
- Education and stakeholder engagement

For each section, users are encouraged to follow a Plan – Do – Check – Act (PDCA) process by setting clear objectives linked with sustainability, defining action items, setting performance indicators, naming the persons responsible, and finally following up by checking and reviewing. The PDCA cycle is the operating system of ISO and many other management standards. Figure 1 provides a sample objective from the SSET where users are asked to reduce the ecological footprint of food. Note that SSET also includes a reference column at the end to allow users to further refer to the relevant guidance standards or best practices.

Figure 1 – Objective 7.1 from the SSET Chapter: Catering, Food and Beverage

Objective	Action Items	Performance Indicators	Person Responsible	Status	References
7.1 Reduce ecological footprint of food	• Source local, organic, seasonal and fair-trade where possible. • Use a high % of fruits, vegetables • Use tap water where possible.	% of local, organic and fair-trade food	Name:	Discussed Documented Implemented Not Applicable	GRI EN 3,6,17,18

SSET was also built following an open-sourced and web-based approach. Beyond the guidelines, one of the primary goals of SSET was to create a living document that would be shared by those working in the sport event management sector and grow through continual updates. The open-source approach has gained wide-spread acceptance with the success of knowledge platforms such as Wikipedia and products such as Firefox and OpenOffice. Using the knowledge and contributions of a large group of individuals reduces the development costs and at the same time creates a community of engaged individuals. SSET exists as both a document and as a type of website called a wiki. Wiki's are editable by users who can add comments, further examples and resources – Wikipedia is probably the best known example of a wiki. One of the other benefits of the web-based approach is that content can be translated by users into multiple languages. SSET has already been translated into English and French, with Spanish and Russian translations under development.

An interesting spin-off of this web-based approach is that a number of organizations have created their own SSET wikis tailored for their users. European Athletics and EventScotland each created customized copies and gave access to thousands of event organisers who work with them. European Athletics encourages their events to not only use SSET, but also contribute to it, and to this end they have created an award for innovations around sustainability.

Guidelines and project management terminology are well and good, but nothing is as effective as seeing the concrete examples and best practices of others. Applications of sustainable principles are unique to each sport, event and location, and therefore require custom solutions. By seeing what is already being done in their country or sport, others will hopefully be encouraged to make similar efforts. Sustainability in sport is still an emerging field, and therefore users of SSET will benefit from adapting, borrowing, using, and contributing content to its development.

Targeting the top of the pyramid: International Sport Federations and National Olympic Committees

Few organizations have the global reach and influence of National Olympic Committees (NOCs) and International Sport Federations (IFs), the governing bodies of sport recognized by the IOC and SportAccord. SSET primarily targets these organizations, and in turn the events they organize, because they are at the very top of the so-called "sport pyramid" (see Figure 2). IFs in particular are unique; contrary to the business world where many organizations compete to deliver the same products and services, in the sport world there is only one IF per sport. They are responsible for setting the rules and managing the structure of their sport.

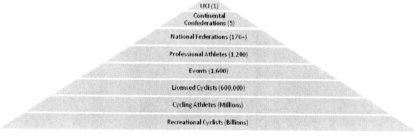

Figure 2 – The Sport Pyramid of Cycling

The International Cycling Federation (UCI) is an example of an IF, which is the highest governing body in the sport of cycling. UCI sets the rules for the seven disciplines of cycling, sanctions the top tier of cycling events and determines the selection procedure for the athletes that take part in the Olympic Games. The next level down are the five Continental Confederations and the 170+ National Federations that are members of the UCI. They in turn influence 1,600 events, 1,200 professional riders, 600,000 licensed riders, millions of cycling athletes and over a billion recreational cyclists, as well as the hundreds of millions of TV spectators of events and the bike manufacturers affected by UCI guidelines.[3] Clearly, programs developed by the UCI that encourage sustainable actions can have enormous reach.

It is also worth mentioning that there are many IFs that do not participate in the Olympic Games. The International Mountaineering Federation is one such IF, and it oversees a variety of disciplines including ice climbing, ski mountaineering and mountain activities such as hiking and trekking. Although the IF has a staff of less than five individuals, they reach more than 1.3 million members across the globe. They actively encourage others to follow sustainability principles and guidelines such as SSET, particularly to protect the natural environments and communities in the mountains. They

---

3.See: International Cycling Union, www.uci.ch, 2010

ask members to respect their sustainability charter and are in the process of setting up a recognition system for these efforts.

While many IFs focus on environmental issues, others emphasize social issues as well. UEFA (the European Union of Football Associations) is an example of an IF that is very serious about their own social responsibility. In particular, they have a number of programs that promote respect, fight racial discrimination, and promote ethical purchasing to ensure fair wages, worker conditions and no child-labor. Criticism UEFA received during the EURO 2008 with regard to alleged Adidas suppliers employing child labor in certain factories in Pakistan (Adidas supplied the footballs for the EURO 2008) highlights the importance of why UEFA is addressing these issues.

One of the challenges IFs face is that many lack the funds or political will to hire a sustainability manager. A recent economic impact study carried out by the AISTS examined the approximately 20 recognized IFs located in the greater Lausanne region in Switzerland. The study found that more than half had an annual budget under five million Swiss Francs, some with a staff of under five people and budgets under one million Swiss Francs.[4] While some IFs make use of committees, volunteers and partners to help them implement sustainability principles and practices, most lack credible expertise and adequate time to invest in doing substantive work in this area. They need affordable solutions and tools that cater to their needs and bring realistic applications to the sport world.

On the other end of the spectrum, a handful of sports such as football, cycling, golf and tennis have large organizations and enough resources to tackle sustainability internally. UEFA, for example, has an annual turnover of close to two billion US dollars. Interestingly, even these sports have only recently begun to see the importance of addressing sustainability in events management and have also expressed a need for planning tools and a solid understanding of best practices in their field.

In 2009, the AISTS sent out a questionnaire that asked 25 IFs about their current views and initiatives in sustainability.[5] Of those reporting, 21 rated sustainability as either "very important" or "the most important issue" for them to manage. Interestingly, just over half had no committee or staff person designated as responsible for this topic. Perhaps not surprisingly then, 19 out of 25 supported a tool like SSET taking a collective approach in order to keep the costs down and encourage knowledge exchange. This also highlights the fact that sport organizations are showing a growing willingness to share information. While in the business sector many keep their best practices a secret to maintain a competitive advantage, perhaps the sport sector sees the advantage that a shared emphasis on this topic will bring. The topic of sustainability is a good candidate for this because it is

---

4.Nassar, V. (2006). *Economic Impact Study of International Sport Federations and Organizations in the Lemanic Arc*; AISTS

5.Dolf, M. (2009). *International Federation Sustainability Scan*; AISTS.

typically not an area seen as a "winner take all" competition (as is the case for securing sponsorship money), but rather a responsibility that all organizations and citizens feel the need to share.

NOCs are at the top of their own sport pyramids. Each country participating in the Olympic Games has an NOC responsible for developing athletes and managing the selection requirements of each sport into the Olympic Games. The Swiss and French NOCs are examples of organizations encouraging sport events to apply sustainable development principles. In 2003, France became the first country to further adapt the Olympic Movement's Agenda 21 to reflect France's commitment to sustainability in sports. Each year hundreds of events apply for and receive a label of support if they follow sustainable development principles.

SwissOlympic, the NOC from Switzerland, has also shown significant leadership. They created a program called EcoSport which awards prizes totaling 30,000 Swiss Francs annually to sport events that undertake environmental initiatives. They have also put in place a number of social development programs such as their Clean and Cool campaign which encourages young athletes to give up unhealthy substances such as cigarettes, alcohol and drugs. SwissOlympic created their own version of an online knowledge base similar to SSET that encourages organisers to plan more sustainable events.

Conclusion

As sustainability in sport develops, so does the need for guidance, standardization and tools to assist sport administrators and event managers. The few sports and countries that have shown leadership in this regard are still only the tip of the iceberg. Sports organizations with limited funding in particular need the tools and support to incorporate sustainability into their operations and events; they are not able to invest a year of one person's time to develop sustainability programs. With new standards under development such as ISO 20121 and tools such as SSET, they will be able to get started more quickly and at the same time benefit from the learning experience of others.

Further guidelines on planning, measuring and reporting specific to sport events are needed, because sport events are in fact a great way to share and compare sustainability due to their similar scope. Virtually all events need to consider the logistics of transportation, accommodation, volunteers, catering, and venue management. While they may vary on aspects such as venue type and length of the event, organizational aspects remain similar enough to follow a standardized approach. These guidelines will also enhance the credibility of efforts by the sports industry and help change the debates around sustainability from "why" to "how".

To effect change, we need to think differently about sharing information. Sport organizations need to realize that rather than protecting best practices as valuable intellectual property, sharing success will lead to a much greater collective benefit. There is no real downside to helping another sport or country do well in this regard, and in fact their experiences can re-inform our own. Once governing bodies are on board with implementing sustainability in a collective way, their reach and impact can lead to rapid change. Sport touches virtually the entire global population and there are no better levers to influence sport than the IFs and the NOCs who in turn influence the rest of the sport pyramid. Using, adapting, sharing and re-creating a tool like SSET will hopefully lead to enormous uptake in environmentally, social, and economically sustainable practices.

Chapter 5

Sustainable Event Management

The Journey to ISO 20121

Fiona Pelham

Introduction

It can be argued that hosting a sustainable event is not achievable, because any event requires temporary materials, energy use, and travel, and can result in potentially negative economic, environmental and social impacts. This debate is not one which will take place herein, but it is important to note that an understanding of the potential negative impacts of an event is required in order to manage, reduce and report these impacts. This chapter will introduce frameworks that support the event industry in developing their understanding of how to identify and manage negative impacts, and report on sustainability more broadly. Specifically, this chapter will review the journey of the ISO 20121[1] standard, which began as an idea by the team preparing the London bid to host the 2012 Olympic Games and Paralympic Games (2012 Games). The review will culminate by describing how ISO

---

1. International Organization for Standardization (ISO) 20121: Sustainability in Event Management (under development as of September 2010)

2012[1] was also in an equally high profile bid by England 2018 to host the 2018 FIFA World Cup™.

The Inspiration for BS8901: Specification for a Sustainable Event Management System

London submitted a 2012 Games bid to the International Olympic Committee (IOC) in 2005 that committed to delivering a *One Planet Olympics*, and achieving the first sustainable Olympic Games and Paralympic Games[2]. This commitment included the use of a sustainable event management system framework to support the delivery of a sustainable event. Existing frameworks at the time were either checklist approaches (limited in their suitability, as it is hard to prescribe generic steps equally applicable across a diverse international event industry) or management systems created for business and focused only on environmental aspects (limited in their suitability as the economic and social aspects are not included, such as with ISO 14001[3]).

A management system is a framework that shapes your way of working. An event requires unique management considerations, including dependency on a supply chain for event delivery and a potential requirement for vast stakeholder engagement, which may not apply to business. Furthermore, the stages of an event include set up, delivery, breakdown and legacy, and do not coincide with the stages of typical business management, which operate on an annual cycle. The London Organising Committee for the Olympic Games and Paralympic Games (LOCOG) would need a process and framework different to traditional business, which meant a new management system approach was required.

Interest from the Event Industry

The event industry is aware that their activities have an associated environmental impact. There are an increasing number of initiatives related to events which are described as *green*, *eco* or *environmental*. For example, the Green Goal™ program implemented by the organisers of the 2006 FIFA World Cup™ in Germany[4] raised the profile of environmental protection as a consideration for the event and other large scale sport events.

---

2. London 2012 bid, *Towards a One Planet Olympics*, February 2005. See London 2012 website (accessed October 2010): http://www.london2012.com/making-it-happen/sustainability/index.php

3. ISO 14001 is an international standard that specifies requirements for Environmental Management Systems.

4. Green Goal™ - Legacy Report, Stahl, H., Hochfeld, C., & M. Schmied (2006). Website (accessed October 2010): http://www.oeko.de/publications/reports_studies/dok/659.php?id=73&dokid=292&anzeige=det&ITitel1=&IAutor1=&ISchlag-w1=&sortieren=&dokid=292

It was a logical step for the event industry to move beyond implementing environmental protection strategies to considering broader sustainability impacts, and developing an understanding that an event could be planned to deliver optimal economic, environmental and social benefits.

Between 2003 and 2010, the event industry's general response to the subject of sustainability was "just tell me what to do to make my event more sustainable". While this response was evidence of the industry's willingness to do something differently, it was also frustrating, because it showed a lack of understanding that sustainability was an emerging and important issue.

During this time the number of sustainable event guidelines in the marketplace began to increase as each event began to share their checklist approach. Although checklists were useful for reference, there was a danger looming; events are unique (e.g., location, size, content) and there is no "one size fits all" response to event sustainability issues. The event industry needed a sustainability management system appropriate for and specific to events.

Strong Champions for Change

Good ideas for change need strong champions for action. The initial idea for a standard for a sustainability management system for events was suggested by David Stubbs, Head of Sustainability for LOCOG, to the team at the BSI British Standards[5] in 2004. LOCOG's support for the development of this standard, which became BS8901, brought attention to the standard and its development process, and supported the work of many event industry individuals passionate for change towards greater sustainability.

A volunteer panel made up of the event industry, standards and sustainability experts worked for almost two years on the development of BS8901. The panel's dedication went beyond attending meetings; many also put the framework into practice and fed back their learning. The event industry representatives understood that business, sport and cultural events had significant planning sequence similarities, and therefore worked to create a management system standard suitable for all event types and sizes. The panel worked to create a management system standard to provide the event industry with a framework for a way of working where sustainability issues were identified and considered at every decision point, not just at bid stage or when the client demanded.

5.BSI British Standards is the UK's National Standards Body. It represents UK economic and social interests across all of the European and international standards organizations and through the development of business information solutions for British organizations of all sizes and sectors. BSI British Standards works with manufacturing and service industries, businesses, governments and consumers to facilitate the production of British, European and international standards. (excerpt accessed October 2010 from BSI British Standards at: http://www.bsigroup.com/en/Standards-and-Publications/About-BSI-British-Standards/)

By 2006 the new standard was being trialed by a number of volunteers, including the Manchester International Festival and the Earls Court and Olympia event venue. In 2008, the Meeting Professionals International[6] European Conference and the Organize This event management company became the first event and event company respectively to be third party certified for the implementation of the BS8901 management system.

BS8901 has enabled the event industry to raise their profile through sustainability leadership and knowledge transfer to other industries looking to address sustainability. BS8901 offers a new way of working for an entire industry that is learning about sustainability and beginning to take responsibility for decisions - an empowering opportunity.

Events as a Catalyst for Change

Major international sport events can serve as a catalyst for change, through investment in local infrastructure, a global viewership of billions of spectators, and an international supply chain keen to win business.

LOCOG worked to harness this power, and implement sustainability within the event supply chain and set a best practice example for the international event industry. I served as Chair of the BS8901 Stakeholder Committee from 2007, and was often told by the more traditional industry figureheads, whom had led the event industry for a significant number of years, that sustainability would not work because it was too expensive and not a priority (both obvious untruths to those who understand the meaning of the word sustainability). I was fortunate enough to witness the power of the Olympic Games to be a catalyst for change first hand when one such figurehead was invited to a presentation on sustainability by LOCOG. Before the end of the presentation, this person was raising his hand to declare that the company he ran was completely committed to the implementation of sustainability. What drove this person to change was not the potential sustainability benefits of using BS8901, but the incentive to become a LOCOG supplier. LOCOG encourages its suppliers to follow BS8901, and this will have positive economic, environmental and social repercussions long after the 2012 Games are over.

It would be incorrect to say the uptake of BS8901 can only be attributed to the influence of the 2012 Games. The BS8901 Stakeholder Committee and wider event industry members who are passionate about sustainability were working simultaneously to provide case studies, presentations and online resources to explain to the event industry how BS8901 could be implemented, and provide constant evidence of its benefits.

Starting in 2007, there was evidence throughout the event industry of the growing importance of implementing, measuring and monitoring sustainability initiatives, with or without the BS8901 framework. Explaining

---

6. Meeting Professionals International is an international association for the event industry.

sustainability credentials became a recognized part of the tendering process for events, and press releases on event sustainability achievements changed from rare to regular. Influencing the procurement process and increasing business are great catalysts for change. Several hotels worked to achieve an environmental label such as Green Globe or Green Tourism Business Scheme, and many events cut the use of bottled water and printing to reduce their environmental impact. The changing economic climate during this time meant the industry began to recognize that avoiding the production of potential waste items (e.g., give aways, handouts, etc.) would save money both in production and waste disposal costs. Change in UK Government regulations at this time (e.g., the UK's Carbon Reduction Commitment) meant the industry needed to start considering how it could demonstrate social and economic benefits, which would offset the negative environmental impacts from events, such as travel. Every small step made a big difference during this period of growing awareness.

The International Growth of Event Sustainability Frameworks

Stakeholders and the event industry took risks, embraced change, and fed back their experiences to benefit the development of BS8901. Within a few years there was tangible evidence within the event industry of the positive benefits of the implementation of a sustainability standard. There was evidence of BS8901 being used outside of the UK, and it was clear that there was the demand for an international standard. Less than three years after its launch, BS8901 was being referred to in international bid documents and used at international events, such as the 2009 United Nations COP 15 Climate Change Conference in Copenhagen:

> *"We worked hard to be architects of an effective, flexible sustainability management system which engaged stakeholders throughout the community. The result is ....a more sustainable Copenhagen, a city which can now claim 53% of all hotel rooms as third party eco-certified, a state of the art public transportation system and affordable access to organic and sustainable foods".*

Jan-Christoph Napierski, Head of Sustainability for COP15

During 2009, BS8901 was proposed as the starting draft for the development of the ISO 20121 international standard. A new chapter started in the life of BS8901 in January 2010; the first meeting was held for ISO 20121, which would use BS8901 as its draft starting point. Over 11 countries were present at the first ISO 20121 meeting held in London, including: Brazil, Canada, China, Denmark, France, Germany, Holland, Japan, Spain, Sweden and the UK. Each country shared their own experience with the implementation of sustainability in the event industry and it was quickly evident that each country had broken new ground with their checklists, community involvement projects and supply chain engagement strategies.

At the time of writing this chapter, the ISO meetings are set to continue into at least 2012, and there are a dedicated number of individuals from over 30 countries who will be contributing the viewpoints of their countries' stakeholder committees.

In addition to ISO 20121, the international event community is also collaborating through the Global Reporting Initiative (GRI) to create a sustainability reporting framework specific for the event sector. A GRI reporting framework outlines sustainability aspects (or issues) to report publicly, and the new Event Organizers Sector Supplement will include some specific to the event industry.

The combination of an international sustainability management system (ISO 20121) and an international reporting framework (GRI Event Organizers Sector Supplement) means the event industry will have a structure for sustainability tailored to its unique industry needs. ISO 20121 is a framework to identify sustainability issues and put action plans in place to address them. The GRI Event Sector Supplement is a framework to report on the issues publicly.

Case Study: How the England 2018 Bid used BS8901 and GRI Reporting

England's bid to host the 2018 FIFA World Cup™ is a good case study to demonstrate how a sustainability management system and reporting framework can work well within a large scale sport event. England began work on their bid to host the FIFA World Cup™ in 2009, just as the development of ISO 20121 and the GRI Event Organizers Sector Supplement had begun. The England 2018 bid team made a commitment that sustainability would be an integrated consideration from the start, and used both international, multi-stakeholder frameworks.

The following steps were taken to identify the key sustainability issues for the bid:

1. Reviewing existing industry best practice;
2. Reviewing previous similar event sustainability issues;
3. Working with UK venue Candidate Host City Stakeholder groups; and,
4. Working with Sustainability Expert Stakeholder groups.

Stakeholder input during the issue identification phase brought transparency to the process and ensured the event team did not overlook issues which may be awkward or difficult to address. Each issue is a potential risk, and it is an obvious step to rank the issues in terms of which are most likely to occur and which could have the greatest negative impact.

The next step was to set objectives and targets to address the top ranked sustainability issues. The objectives and targets were shared with key stakeholders. Over 25 targets were set and a commitment was made to regularly report on the progress to achieve them. In 2009, event sustainability reporting using the internationally recognised GRI framework was limited; the exception to this was the Organising Committee for the Vancouver 2010 Olympic and Paralympic Winter Games (VANOC), who based their event reporting on the GRI Guidelines with some necessary modifications applicable for an event. This meant that the England 2018 team did not have baselines from existing best practice to guide them, so a commitment was made to measure baselines, and reduction targets were aligned with UK Government or international event best practice.

In 2009, the UK Government's commitment for carbon emissions reduction was 40% by 2020 based on 2007 figures. The England 2018 bid commitment became a 40% reduction by 2018, and an estimated carbon footprint of the event and a basic reduction strategy was developed to support this commitment.

The bid team used the (then in development) ISO 20121 framework to ensure that sustainability was considered at every point, and this shaped their bidding process. Potential venue Host Cities attended a sustainability workshop to learn how to identify their sustainability issues, and objectives and targets were set to address these issues. Embedding the ISO 20121 framework into England 2018's bidding process was a successful way to ensure all areas of the bid recognized and addressed sustainability issues.

England 2018's bid details a clear commitment to delivering an event which identifies, addresses and measures its sustainability impacts. It is hoped that the bid team's use of the ISO and GRI frameworks will encourage the event industry to use this approach, and for it to become common practice in future international bids.

The Future of Event Sustainability Frameworks

It is possible that the event industry will have been transformed in the span of just ten years. Every step towards sustainability makes a positive difference, and the ISO 20121 and GRI Event Organizers Sector Supplement frameworks have the potential to turn those steps into a continuous process of improvement.

The international input from dedicated industry stakeholders into the development process of trialing, testing and using both frameworks is at a crucial point. The enthusiasm and passion of the event industry for the concept of sustainability has lead to stakeholders taking a proactive role in shaping their business, rather than waiting for regulation or client pressure to change it for them. The event industry now has the credible frameworks to ensure that sustainability issues move from being perceived as risks to being understood, addressed and reported on, and seen as opportunities. There is a framework to provide an understanding of sustainability issues and a system to address and transparently report on them and the support for transformational industry change is there.

Chapter 6

Greening Sport and Inspiring Societal Change

An ENGO Perspective from the Vancouver 2010 Olympic and Paralympic Winter Games

Deborah Carlson and Paul Lingl

Introduction

Environmental non-governmental organizations (ENGOs) have tradition-ally lobbied governments directly for changes in law and policy, or used boy-cotts or demonstrations to create pressure for change. However, it is now clear that deeper public engagement is also necessary to bring about lasting societal transformation and environmental sustainability.

From 2005 to 2010 the David Suzuki Foundation was involved in a cam-paign to reduce the climate impact of the Vancouver 2010 Olympic and Paralympic Winter Games (Vancouver 2010), to promote best practices in carbon management for event organizers and businesses, and to use the pro-file of Vancouver 2010 to strengthen public support for action on climate change. We engaged with athletes, the Vancouver Organizing Committee for the 2010 Olympic and Paralympic Winter Games (VANOC), its spon-sors, and with professional sports organizations. We also reached out direc-tly to the public. What follows is a brief account of our experiences and an assessment of the results of our efforts. We conclude with thoughts on ways for the Olympic Games and other sporting events to improve their environmental performance, and inspire further societal change.

Getting Started

As mentioned previously our Vancouver 2010 campaign was a project of the David Suzuki Foundation, a Canadian ENGO headquartered in Vancouver. The Foundation works with government, business and individuals, and one of its long-standing priorities is climate protection.

Given the prominence of the Olympic Games generally, it was clear that Vancouver 2010 presented an opportunity to communicate environmental messages to an audience of hundreds of millions of people in Canada and around the world, including people not typically engaged by ENGOs. With climate change quickly becoming the defining issue of our generation – and the very future of Winter Olympic and Paralympic Games at stake due to warming temperatures – we decided to focus our campaign on solutions to climate change.

We settled on a goal of ensuring that Vancouver 2010 was carbon neutral – in other words, that they would have no net climate impact. This would involve VANOC measuring the climate impact of the event, reducing emissions as much as possible, and then investing in carbon offsets to neutralize remaining emissions. Carbon neutral initiatives have the advantage of encompassing all aspects of an organization's climate impact, such as how energy-efficient its buildings are, the type of energy used, transportation, and even waste. Moreover, the three requirements of carbon neutral initiatives – measuring, reducing and offsetting – provide a simple model that any individual, business or organization can use to minimize their climate impact.

The Vancouver 2010 Bid Book presented to the International Olympic Committee (IOC) provided an opening for our campaign, as it included an aspirational goal to "move towards a zero net emissions Games that is climate neutral." We decided to work to ensure that VANOC actually *achieved* carbon neutrality, and did so in a way that utilized best practices, including the use of high quality, Gold Standard[1] carbon offsets. We also wanted VANOC to implement an effective public outreach program to promote its efforts to reduce its climate impact, which we hoped would inspire spectators and the general public to manage their own carbon footprints as well.

The campaign began with the publication of our report, *Meeting the Challenge: A Carbon Neutral 2010 Winter Games Discussion Paper*[2]. We worked with VANOC to prepare this report, and estimated that total greenhouse gas

---

1. The Gold Standard. Website: http://www.cdmgoldstandard.org/

2. *Meeting the Challenge: A Carbon Neutral 2010 Winter Games Discussion Paper*. The David Suzuki Foundation. January 2007. Website: www.davidsuzuki.org/publications/reports/2007/meeting-the-challenge/

emissions from the Vancouver 2010 event would be over 300,000 tonnes of CO_2 equivalent – about the same amount generated by 60,000 cars on the road for a year. By far the largest emission source – at roughly half of the total – would be travel to Vancouver by spectators, mostly by air.

In addition to making detailed recommendations on how VANOC could make the Games carbon neutral, *Meeting the Challenge* also described environmental initiatives from previous Olympic and Paralympic Games. Notable advances in environmental protection efforts in the Olympic Movement over the past twenty years include the following: the first environmental initiatives taken at the 1994 Lillehammer Games; the subsequent decision in 1994 by the IOC to establish the *Environment* as the third pillar of the Olympic Movement (along with *Sport* and *Culture*); the innovative "Green Games" held in Sydney in 2000; and the Salt Lake City 2002 Games, which were the first to measure and offset climate impacts. Our report emphasized that environmental concerns were becoming ever more urgent, and each successive Games Organizing Committee should be raising the bar in adopting and promoting solutions. Unfortunately, this has not always happened – many observers felt the 2004 Olympic and Paralympic Games in Athens, for example, could have done more.

We presented *Meeting the Challenge* at a joint news conference with VANOC, and offered its recommendations as a challenge for VANOC to meet. VANOC publicly accepted our challenge.

Working with Athletes

In 2006, we received an email from Olympic alpine skier Thomas Grandi, who was interested in our work to address climate change. He and his wife, Sara Renner (also one of Canada's top Olympic athletes), were already seeing the impacts of climate change in the mountains where they were competing, and they wanted to take action. We had hoped to work with athletes on our Vancouver 2010 campaign, so this expression of interest from two Olympians was an amazing opportunity. Together with Grandi and Renner, the David Suzuki Foundation launched the *Play It Cool* program at a packed news conference later that year.

The concept of *Play It Cool* is simple: participating athletes work to reduce their own climate impact – for example, by driving less or offsetting the emissions from their travel to compete and train. As role models, these athletes would also share climate solutions with the general public through media interviews and public presentations. *Play It Cool* athletes are also working to green their sports. An example is Olympic medalist Kristina Groves, who has been engaging staff, athletes and sponsors at Speed Skating Canada around sustainability issues.

After its launch, the *Play It Cool* program gained momentum and eventually more than 70 elite athletes were participating, making the program a major driver in our Vancouver 2010 campaign. In early 2009, *Play It Cool* athletes signed an open letter to VANOC's CEO, John Furlong, asking him to follow the recommendations in *Meeting the Challenge* to ensure Vancouver 2010 would be a carbon neutral event. To our knowledge, it was the first time athletes had intervened in this way regarding Olympic sustainability, and VANOC officials later told us that it provided a major boost to their efforts.

Working with the National Hockey League Players' Association

While launching *Play It Cool*, we met National Hockey League (NHL) player Andrew Ference. Ference envisioned a similar initiative for NHL players, and, as a representative to the National Hockey League Players' Association (NHLPA), he was able to convince his fellow player representatives and the NHLPA administration to create the NHLPA Carbon Neutral Challenge, in partnership with the David Suzuki Foundation.

The Carbon Neutral Challenge was a huge success, with 523 players representing every team in the league participating in the first year – making it, as far as we know, the largest player-driven environmental initiative in professional sports history. Andrew Ference appeared on the iconic Canadian TV show *Hockey Night in Canada*, where he described the initiative and his efforts to protect the planet for his young daughter's generation.

Together with *Play It Cool*, the NHLPA initiative set an important precedent for the Olympic Movement by featuring athletes and sports organizations taking responsibility for their climate impact.

Winter Sports and Climate Change

To keep the pressure on VANOC for a carbon neutral Vancouver 2010 event, the David Suzuki Foundation published its report *On Thin Ice*[3] in 2009. The report discussed the vulnerability of winter sports, including the Olympic and Paralympic Winter Games, to climate change, and recommended ways for sporting events and organizations to play a leadership role. At the time, VANOC was co-hosting the World Conference on Sport and the Environment, and we held our media event for the report's release at the same location as the conference to gain the attention of delegates and media. Eminent environmentalist Dr. David Suzuki joined three of Canada's top competitive skiers and snowboarders, who described their firsthand experiences of climate change, such as race cancellations due to lack of snow. They collectively called on VANOC to take responsibility for the climate impact of Vancouver 2010. After our media event, CEO John Furlong (who was attending the conference) told the assembled reporters that VANOC was very confident it would make Vancouver 2010 carbon neutral

---

3.*On Thin Ice: Winter Sports and Climate Change*. The David Suzuki Foundation. March 2009. Website: www.davidsuzuki.org/publications/reports/2009/on-thin-
-ice-winter-sports-and-climate-change/

by offsetting all major greenhouse gas emissions, including those from spectator travel. This was the first time that this specific commitment had been made publicly.

Engagement with Olympic Sponsors

While athletes are the main attraction at sporting events, corporate sponsors are also key players in amateur and professional sports. They contribute hundreds of millions of dollars to the Olympic Movement, and in many cases play a significant communications role through advertising and media coverage. In late 2009, VANOC forecast that air travel by Vancouver 2010 sponsors and partners would be responsible for about eight per cent of Vancouver 2010's total emissions. Because of these factors, we felt their participation in the Vancouver 2010 carbon neutral initiative was important.

VANOC circulated *Meeting the Challenge* directly to Vancouver 2010 sponsors, which lead to representatives from Coca Cola Ltd. (Coca-Cola in Canada) contacting the David Suzuki Foundation for guidance. Coca-Cola is the longest continuous sponsor of the Olympic Movement, and was also a co-sponsor of the Vancouver 2010 Torch Relay. We held a series of meetings, and in early 2009 the company committed to measuring and reducing greenhouse gas emissions for its Vancouver 2010 operations, including those from air travel, vehicles, energy use and the Torch Relay. Remaining emissions would be offset using Gold Standard carbon offsets, making this Coca-Cola's first major carbon neutral event.

Coca-Cola's initiative lent momentum to VANOC's carbon management program by showing that at least one prominent sponsor supported climate action at the event. VANOC subsequently announced a voluntary offset program for Vancouver 2010 sponsors and government partners, known as Carbon Partners. Coca-Cola participated in this program, as did more than 30 others, including McDonald's, Samsung, and Visa. As far as we know, this was the first time Olympic sponsors had participated in an organized program to measure and offset their Games-related greenhouse gas emissions, and we hope it will be a model for future Games. Ideally, participating sponsors will use their Vancouver 2010 experience as a starting point for more comprehensive carbon management activities within their organizations.

The Results of Our Campaign

Throughout our campaign we encouraged VANOC to measure, reduce and offset its climate impact using best practices, and strengthen public support for action on climate change through an effective outreach campaign. Overall, the results were mixed.

VANOC made progress in addressing its climate impact and has estimated it reduced its emissions by at least 15 per cent below business as usual, through energy-efficient venues and other initiatives. VANOC committed to offsetting unavoidable emissions from its own operations, the Torch Relay, and travel and accommodations for all 6,850 athletes and team officials. Although VANOC inventoried spectator travel – estimated to be 128,000 tonnes – it did not offset these emissions, notwithstanding John Furlong's comments to the media during the World Conference on Sport and Environment. In fact, only a fraction of the event's overall indirect emissions were offset, mostly through the voluntary sponsor program.

Vancouver 2010 did set several precedents with respect to carbon management. They were the first Olympic and Paralympic Games to measure and publish the climate impact for both the Olympic Games and Paralympic Games, including emissions from the start-up of operations in 2003 until the conclusion of the events in 2010, instead of just the few weeks during "Games time". They were also the first to feature carbon-neutral athletes and a carbon-neutral Torch Relay. Moreover, they created a new official sponsorship category for carbon offsets – a precedent that we hope will make financing environmental initiatives easier for future event organizers.

Despite these achievements, a high-profile public engagement program never materialized from Vancouver 2010 – a major disappointment from our point of view. Nonetheless, VANOC's relatively limited efforts in this area offered a glimpse of the types of public engagement activities that are possible, including a sustainability contest for youth, and videos shown at pavilions during Vancouver 2010 describing VANOC's carbon management program. A more ambitious program might have included working with media sponsors to reach out to the event's vast television audience, and using the opportunities presented by the 2010 Torch Relay to engage Canadians in communities across the country.

The David Suzuki Foundation held another media event a few days before the opening ceremonies of Vancouver 2010 to release our *Climate Scorecard for the 2010 Winter Games*[4]. This report looked at VANOC's performance across 10 climate-related categories, including venue design, energy use, and transportation. We awarded Vancouver 2010 a bronze medal overall for their efforts. The report received enormous media coverage from around the world, with Vancouver's record warm winter and images of snow being trucked in from 200 kilometres away to one of the mountain venues driving home the message about the vulnerability of winter sports to a warming climate.

Recommendations for the IOC and Other Sports Organizations

One important lesson from our Vancouver 2010 campaign is that change comes slowly to institutionalized sporting events like the Olympic and Paralympic Games. Even though the *Environment* has been the third pillar of the

---

4. *Climate Scorecard for the 2010 Winter Games*. The David Suzuki Foundation. February 2010. Website: www.davidsuzuki.org/publications/reports/2010/climate-scorecard-for-the-2010-winter-games/

Olympic Movement since 1994, it still appears to be a relatively low priority for both the IOC and many Organizing Committees. To improve the performance of future Games in reducing their climate and other environmental impacts, and to realize their potential to catalyze change, the IOC will need to implement some changes. Our recommendations below could also be applied to other major sporting events and associations.

First, the IOC should set environmental performance requirements for all Organizing Committees, in areas such as carbon management, waste, water use, clean energy, and transportation – and then ensure that these are integrated into the bid, planning, and implementation stages. For example, all Games should have a comprehensive carbon management plan that ensures climate impacts will be measured, reduced and offset according to global best practices. By leaving the specifics of environmental performance up to the discretion of event host cities, the IOC is effectively assigning environmental protection a much lower importance relative to other aspects of staging the event – such as venue construction and sponsorship deals – most of which are subject to rigorous IOC specifications and oversight. Requiring the use of environmental best practices for the Games would help enable consistently high performance.

Second, the IOC should develop guidelines for Organizing Committees to integrate public outreach around environmental solutions into every Games, just as it requires host cities to put on a high-profile festival of the arts as part of the *Culture* pillar of the Olympic Movement. Ideally, this outreach would involve athletes and sponsors – including TV and other media sponsors – and would target local, national and international audiences with inspiring environmental messages.

Third, having an independent watchdog for every Games would increase monitoring capacity and help ensure greater public accountability. While Games bids now typically include aspirations to be the "greenest Games ever", there has been little evidence of IOC or other oversight to ensure that host city commitments around sustainability are in fact met. One noteworthy exception is the Commission for a Sustainable London 2012, which provides assurance to the Olympic Board and the public that the London 2012 Olympic and Paralympic Games are meeting their sustainability commitments.

Finally, because not all host cities or countries have the same financial means, the IOC could work with its partners to create an environmental fund, with financing from a new worldwide environmental sponsorship category, media-rights revenues, or other sources. This fund could help ensure that all Olympic Games organizers are able to take responsibility for their environmental impact.

Conclusion

For generations, the Olympic and Paralympic Games have inspired athletes to strive for excellence while captivating the public imagination, but they have also been agents for change and have contributed to breaking down racial and social barriers. Now, as we face the urgent global challenge of climate change, we have an opportunity to use the power of sports and the Olympic Movement to champion and inspire action on this important issue.

In 2007, a cover story on climate change in *Sports Illustrated* noted that it is "time for our teams and athletes to take the lead, galvanize attention and influence behavior." At the David Suzuki Foundation, our work with *Play It Cool* has made it clear how effective athletes can be in communicating to the public about climate change. Not only are they passionately committed, but they are able to draw a compelling connection between their firsthand experience of climate impacts and the need to take action.

Along with athletes, sporting events like the Olympic and Paralympic Games can demonstrate leadership and inspire broad audiences to become involved in environmental solutions. Our own experience with Vancouver 2010 suggests that there is a strong business case for Organizing Committees to reduce their event's environmental impacts, including cost savings from energy-efficient venues, and positive public relations. However, large events like the Olympic Games still have a long way to go to reduce their climate impact, and greening the Olympic Movement will require more decisive action from the IOC and Organizing Committees. We hope that future sporting events, including the London 2012 Olympic and Paralympic Games, pick up where Vancouver left off, and raise the bar on carbon management even further.

In closing, we are grateful to our funders, the Bullitt Foundation and the Claudine and Stephen Bronfman Family Foundation, for recognizing the opportunities associated with putting the spotlight on climate change at Vancouver 2010. We would also like to thank the VANOC sustainability team and all the athletes involved in *Play It Cool* and the NHLPA Carbon Neutral Challenge, and in particular Sara Renner, Thomas Grandi and Andrew Ference.

Chapter 7

One Planet 2012

How NGOs Can Help to Transform Sustainability in Sport

Sue Riddlestone

Introduction

When I heard in the summer of 2003 that London was putting together a bid to host the 2012 Olympic and Paralympic Games (2012 Games), my first reaction was: "what a terrible idea". As an environmentalist, for me this conjured up visions of spectators flying in to London from around the world, and a lot of money to be spent on resource intensive sport buildings and infrastructure which would turn out to be wasteful follies. But I became involved in helping London to win the bid and then to deliver on its sustainability promises; today I feel part of the team and am very proud of what we have achieved together. We will have to wait until 2013 or later to see the ultimate sustainability outcomes from hosting the event, but the signs are good and many people are working to see the 2012 Games set a new benchmark for sustainability. In this chapter, I will tell the story of how sustainability NGOs worked together with the London 2012 bid team, the London 2012 Organising Committee for the Olympic and Paralympic Games

(LOCOG), the Olympic Delivery Authority (ODA), and others, and some of the lessons we have learned. The aim is to provide useful insights which others can apply.

Personal roles and responsibilities

I am the Director of a London based social enterprise and charity called BioRegional Development Group (BioRegional). We work with partners to build real-life sustainable communities such as the BedZED eco-village in London and many international projects. We also set up sustainable supply chains and enterprises like our kerbside recycling company *The Laundry*. We take a practical and solutions-focused approach to our projects, which are aimed at helping us to live more sustainably.

I originally became involved in the 2012 Games as a member of the London Sustainable Development Commission (LSDC), which is an independent, voluntary body which plays a critical friend role to the Mayor of London. In 2003, the then Mayor of London, Ken Livingstone, asked the LSDC to advise the London 2012 bid team on the sustainability of their plans. The bid masterplanners presented their outline plans for an Olympic Park, which encompassed an area known as the Lower Lea Valley, to the LSDC in September 2003. Those of us that wanted to help then visited the site in East London, close to the former docklands. As the masterplanners had explained, the community had suffered from lack of investment and was criss-crossed with roads, railway lines, electricity pylons, rivers and canals. The many derelict sites sported beer cans and buddleia bushes and recycling yards abounded. Yet the rivers and canals were lovely and a visit to the local pub confirmed what a great community it was. We could see, just as Mayor Livingstone had pointed out, that a 2012 Games-led regeneration could bring a sense of local pride, create jobs and a better, more sustainable community for the local people. This is what made me and many others want to get involved in the bid.

Mayor Livingstone had given the LSDC the authority to review and influence the bid plans. The bid team had actually been doing a good job, but we were able to make suggestions for improvements to the Masterplan, the Sustainability Statement and the Environment theme of the bid candidature file to be submitted to the International Olympic Committee (IOC). We carried out training sessions and sustainability workshops with the bid team. On reflection, it was important that the Mayor placed such high importance on sustainability and gave the LSDC the necessary access and authority. The bid team organised consultation meetings and workshops where many organisations were able to contribute to the plans and proposals. A lot of input was given freely by these NGOs and stakeholders and this built support for the bid. There was a tremendous amount of goodwill.

In 2004 David Stubbs, an experienced professional in sport and the environment, was appointed as Head of Sustainability for the London 2012 bid. Through BioRegional's engagement at NGO consultation meetings, we started to work with David and began to develop the idea of using the one planet living sustainability framework and principles (see Figure 1) – which we had developed from our work on sustainable communities – and applying it to the London 2012 bid. BioRegional and WWF-UK worked together with David and presented what we called the "One Planet Olympics" to Lord Sebastian Coe, Sir Keith Mills and other senior staff at the London 2012 bid company. They liked it! BioRegional was then commissioned to write the sustainability strategy for London's 2012 Games bid.

Figure 1: Ten principles of one planet living

I believe there were at least four reasons why the London 2012 bid team decided to work more closely with BioRegional and WWF-UK to develop their sustainability strategy. Firstly, a good working relationship had already been established and we had demonstrated we were knowledgeable and could be helpful. Then there was the halo effect of the bid being associated with charities. WWF and their panda logo are one of the most trusted environmental brands in the world with an international reputation. This tripartite relationship gave the bid team access to cost effective expertise, including BioRegional's practical experience in developing innovative solutions for sustainability in the built environment and in sustainable business operations. Finally, the simple and holistic framework and communications story of "one planet living" worked well for the 2012 Games bid.

Lord Coe and the 2012 bid company agreed through a Memorandum of Understanding to work with BioRegional and WWF-UK, and to use the One Planet Living (OPL) approach and its ten principles, which were developed by BioRegional and WWF. This gave BioRegional the mandate to develop the sustainability strategy in those terms. Many good commitments had already been made up to that point, which we drew into the new strategy. But we were also able to add to it by using the OPL framework. For example, we included a commitment to procure sustainable food for the 2012 Games, which would be the first time this would be done for any Olympic and Paralympic Games (2005, London 2012, BioRegional & WWF-UK). We worked in partnership with David to develop the strategy, and he would then check with the bid company as to what they felt was achievable. We organised workshops on themes such as zero waste with other NGOs and stakeholders to get the benefit of their views and experience. This process and the work that had already been done in engaging NGOs meant that the strategy and the bid became stronger and everyone felt an ownership of it. This is important if you want a strategy to be delivered!

Gains and losses

Some things we pushed for were not included in the bid, such as zero carbon in event building energy use. The 2012 Games' approach instead became a strategy for a "low carbon Games" (2005, London 2012). We stood firm on what sustainability meant, but for carbon and some other issues, the bid team did not have the confidence that they could deliver them technically or cost effectively.

The LSDC wanted to ensure that the commitments made in the bid would be followed through if London won the right to host the 2012 Games, and therefore pushed forward the idea of creating an independent sustainability assurance body. It took some months of dedicated effort before and after the bid was won to secure agreement and funding for this assurance organisation. Crucially, the assurance body was referred to in London's bid candidature file. In 2007, the assurance body was established as the Commission for a Sustainable London 2012 (CSL). CSL has played a vital role in holding the many delivery bodies to account, and reminding them what was promised at an early enough stage to allow, in most cases, for corrections and improvements to be made. The CSL Chair and the leader of the CSL Secretariat Team Leader came from the LSDC and BioRegional respectively, and were involved since the bid stage, so they have an almost encyclopaedic grasp of their subject.

While the sustainability strategy was set out in the Environment theme of the candidature file, the bid team felt it was important to also produce an easy to read brochure to highlight the holistic sustainability framework. This brochure was called *Towards a One Planet Olympics* and was given to those who were most interested in this topic and to the IOC.

The sustainability strategy that was presented to the IOC in February of 2005 represented a step forward for sustainability at major sporting events. *Towards a One Planet Olympics* was acclaimed as "the best and most holistic sustainability strategy of all the bids" by environmental expert David Crawford (2005). The Chief Executive of WWF-UK at the time, Robert Napier, personally presented the strategy to the IOC on behalf of the bid team, WWF-UK and BioRegional. This involvement of NGOs and the innovative approach we brought added to the weight and credibility of the bid.

On the 6th July 2005, we gathered to watch the IOC's decision on television as the IOC President Jacques Rogge said: "the Games of the thirtieth Olympiad in 2012 are awarded to the city of ... London"! We were amazed, delighted and so proud of the fantastic professional team who had worked on the bid. It was an unforgettable moment for our country and in my life, and just shows how sport can bring people together. Everyone was pleased with what had been achieved and the Olympics Minister Tessa Jowell wrote to thank us and confirmed the commitment to the One Planet Olympics.

Looking back five years later, that moment was the high point, so far at least, of the influence of NGOs on the sustainability of the 2012 Games. I believe it was crucially important to have been involved at the earliest stages of the bid. We received the support of senior decision makers, and influenced the bid strategy and plans. Because these were included in the 2012 Games bid, they would have to be delivered as a binding commitment made to the IOC, and assured by the new independent body CSL.

As soon as London had won the right to host the 2012 Games, BioRegional and WWF-UK were in a much different position. The Olympic Park regeneration project turned quickly into a large commercial construction project with many companies working on it, multiple stakeholders to keep happy and an immovable deadline. It took six months after the bid was won for the Chief Executives of LOCOG and the ODA to be appointed, and during that time nobody we spoke to felt able to make commitments about how we as NGOs could work with them. We continued to attend meetings when invited and commented on plans and proposals while we waited for LOCOG and the ODA to get up and running. We thought about fundraising to support our work, but charitable funders did not see the 2012 Games as a suitable use of charitable funds, as LOCOG would be raising large amounts of private sponsorship funding. We therefore continued our work pro bono.

We met with the ODA's Chief Executive David Higgins and LOCOG's Chief Executive Paul Deighton in late May of 2006, which was ten months after London won the right to host the 2012 Games. The two CEO's were very friendly, stated their commitment to sustainability and said that they were delighted to have us inside the tent. I think the ODA and LOCOG were open-minded about how WWF-UK and BioRegional could continue to work with them, but perhaps they weren't sure what to do with us. At the time, there seemed to be a conflict between the idea of us as NGOs becoming independent arbiters of how well they were doing, versus having us work with the delivery team and help them, at which point we would not be seen as independent. From our point of view, we wanted to continue to work with them and help to make the 2012 Games the first sustainable Olympic and Paralympic Games, which was promised during the bid.

In effect what has happened is that both WWF-UK and BioRegional have continued to engage and work with the ODA and LOCOG on the sustainability of this huge project in an unofficial capacity as high level stakeholders. BioRegional have used our own funds and have won grant and consultancy funding working on aspects of the 2012 Games. For example, BioRegional raised some government funding to support reclamation and reuse of demolition materials, and we chose to direct some of these funds towards the demolition activities on the Olympic Park. On a site visit, we saw that buildings were being demolished in such as way that materials could not be reclaimed for reuse (versus downcycling through crushing), and alerted the ODA to this. The ODA allowed us to work on site to survey the remaining buildings and work with the demolition team to facilitate reclamation and reuse. We also gave talks to designers working on the Olympic Park venues to help them to think ahead about reusing the demolition materials in their designs. We then convinced the ODA to allow BioRegional to document this work and key learning as part of the learning legacy. At the time of writing this chapter, the report is awaiting publication by the ODA.

WWF-UK has supported a full time member of staff at both BioRegional and WWF-UK to work alongside the 2012 Games organisers and stakeholders on aspects of sustainability since 2007. This allows BioRegional to continue to input and advise on the 2012 Games programme, for example on the London 2012 Sustainability Plan *Towards a One Planet 2012* (2007, revised in December 2009) or to assist with research on topic areas such as alternatives to PVC. We have a good working relationship with the 2012 Games delivery team, but post bid there continues to be a question as to our role as NGOs.

Where are we going?

So now, with less than two years to go until the 2012 Games begin, we can consider: Have NGOs helped to transform the sustainability of the 2012 Games, and what has worked well?

The 2012 Games does look set to reach new heights in sustainability which we hope will leave a lasting legacy for other sporting events. The NGOs helped to set binding, stretching, innovative, yet realistic targets at the earliest stages by working closely with the bid team. This, combined with the halo effect of association with sustainability charities, can only have helped London to win the right to host the 2012 Games. NGOs have been helpful and constructive, with many NGOs contributing through consultation meetings and at their own expense. NGOs have also worked as part of the delivery team and in a professional and business-like manner, sometimes bringing their own resources to enable this. NGOs in the 21st century are increasingly social entrepreneurs who bring credibility and expertise, taking a much more constructive, solutions-focused approach. NGOs have also played a critical friend role; for example, when some tenders went out in the early days after the bid was won without reference to sustainability, we noticed it and put pressure on to get mechanisms quickly in place to address this issue. At the time of writing we are briefing newcomers to the project on the Legacy commitments made in the bid, and again offering our help to deliver on these promises.

But there is always room for improvement. After the bid was won it would have been better to define clear roles and responsibilities for the NGOs who had worked so hard alongside the bid team. The assurance body CSL has the authority to point out issues that need remedying; but unlike at the bid stage, NGOs are no longer a required element for the delivery bodies, and may even seem to the delivery bodies like a liability to be managed.

Because we decided we still had something unique to offer and wanted to follow through on what we had started during the bid, we have found a way to play a useful role in delivery. But the effectiveness of our efforts has been reduced because of our unofficial role.

Conclusion

To conclude, NGOs can bring something extra to the creation of sustainable sporting events. Their motivation is to work for the good of society rather than their personal profit, and if you get NGOs on-side they will work hard and can mobilise the wider society and stakeholders. Don't expect them to always work for nothing; NGOs still have to pay the rent. It is also useful for event organisers to check NGO credentials prior to engaging, as some NGOs will be more useful than others. NGOs can bring credibility and high levels of expertise. Based on my experience, I recommend that event organisers seek out NGOs with the skills and experience you need and get them involved early on at the planning stage. Consultation meetings and workshops can be a useful way to draw in suitable partners. If you can find a way, work them into the delivery and evaluation. Working with organisations who want to make the world a better place can only enhance the quality of a sporting event.

References

London 2012 Candidate City (2005) *Towards a One Planet Olympics* – achieving the first sustainable Olympic and Paralympic Games http://www.bioregional.com/what-we-do/our-work/one-planet-2012/

David Crawford (2005) *2012 Olympic Bids and Sustainability*, Analysis by David Crawford. Posted: Saturday, June 25, 2005 on http://www.aroundtherings.com

London 2012 (2005) Environment and Meteorology Volume 1 Theme 5, pages 74-87 http://www.london2012.com/documents/candidate-files/theme-5-environment.pdf

London 2012 (2007) *Towards a one planet 2012* – London 2012 Sustainability Plan http://www.london2012.com/documents/locog-publications/london-2012-sustainability-plan.pdf

Chapter 8
The European Healthy Stadia Network

Sports Stadia, Public Health and Sustainability

Matthew Philpott and Russell Seymour

Introduction

In this chapter, the authors will introduce the Healthy Stadia concept, its origins, and how the concept has been adopted in practice. The chapter will then chart the rising importance of environmental sustainability to the Healthy Stadia agenda and the links between sustainability and public health. Finally, the authors will give examples of sustainability initiatives embraced by sports stadia, moving on to a case study of the Lord's Cricket Ground (UK) detailing their waste management and recycling schemes and wider sustainability strategy.

Sports Stadia and Health

There has been a long standing acknowledgment of the health benefits and societal gains to be made through participation in physical activity and sports[1]. Through advances in sports science, nutrition and training tech-

---

1. WHO (World Health Organisation) 2003

niques, we now have the fittest and fastest generation of athletes on the playing field, track and in the pool. However, there has only been limited attention[2] paid to the role that both professional and amateur sports clubs, and in particular *their stadia* as hubs of the community, can contribute to raising the levels of public health and wellbeing, social cohesion and – of specific interest to this paper–environmental sustainability.

For many years the idea of utilising a 'setting' to promote health and reduce health inequalities has been applied to a number of everyday environments. The settings approach developed quickly after the World Health Organisation's (WHO) Ottawa Charter[3] laid the foundations for much of modern health promotion, shifting the emphasis away from the individual and concentrating on the living environments and organisational structures as a medium to promote health. This approach has already seen success in contexts of schools, workplaces and even hospitals and prisons, and has been used by public health agencies[4] (in particular the WHO) to deliver interventions aimed at tackling lifestyle issues associated with smoking, diet and even substance misuse. Over the last five years, the potential for using sporting stadia as health promoting settings has started to be realised, not only to the benefit of local communities, but also to help achieve the corporate objectives of the clubs and stadia involved[5]. In the UK alone, a wide range of projects aimed at helping sports stadia to promote initiatives that fans and staff can *opt into* concerning lifestyle choices and social and environmental issues have been rolled out on a local and national level[6].

One of the most significant developments in this field in the last five years, certainly in terms of its geographical reach, has been the formation of a European Healthy Stadia Network. This Network, coordinated by UK based cardiovascular disease prevention charity Heart of Mersey and part-funded by the World Heart Federation, now consists of over 170 stadia and organisations and is the continuation of a public health pilot project, co-funded by the European Commission between July 2007 and December 2009. To date, the Network has brought together representatives from twelve European partner countries, and a mix of organisations involved in

---

2. For articles relating to professional sports stadia, see: Jackson et al. (2005). Crabb and Ratinckx (2005). For articles relating to health promotion through amateur clubs, see: Dobbinson et al. (2006). Kokko (2010).

3. WHO (World Health Organisation) (1986).

4. For introductory texts to the concept of health settings and health promotion using specific types of settings (hospitals, schools, prisons), see: Dooris (2004). Whitelaw et al. (2001). Pelikan et al. (2001). Lister-Sharp et al. (1999). Whitehead (2006).

5. For introductory texts to professional sport and CSR, see: Smith & Westerbeek (2007). Babiak & Wolfe (2009).

6. Within the UK, a number of governing bodies of sport and professional leagues have started to address the potential role of health promotion through sports stadia and professional sport, in particular: Premier League Health (football Premier League); Something to Chew On (Rugby Union's Premier Rugby); and, Clubs That Count (Business in the Community).

both sports and health. These include governing bodies of sport such as UEFA (Union of European Football Associations), health agencies such as the European Public Health Alliance and the World Heart Federation, and many well known clubs and stadia, including Liverpool FC's stadium Anfield (UK), Milan's San Siro Stadium (Italy), and the Aviva Stadium (the new national stadium for Ireland).

Healthy Stadia – Concept and Implementation

The concept of a 'Healthy Stadia' can be traced back to the modernisation of UK sporting stadia in light of the Bradford and Hillsborough tragedies of the late 1980's. Not only was there an imperative for stadia to become *safer* places for supporters to visit, but it was also recognised that there was a real opportunity for stadia to become viable healthy settings for both fans *and* employees.

Food and drink choices both inside and immediately surrounding the stadia are, in general, high in saturated fats and sugar[7]. Similarly, green transport access routes to stadia are often very poor, with cycle parking rarely offered, whilst the excellent fitness facilities inside stadia and training grounds are generally not accessible to the surrounding communities. In addition, the considerable marketing potential of playing staff is often used by companies promoting less healthy product lines, generally at odds with the nutritional intake of the athletes on the pitch. Whilst this conventional view of stadia and their 'offering' is still often the case, there are clear signs of change and huge opportunities ahead, and this assertion is backed up through a European audit of current 'Healthy Stadia' practice (see next section). Sports stadia play iconic roles in communities and are capable of reaching large numbers of people, both in the grounds and surrounding areas. Furthermore, the demographic and age-group of fans visiting stadia – middle aged, working class males – are exactly those who are the most susceptible to growing health problems such as obesity, cardiovascular disease, testicular cancer and mental health issues.

Realising these opportunities, from 2005 onwards a number of projects and initiatives in the North West of England have worked with local stadia to adopt healthy initiatives aimed at fans, visitors and staff[8]. As a result of these regional projects, a working definition of a 'healthy' stadium has been established, namely:

> *'Healthy Stadia are .....those which promote the health of visitors, fans, players, employees and the surrounding community... places where people can go to have a positive healthy experience playing or watching sport'*

---

7. For a useful discussion of food supply in stadia and football fans attitudes to food choices, see: Ireland and Watkins (2010).

8. Crabb & Ratinckx (2005). Haig & Crabb (2006).

In the case of a sub-regional pilot project run with stadia in the Merseyside area of the UK – including stadia representing football (Everton, Liverpool and Tranmere FCs), rugby league (St Helens and Widnes RLFCs) and horse racing (Aintree Race Course) – the healthy stadia approach has been firmly based on a commitment to partnership-working with local agencies, encompassing health services, urban regeneration agencies, emergency services, education, transport authorities, and food and drink suppliers. Many successful healthy lifestyle initiatives have been developed over a five year period and embedded within stadia, examples of which include:

- Displaying and promoting the fruit and vegetable 5-a-day message to supporters and visitors. For one stadium, this includes a fruit delivery scheme in the main reception area, with a range of healthier food choice options now available in staff canteens.
- Players' diets and healthy eating messages are included on the club websites in a 'Healthy Stadia' section. Players now regularly endorse healthy eating messages in the work they do with local communities.
- Initiatives have been rolled out that are aimed at increasing physical activity in children through various community schemes, and use of stadia training facilities.
- Local health walks have been developed to and from stadia with encouragement to progress to more advanced exercise, with pedometers provided.

Even at this early stage in the development of the Healthy Stadia concept, it was recognised by sports clubs and local partner agencies that there were distinct opportunities for sports stadia to make a positive impact on the overlapping areas of public health and environmental sustainability, and this will be discussed in further detail in later sections of this paper. Therefore, in addition to the lifestyle initiatives already described, stadia in Merseyside also adopted green travel plans to encourage walking and cycling to stadia, including cycle storage made available at some sites, whilst all stadia became smoke free before UK legislation came into effect, with many now looking to support those wishing to quit smoking through smoking cessation drop-in clinics.

European Programme of Work

Following the success and interest generated by the Merseyside Healthy Stadia Programme, a successful proposal for a 'Sports Stadia and Community Health' project was made to the European Commission in the framework of its Public Health Programme[9]. This project worked with an initial group of partner agencies in Finland, Greece, Italy, Latvia, Ireland, Poland,

---

9.Parker & Ireland (2007).

Spain and the UK, and was tasked with piloting the Healthy Stadia concept with stadia in a cross-section of European countries and developing suitable guidance documentation to further the future roll out of healthy initiatives. One of the key activities for the European programme has been to establish a benchmark of current practice concerning Healthy Stadia initiatives across Europe. Following an initial literature review, in March 2008 a questionnaire enquiring into the stadium's age, ownership, capacity and range of 'healthy' initiatives was disseminated by European project partners for an eight month period, resulting in returns from 10 different countries, representing over 12 different sports. Of the returns, 51% of respondents were involved in community engagement, with 55% participating in partnership-working, whilst an impressive 70% of stadia and clubs had players working as 'health champions' within their communities. The majority of initiatives focused on the themes of tobacco control in stadia and smoking cessation, and healthy food and drink choices, whilst there was also substantial work in the areas of physical activity, mental health and, of particular significance to this paper, green transport planning, promotion of public transport and car pooling, water and/or energy saving schemes and stadia-based recycling programmes.

Building on this initial evidence base, the key product that has been created through the European project is a Healthy Stadia 'Toolkit'. This guidance document is aimed at stadia management and intermediary partner agencies, and has drawn heavily on pilot projects that have been run with sports stadia in Finland, Ireland, Spain and Latvia. The Toolkit provides users with a walk-through of the basic steps needed to role out Healthy Stadia initiatives, such as putting an action plan together, locating partners, evaluation and mainstreaming of healthy initiatives. This set of guidance is also supported by a host of case studies drawn together from stadia participating in the Programme, and these have been grouped together under the three themes of Lifestyle, Social and Environmental. The Toolkit and a selection of its case studies are available as a hard copy document and as an online toolkit available at: www.healthystadia.eu.

In order to disseminate much of the learning and results from this programme of work, a European conference was held in Liverpool (UK) in September 2009, where the Healthy Stadia Network was officially launched. In addition to keynote speeches from UEFA, the European Commission and major sports stadia such as Anfield (Liverpool FC) and the Amsterdam Arena, the findings from the audit of current practice, the piloting of the Toolkit and case studies generated through the European programme were disseminated to over 250 delegates[10].

---

10. To access conference presentations, conference report and all published documents produced by the EU funded programme of work, please see: www.healthystadia.eu/index.php/resources/downloads.html

Environmental Sustainability & Public Health

Charting the growth of the Healthy Stadia Network since 2005, firstly within the UK and then in other European countries, it is interesting to note that what started as a project predominantly focussed upon sports stadia and lifestyle initiatives, has increasingly seen greater interest from stadia in adopting environmental sustainability initiatives that also have a positive affect on health. The interrelationship between health, the environment and health inequalities has been brought keenly into relief in recent years, and is now recognised as a key theme across all sectors of society; from businesses such as sports stadia to the fans and employees that utilise them, there is a growing recognition that in order to promote good levels of health and to reduce health inequalities, there is also an overwhelming responsibility to promote a healthy environment[11].

In addition to traditional conceptions of health, such as freedom from disease and positive lifestyle choices, there is now recognition of key environment and health 'interfaces'[12], including, good quality and well located housing, green transport options (safe walking and cycling routes), protection of clean air and water, low exposure to noise, and as discussed in the following case study, minimisation of waste. Within the context of sports stadia, many of these *joint* environment and health themes have now been recognised as areas of intervention from the perspective of environmental impact. In addition, there is also a growing recognition amongst sports clubs and major sporting events that they can use their iconic status at both local and global level to promote environmental responsibility amongst end users – fans, viewers, staff and residents in local communities[13].

Over the course of Healthy Stadia's European programme of work, a wide range of environmental-based initiatives have been set up to positively affect the health of fans, employees and local communities[14]. As a direct result of the programme, stadia in Ireland have promoted walking routes to stadia with the additional supply of safety walking lights to school children during winter months, whilst a collection of stadia in Finland have developed a widely adopted car pooling scheme for professional players, staff and fans alike. In Latvia, stadia have used the powerful voice of local sports stars from basketball and volleyball to promote environmentally friendly lifestyles to local school children, and in the UK clubs such as Liverpool FC have rolled out initiatives that both engage and incentivise local children to clear away litter from areas surrounding the stadium on match days.

---

11. Griffiths & Stewart (2008). Griffiths et al. (2009).

12. See, Donaldson & Donaldson (2003). in particular Chapter 10.

13. Smith and Westerbeek (2004). Schmidt (2006).

14. Please refer to the European Healthy Stadia Network's website 'Case Studies' for further information – www.healthystadia.eu

It is widely recognised that numerous new-build stadia have 'designed-in' sustainability features – e.g. rain harvesting systems – as part of their everyday operations[15], whilst existing stadia are already working towards environmental standards accreditation aligned to their operations, for example the ISO 14001 certification (Environmental Management Systems), and more recently in the UK, the BS8901 certification in Sustainable Event Management. Examples of this work include systems leading towards a lowering of CO_2 emissions and energy consumption, water conservation techniques, and recycling and waste management schemes. An example of a newly built stadium that personifies an integrated approach taken to environmentally sustainable operations that has recently joined the European Healthy Stadia Network is the Aviva Stadium in Dublin, Ireland. In addition to the stadium's design supporting extensive use of natural light, and the development of a rainwater harvesting system that can store up to 32,000 litres of water for pitch irrigation, the Aviva Stadium has taken an innovative 'peer approach' to promoting water and energy efficiency. In the spirit of transparency and peer motivation, the Aviva Stadium now discloses its energy and water consumption behavioural patterns and utility related footprint to ensure a best practice approach in all areas of operation. Not only is this practice a useful self-monitoring strategy for the stadium, but this is also intended to encourage other stadia to become equally transparent and participate in similar activities.

Finally, it should be noted that in addition to the public health, social and environmental benefits of adopting a Healthy Stadia approach, it has become clear from engagement with stadia across Europe that there is also a coherent *business case* to be made to stadia management and partner organisations involved in delivering Healthy Stadia initiatives. Engaging with the *wider* Healthy Stadia agenda can help build a positive corporate profile, engage with a broader audience, nurture new partnerships, uncover further business opportunities and help secure additional sources of funding. It is hoped that the growing recognition by sports clubs and stadia to engage positively with the burgeoning corporate and social responsibility movement will act as a vehicle to allow public health and its links with environmental sustainability to flourish in the years ahead.

To finish this chapter, and for the reader to understand the strategic and day to day considerations of stadia management engaged in environmental sustainability, there now follows a case study from Lords Cricket Ground in the UK. This case study is from a first person perspective, and offers a unique insight into the development of an integrated waste management system at an historic sports stadium, including its key considerations, challenges and successes to date.

---

15. For an introduction to architectural design of stadia and the imperative of environmental sustainability, see: John, G. et al. (2007).

Lord's Case Study

Dr Russell Seymour, Sustainability Manager – Lord's Cricket Ground, UK

In recent years, sustainability has become a significant political and social issue. Rising energy and water costs, increasing insurance premiums, variation to business because of climate impacts, and the likelihood of further regulation and reputational issues mean that forward-thinking businesses are addressing sustainability and will continue to do so. The Marylebone Cricket Club (MCC) and Lord's Cricket Ground believe that sports stadia should be no exception; it could be argued that, with its need for a clean and healthy environment for athletes to train and compete in and its expectation of fair-play, sport is closer to these issues than many other businesses.

To substantiate this argument, in a recent (2010) survey of spectators at Lord's Cricket Ground, more than 80% thought that sports venues should behave in an environmentally friendly way and 95% said that they would be willing to cooperate with a venue's efforts to be more environmentally friendly. So how should we meet these expectations?

The first step is to understand exactly what it is you are confronting. Sustainability is broad and it pervades everything that you do. It should never be a 'bolt-on' at the end of the process; it has to be part of the process, part of what you do, which often requires a change of attitudes and this can take time. In my current position as Sustainability Manager at Lord's, I consider issues in relation to seven categories; waste, utilities use (including greenhouse gas emissions), materials and procurement, transport and communication, health and welfare, community and charity, and biodiversity. An overarching factor is management and education. Some of these areas are not my direct responsibility and some have more significant impacts than others. The 'maturity' of each category is considered in terms of a sustainability progression; the steps are not necessarily exclusive, but they do give a logical progression in improving performance. An example for waste management is given in the table below:

1. Do nothing	No attempt to reduce the amount of waste; mingled waste; no recycling; all waste going to landfill.
2. Internal management	
2a. Manage the end of the process	Set targets to reduce waste; dispose of waste in separated waste streams, maximise recycling and minimise landfill.
2b. Manage the whole internal process	Manage waste production (not just disposal). Staff self-sort waste. Consider waste production in procurement decisions.
3. External engagement	
3a. Engage business stakeholders	Inform stakeholders. Require contractors to use environmentally friendly, recycled and/or recyclable materials. Reduce and/or send back packaging to suppliers.
3b. Engage public, media and community	Publicise performance. Publicly report and feedback information. Create recycling initiatives for the local community.

We have had some success in recent seasons at Lord's in improving our waste management. We have three interlinked objectives: to reduce the amount of waste produced (measured per spectator); to increase recycling; and, to reduce waste to landfill. Along with our waste management contractor we have achieved zero waste to landfill for the 2010 season (notwithstanding an inert fraction of ash that does go to landfill). Waste that previously went to landfill now goes to produce 'refuse derived fuel', a waste-to-energy initiative that reduces the use of fossil fuels in generating electricity. Of course, incineration of waste does throw up other environmental issues; but, in terms of carbon dioxide, the fuel replaces equivalent quantities of fossil fuel effectively off-setting the emissions.

Our challenge now is to increase recycling; no easy task as this requires affecting the behaviour of a crowd that may not be expecting to see self-sort recycling stations in a sports ground. With landfill taxes increasing annually, there is a clear business case for managing waste more effectively, and this is generally true across the board for all sustainability issues as initiatives generally relate to greater efficiency.

The other six categories are developed to a greater or lesser degree of maturity; we are by no means perfect and there are always opportunities to improve. Ultimately, for Lord's Cricket Ground – and potentially other sports stadia – sustainability equates to efficiency, responsible stewardship and longevity; it is a way of thinking that encompasses economic, environmental and social issues to ensure future survival.

References

Babiak, K & Wolfe, R. (2009). Determinants of corporate social responsibility in professional sport: Internal and external factors. Journal of Sport Management, 2009, 23, 717-742.

Crabb, J & Ratinckx, L. (2005). The healthy stadia initiative. North West Public Health Team, Department of Health (UK).

Dobbinson, S.J. Hayman, J.A. Livingston, P.M. (2006). Prevalence of health promotion policies in sports clubs in Victoria, Australia. Health Promotion Int, 21, 121-129.

Donaldson, L & Donaldson R. (2003). Essential Public Health, Second Edition (Revised). Oxford: Radcliffe Publishing.

Dooris, M. (2004). Joining up settings for health: a valuable investment for strategic partnerships? Critical Public Health, 14, 37-49.

Griffiths, J. Rao, M., Adshead, F. and Thorpe, A. (Eds). (2009). The Health Practitioner's Guide to Climate Change: Diagnosis and Cure. London: Earthscan.

Griffiths, J. & Stewart, L. (2008). Sustaining a Healthy Future. London: Faculty of Public Health.

Haig, M & Crabb, J. (2006). Healthy Stadia Report 2005/06. Liverpool: Heart of Mersey.

Ireland, R & Watkins, F. (2010). Football fans and food: a case study of a football club in the English Premier League. Public Health Nutrition, 13:682-687. Cambridge University Press.

Jackson, N.W. Howes, F.S. Gupta, S. Doyle, J.L. Waters, E. (2005). Policy interventions implemented through sporting organizations for promoting healthy behaviour change. Cochrane Database of Systematic Reviews, 2, CD004812.

John, G. Sheard, J and Vickery, B. (2007). Stadia: A Design and Development Guide (4th Edition). Oxford: Architectural Press (Elsevier).

Kokko, S. (2010). Health Promoting Sports Club. Studies in Sport, Physical Education and Health 144. Jyvaskyla: University of Jyvaskyla.

Lister-Sharp D, Chapman S, Stewart-Brown S, Sowden A. (1999). Health promoting schools and health promotion in schools: two systematic reviews. Health Technology Assessment 1999;3 (22).

Parker, M & Ireland, R. (2007). Sports Stadia and Community Health. Annexe 1: Description of the Action. Proposal to the Public Health Executive Agency of the Health and Consumer Protection Directorate of the European Union. Unpublished.

Pelikan, J.M. Krajic, K. Dietscher, C. (2001). The health promoting hospital (HPH): concept and development. Patient Education and Counselling, 45, 239-243.

Schmidt, C. (2006). Putting the Earth in Play: Environmental Awareness and Sports. Environmental Health Perspectives. 2006. 114(5): A286–A295.

Smith, A. & Westerbeek, H. (2004). The Sport Business Future. London: Palgrave Macmillan.

Smith, A. & Westerbeek, H. (2007). Sport as a Vehicle for Deploying Corporate Social Responsibility, Journal of Corporate Citizenship, 7(25): 43-54.

Whitehead, D. (2006). The health promoting prison (HPP) and its imperative for nursing. International Journal of Nursing Studies, 43, 123-131.

Whitelaw, S. Baxedale, A. Bryce, C. Machardy, L. Young, I. Witney, E. (2001). 'Settings' based health promotion: a review. Health Promotion International, 16, 339-353.

WHO (World Health Organisation) (1986). Ottawa Charter for health promotion. Copenhagen: WHO European Regional Office.

WHO (World Health Organisation) (2003). Health and Development through Physical Activity and Sport. Geneva: WHO.

Part III

Sustainability and the Olympic Games and Paralympic Games

Chapter 9

Do the Olympic Games Lead to a Sustainable Increase in Grassroots Sport Participation?

A Secondary Analysis of Athens 2004

Athanasios Pappous

Introduction

Hosting the Olympic Games is a notoriously expensive operation, and the International Olympic Committee (IOC) and host national governments have to justify the huge cost and investments. The Athens 2004 Olympic and Paralympic Games (2004 Games) had an overall cost to the Organising Committee of US $11 billion, almost double the initial stated budget. Six years later, Greece has just requested a €45bn bailout package from the EU and International Monetary Fund to avoid bankruptcy. Currently, criticism of the Greek fiscal policy has sharpened and voices are raised arguing that the 2004 Games spending played an important part in helping Greece fall into debt crisis (Gatopoulos, 2010). Other Olympic and Paralympic Games (Games) host cities' concerns centre around the huge investments governments put into Olympic and Paralympic sport. This is highlighted by the organisers of the forthcoming London 2012 Olympic and Paralympic Games (2012 Games), who have recently announced that US $39 million is to be cut from the 2012 Games budget (Associated Press, 2010). Under the uncertain economic climate and the growing criticism against the economic sustainability of the Games, an important question needs to be answered: Does hosting of sport mega events, such as the Games contribute to sustainable economic and social development, making them worthwhile governmental investments?

This question is particularly pertinent today, as most countries are facing severe economic constraints (e.g., recession, inflation, currency de-valuation). The most commonly stated argument for hosting the Games involves the notion of *sustainability* and the social benefits and legacies of the Games.

Sustainable development is the policy agenda of our time and it is becoming a hot topic in the interdisciplinary research agenda. However, sustainability is a complex term that is difficult for the general public to understand. The editors of this book suggest that sustainability refers to "a holistic perspective that harmonises social, economic and environmental dimensions and systems and balance opportunities and constraints". Indeed, sustainability is an ambiguous umbrella term that encompasses a wide range of definitions. Most of the discussion and information around sustainability that we read, listen to and watch in the media use anecdotal rather than empirical evidence (Murphy and Bauman, 2007). Despite the wealth of information about the Games, empirical research around the social legacy of the Games is surprisingly scarce.

Given the plethora of sustainability indices and dimensions available, the present study will focus on whether the 2004 Games inspired people to lead a more active lifestyle. According to the typology developed by Laura Keogh (2009), the sport participation dimension constitutes a *soft* legacy:

> "A hard legacy may comprise the construction of sporting venues and associated infrastructure and soft legacies may relate to increased sporting participation". (p.8)

In this chapter, secondary sources from Eurobarometer surveys are used to examine whether grassroots sport participation of the Greek population was boosted as a result of hosting the 2004 Games.

Grassroots participation after the Games: From Athens to London

> *"We want the Games, are eager for the Games. We love our country and we love the Games. For us, the Olympics is a way of life."*
> (Gianna Angelopoulos-Daskalaki)

These were the words of the president of the Greek 2004 Games bid committee, Gianna Angelopoulos, in August 1997 (Longman, 1997), just one month before the IOC awarded the city of Athens with the right to host the Games of the XXVIII Olympiad. This kind of rhetoric regarding the Olympic tradition provided the members of the IOC the sentimental choice to return them to their birthplace.

However, at the time when Athens was bidding for the Games, several studies were indicating that instead of an *Olympic way of life,* contemporary Greeks were adopting a rather sedentary lifestyle which was becoming a serious epidemic. In 1999 a Pan-European study (De Almeida et al. 1999) concluded that, together with Portugal, Greece shared the highest inactive population in Europe. This finding was confirmed a couple of years later by a random, multi-stage sample survey which took place in the Greek province of Attica, which highlighted that half of the interviewees reported being physically inactive (Pitsavos et al. 2005). So the question remains: Did the staging of the 2004 Games in Athens lead to any sustainable change in the lifestyle of Greeks by increasing participation in sport and physical activity?

The above question is particularly salient at present, two years prior the celebration of the 2012 Games, and form part of a timely research agenda regarding the Social Sustainability of the Games. Media attention and re-search scholars are currently questioning the possible effects that mega sport events might have in increasing the sport participation of the host population. Indeed, one of the most prominent key pledges from the organiz-ers of the 2012 Games is to "make the UK a world-leading sporting na-tion" and "to increase sport participation"[1]. The goal set by the UK Govern-ment is to increase the physical activity level by at least two million in Eng-land by 2012 (NHS, 2009); a target that is regarded as being extremely am-bitious (Coalter, 2004). In fact there are several voices alleging that the 2012 Games may fail to deliver on its promise to promote the nationwide pop-ularity of physical activity, as it has been claimed. The 2012 Games organ-izers and Government are frequently being criticized by those critical of the 2012 Games for supposedly constructing an elitist project, instead of provid-ing a detailed plan for improving participation in grassroots sport. Lord Se-bastian Coe, Chairman of the London 2012 Organising Committee of the Olympic Games and Paralympic Games (LOCOG), contested these allega-tions by stating that:

> *"I will fight the nostrum that this is just about elite sport. The challenge is not whether we finish fourth or 20th in the medals table but what we do to convert big British mo-ments into 10,000 more kids picking up sport."* (Beard, 2008)

However, evidence for the impact of the 2012 Games on sustained particip-ation in sport is open to doubt. Research does not offer clear results to ar-gue that mega sport events increase long-term sport participation.

This issue is addressed herein by evaluating whether there has been any long-term increase in sport participation following the 2004 Games. In or-der to carry out this task, a three period analysis based on Eurobarometer surveys from one year prior to the 2004 Games (EORG 58.2), just after the

---

1.*London 2012 Legacy Vision Presented to IOC* (12 June 2007). London 2012. See: ht-tp://www.london2012.com/press/media-releases/2007/06/london-2012-legacy-vis-ion--presented-to-ioc.php (accessed November 2010).

2004 Games (EORG 62.0) and five years following the culmination of the 2004 Games (EORG 72.3) are utilized.

Eurobarometers

Eurobarometers are surveys across European Union member states where all participants are aged 15 years and over, and are interviewed face-to-face in the respondent's home and in their corresponding national language. The sample design which is applied in all member states is a multi-stage, representative sample of each country.

According to Abel (2004, as cited in Tzormpatzakis, 2007), the Eurobarometer 58.2 was the first survey at a European level to investigate health-enhancing physical activity. Following the pioneer survey 58.2 which took place in 2002, the Sport Unit of the European Union renewed the census in 2004 and in 2009 and commissioned polls 62.0 and 72.3 respectively. Despite the slight modifications in the questionnaires which took place in the three waves of the survey, the majority of the questions are comparable and set the ground for long term assessment. In the following sections there will be an examination of the responses to the survey questions which are related to sport participation.

Results

Figure 1 shows the percentage of the Greek respondents who stated that they exercise regularly. The results are broken down for three periods corresponding to the three waves of the above mentioned Eurobarometers: before the 2004 Games (2003), just after the 2004 Games (2004) and five years after the 2004 Games (2009).

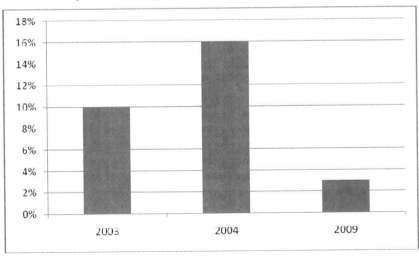

Figure 1. Greek respondents who declared they exercise regularly

The bar graphs corresponding to the 2003 and 2004 surveys highlight a significant upward trend (+6%) in levels of physical activity following the 2004 Games in 2004. However, the number of interviewees affirming that they do sport three times or more per week decreased significantly in 2009, five years after the celebration of the 2004 Games. Indeed, the data from the 2009 survey reports that Greece, together with Italy and Bulgaria, had the lowest number of citizens who play sport regularly (3%) in the European Union.

Important findings on the impact that hosting the 2004 Games might have had on the grassroots sport participation can be also drawn from comparing the percentage of those respondents who in 2003, 2004 and 2009 said that they <u>never exercise</u> (Figure 2). Did the celebration of the 2004 Games inspire the most sedentary part of the Greek society to become more physically active?

Figure 2 illustrates the percentage of Greek citizens who reported being completely sedentary. The first element that immediately draws attention is the significant decrease, from an average of 75% of the population in 2003 to 57% in 2004. As noted in the Eurobarometer report:

"The evolution compared to last year [2003] turns out to be especially positive in the country organising the most important sports event of the year, the Olympic Games. In fact, the proportion of interviewees who claim to never play a sport has decreased by 18 points in Greece compared to the results of 2003 (from 75% to 57%)". (EORG, 72.3).

However, as can be seen on the third bar corresponding to the 2009 data, the decrease in the percentage of the inactive people did not last. Five years after the closing ceremony of the 2004 Games, the percentage of Greeks reporting they were completely sedentary increased to 67% (+10).

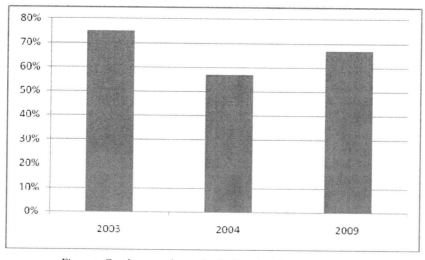

Figure 2. Greek respondents who declare that they never exercise
(census 2003, 2004 and 2009)

Discussion and Conclusion

Data from the 2003 and 2004 Eurobarometer questionnaires referring to sport participation indicate a significant increased number of Greeks reporting exercising regularly (from 10% in 2003 to 16% in 2009), while at the same time the representative sample of people responding that they never exercise decreased significantly (from 75% in 2003 to 57% in 2004).

Before assuming a direct correlation between hosting the 2004 Games and the overall more positive attitude of Greeks towards sport participation in 2004, some important national and international contextual parameters which might have influenced this upward trend need to be considered. During the summer of 2004, Greece was the protagonist of one of the biggest surprises in sport history. Against the odds they won the Euro 2004 Football Championship, which generated an overwhelming sense of excitement and sporting euphoria amongst the Greek population that might have sparked enthusiasm for being active – as recorded in the 2004 Eurobarometer results. Another element that might have influenced the results is the fact that the European Parliament had established 2004 as the European Year of Education through Sport. This resulted in an abundance of initiatives in Greece designed specifically to raise awareness about the importance of physical activity and involved active sport promotion. Thus, precautions have to be taken when comparing data on sport participation chronologically, since several other extraneous factors may have positively or negatively influenced sport/physical activity participation statistics.

Moreover, a closer examination of the 2009 data indicates that the sport participation increase between 2003 and 2004 was only temporary, with no long-lasting effect on the overall sport participation of the host country. As can be observed in the 2009 Eurobarometer survey, five years after the Games, the percentage of people affirming that they exercise regularly had plummeted to a level that was significantly lower than the period before the 2004 Games (from 10% in 2003 to 3% in 2009); this result classified Greece as one of the most sedentary countries in the European Union. The lack of literature in this area makes it a difficult task to compare the findings of this secondary data analysis. However, the transient increase in sport participation recorded in the Greek population during the 2004 Games period corroborates an earlier study commissioned by the London Assembly, which examined the long-term impact on sports participation that the hosting of the Games had in Barcelona (1992 Games), Atlanta (1996 Games), Sydney (2000 Games) and Athens (2004 Games). In agreement with the findings expressed above, the 2007 London East Research Institute's report on previous Games indicated that there is evidence only of short-term increases in sports participation following the Games:

> "Sports participation increases are often assumed very readily by host cities. Both Barcelona and Sydney provide evidence for some positive short term impacts. However there is doubt about the sustainability of Olympic effects and Sydney evidence is ambiguous. There is a tendency prior to hosting the Games to presume a large positive impact on participation rates. However,

Olympic impact on sports participation, within the host city and more generally is reported to be positive only anecdotally. More detailed research has
been largely inconclusive, for example in Sydney" (London Assembly, London
East Research Institute, 2007, p.47)

The findings of this study are also consistent with the EdComs literature review (2007). This review observed that the benefits in terms of encouraging
participation in physical activity were short-term in nature.

In summary, this simple tripartite comparison of the Greek respondents
to the Eurobarometer surveys prior (2003), immediately after (October
2004) and five years after (2009) hosting the 2004 Games reveals that instead of producing a lasting impact on a generation of people who are ex-
cited about sport, the 2004 Games had a temporary impact on sport/phys-
ical activity participation.

Interviews conducted with Greek respondents in the Special Eurobarometer 213 "Citizens of the European Union and Sport" survey, conducted
between October 11 and October 31 of 2004, when respondents still had
vivid memories of the European football competition and the 2004 Games,
translated in 2004 to a significant upward trend (+6%) in sport participation. However, the 2009 data for this population suggests that if a broader
strategy towards an active lifestyle is not implemented, the sporting excitement will apparently not sustain participation, leading to a reduction and
possibly a 'rebound effect', where participation drops to levels lower than
during the pre-Games period (from 10% in 2003 to 3% in 2009).

Despite these discouraging long-terms trends, there appears to be a critical difference with the culture in the UK as it prepares to host the 2012
Games that may make a difference in avoiding the same fate as that seen
in Greece. The organisers of the 2004 Games did not prioritise an increase
in sport participation of the general population. Their main concern was to
ensure the security of the 2004 Games (Samatas, 2007). The 2004 Games
were the first to take place since the September 11th 2001 terrorist attacks
in the United States, and it was the risk of a terrorist attack which mono-
polised the interest of the organizers. As a result the security expenses of
the 2004 Games were colossal – three times the amount of money and security personnel than was used for the 2000 Games in Sydney. LOCOG and
the UK Government have established that the grassroots sporting legacy
should be a top priority and increasing participation in sport is a key legacy promise for the 2012 Games. In this sense, this will be a pioneer effort.
As Weed et al. (2008) noted, "no previous Games has employed strategies
towards raising physical activity or sport participation. As such, the use of
an Olympic Games to raise physical activity and sport participation has not
been attempted in any real sense." (p.8).

In that respect, it will be interesting to see if LOCOG and the UK
Government achieve their ambitious plans and manage to turn the UK into
a more active nation, or whether the results will have the same "firework
effect" reported in previous host cities, most notably in Athens in 2004,
where participation increased dramatically in the short-term, but was not
sustained.

References

Associated Press. (2010, May 24). Olympic organizers face $39 million cut in new government spending plans. *The Republic*. Retrieved from: http://www.therepublic.com/view/story/3f583244f86c4168b713-f75dd1035972/OLY--London_Budget_Cuts/

Beard, M. (2008, July 25). 2012 Games 'will fail to boost grassroots sport'. *London Evening Standard*. Retrieved from: http://www.thisislondon.co.uk/standard-olympics/article-23514159-2012-games-will-fail-to-boost-grassroots-sport.do

Coalter, F. (2004) Stuck in the Blocks? A sustainable sporting legacy. In A.Vigor, M.Mean and C.Tims (Eds.) After the Gold Rush: A sustainable Olympics for London. London: IPPR/Demos.

De Almeida M, Garcia P, Afonso C, D'Amicis A, Lappalainen R, Damkjaer S (1999). Physical activity levels and body weight in a nationally representative sample in European Union. Public Health Nutr 2: 105–13.

EdComs (2007). London 2012 Legacy Research: Final Report. London: COI/DCMS.

European Opinion Research Group (2003). Special Eurobarometer 183–6/Wave 58.2 "Physical activity". Brussels: European Commission.

European Opinion Research Group (2004). Special Eurobarometer 213/Wave 62.0 "The citizens of the European Union and Sport". Brussels: European Commission.

European Opinion Research Group (2009). Special Eurobarometer 334/Wave 72.3 "Sport and Physical Activity". Brussels: European Commission.

Gatopoulos, D. (3 June 2010). Did 2004 Olympics spark Greek financial crisis? The Associated Press

Jere Longman, Published: August 3, 1997, "Athens Pins Olympic Bid to World Meet". http://www.nytimes.com/1997/08/03/sports/athens-pins-olympic-bid-to-world-meet.html

Keogh, L. (2009). London 2012 Olympic legacies: Conceptualising legacy, the role of Communities and Local Government and the regeneration of East London. Department for Communities and Local Government: London

London Assembly- London East Research Institute. (2007). *A lasting legacy for London? Assessing the legacy of the Olympic Games and Paralympic Games*. Retrieved from: http://legacy.london.gov.uk/assembly/reports/econsd/lasting-legacy-uel-research.pdf

National Health Service (2009). *Go London: An active and healthy London for 2012 and beyond*. Retrieved from: http://www.thinkfeetfirst.com/webfiles/docs/Go%20London_16-07_LR_Web.pdf

Murphy, N. M., & Bauman, A. (2007). Mass sporting and physical activity events—are they "bread and circuses" or public health interven-

tions to increase population levels of physical activity? Journal of
Physical Activity & Health, 4(2), 193-202.

Pitsavos C, Panagiotakos DB, Lentzas Y, Stefanadis C. Epidemiology of
leisure-time physical activity in socio-demographic, lifestyle and
psychological characteristics of men and women in Greece: the
ATTICA Study. BMC Public Health 2005; 5:37

Samatas, M. (2007). Security and surveillance in the Athens 2004
Olympics: Some lessons from a troubled story. *International Criminal Justice Review, 17*, 220-238.

Tzormpatzakis, N., Sleap, M. (2007). Participation in physical activity and
exercise in Greece:a systematic literature review. International
Journal of Public Health, 52: 360–371

Weed, M. ,Coren, E., Fiore, J., Mansfield, L., Wellard, I., Chatziefstathiou,
D., Dowse, S.(2009). A Systematic Review of the Evidence Base
for Developing a Physical Activity and Health Legacy from the
London 2012 Olympic and Paralympic Games. Retreived from:
http://www.london.nhs.uk/publications/independent-publica-
tions/independent-reports/a-systematic-review-of-the-evidence-
base-for-developing-a-phsyical-activity-and-health-legacy-from-
the-london-2012-olympic-and-paralympic-games

Chapter 10

Vancouver 2010

Raising the Bar for Sustainable Olympic and Paralympic Winter Games

Ann Duffy

Introduction

How will the Vancouver 2010 Olympic and Paralympic Winter Games (Vancouver 2010) be remembered when it comes to sustainability, and against what benchmark and according to whom? The Sustainability Team at the Vancouver Organizing Committee for the 2010 Olympic and Paralympic Winter Games (VANOC) understood that this question was not only fair, but would prevail from the bid phase throughout the seven year project and well into the future.

In light of the high expectations identified in the bid phase by community, business, and governmental stakeholders, VANOC took sustainability seriously and raised the bar in the Olympic Movement for hosting sustainable Olympic and Paralympic Games (Games). It mounted a comprehensive approach to managing environmental, social, and economic impacts and opportunities of the Games and its legacies through unprecedented participation with sponsors, government partners and community-based organizations. It is hoped that future Games will be inspired to build on VANOC's experience, performance and lessons learned.

Sustainability was a VANOC bid commitment to the International Olympic Committee (IOC), and it became its mandate. The term *sustainability* meant managing the environmental, social and economic impacts and opportunities of the Games to produce lasting legacies, locally and globally. It was embedded as a core value, a strategic objective and an enduring ethos that influenced the many decisions made on a daily basis over the seven year project. VANOC invited ongoing input from an array of key stakeholders and partners and fostered a culture of collaboration and innovation. Six sustainability performance goals defined VANOC's sustainability program:

1. Accountability
    *   To behave ethically, set measurable performance targets and communicate openly about our progress and challenges
    *   To consult with external groups affected by our activities

2. Environmental Stewardship and Impact Reduction
    *   To conserve natural environments and manage, mitigate and offset negative impacts

3. Social Inclusion and Responsibility
    *   To convene accessible Games that have a positive impact on socially and economically disadvantaged groups that otherwise might not benefit
    *   To care for our workforce, protect human rights and ensure health and safety

4. Aboriginal Participation and Collaboration
    *   To work with our partners to achieve our goal of unprecedented Aboriginal participation in the planning and hosting of the Games, and in the creation of Games legacies

5. Economic Benefits
    *   To demonstrate that sustainable innovation and practice makes good business sense

6. Sport for Sustainable Living
    *   To use sport and growing athlete and public interest in living more sustainably to inspire action on local and global sustainability challenges

Accountability

Each of the six sustainability goals were addressed and implemented through VANOC's Sustainability Management and Reporting System (SMRS). As issues and input relating to these themes emerged, VANOC responded where it could, monitored its performance, and communicated and reported information regularly.

Table 1. Outlines the key components of VANOC's SMRS

Corporate Sustainability Policy	The policy defined terms of reference, governance and outlined the six performance goals based on local bid commitments and global standards.
System for Integrated Delivery and Cross-Organizational Responsibility	Ten corporate-wide (implementing) procedures linked with VANOC's Games planning and management approach. It included seven environmental standard operating procedures, a licensee code of conduct, supplier code of conduct, business plans, master schedules, sustainability deliverables and targets, and communications and training.
Annual Sustainability Performance Report	Annual progress, key performance measures and outcomes were tracked and reported on in alignment with the GRI G3 guidelines (see below).
External Board Advisory Committee on Sustainability Performance (BACSP)	The BACSP reported to the Sustainability and Human Resources Committee (SHRC) of the VANOC Board of Directors.
Feedback and Input	Partners and internal and external stakeholders were invited to provide input regularly.
Monitoring	Key performance information was provided to the VANOC senior executive team, BACSP, SHRC, VANOC Board of Directors on a quarterly basis.
Pre-Games and Games-Time Operating Support	Environmental management and sustainability guidance was embedded in sport event planning, venue operating plans, and functional operating plans, job-specific and venue-specific training plans.
Assurance	Annual stakeholder engagement took place and third-party assurance for the final two (of five) annual sustainability reports was conducted.
Communications	Stories and innovations were highlighted in e-newsletters, on Vancouver2010.com, in presentations, workforce training, community outreach, athlete, youth and public engagement initiatives.

The SMRS was informed by the AA1000 Accountability principles for materiality, responsiveness and completeness[1]. This in turn helped to guide VANOC on who to engage with and how. Input was sought from internal and external stakeholders on a regular basis through open house sessions, on-line resources, focus groups and workshop-style meetings. The ISO

---

1. AccountAbility is a not-for-profit organization leading the AccountAbility's AA1000 series of standards for sustainable development. Website: http://www.accountability.org/aa1000series (accessed 1 July 2010).

14000 series Environmental Management Systems standard was adapted to support the structuring of the corporate policies and procedures for planning, implementation, checking and continual improvement[2]. The Global Reporting Initiative's (GRI) G3 Guidelines informed VANOC's approach to identifying, tracking and reporting sustainability performance including guidance on performance measures, providing balance and conducting assurance[3].

In 2009, VANOC was recognized for its innovative approach to sustainability reporting as a mega sport event entity by CERES (an independent network of investors and public interest organizations for sustainable prosperity) and the Association of Certified Chartered Accountants (ACCA).

Two enduring legacies designed to support emerging management practices for sustainable events include the on-line and open-source Sustainable Sport and Event Toolkit (SSET) and a new national sustainable event management standard. SSET was created in partnership with the International Academy of Sport Science and Technology (AISTS) in Lausanne, Switzerland. The toolkit includes practical guidance, examples and resources for federations, organizing committees, host cities and sponsors interested in the social, environmental and economic impacts and opportunities of their sport and events[4]. VANOC also worked with the Canadian Standards Association (CSA) to establish Z2010 – Canada's first sustainable event management standard – in collaboration with sport, business and culture event sector stakeholders and the CSA. In its last year of operation, VANOC also contributed to the GRI's preparation of a sector supplement for sustainable event reporting.

Lessons learned focus on the benefits of reporting and communicating Vancouver 2010's sustainability plans and performance early. Through reporting VANOC could articulate its spheres of control and responsibility as well as areas of influence. Through GRI reporting, VANOC demonstrated transparency and balance on its sustainability plans and performance. Through continual stakeholder engagement, interest groups, partners, sponsors and the public at large provided valuable input and feedback that VANOC could respond to. Where possible and practical, VANOC could make changes to plans, operations, programs, Games-time events and legacies. By using internationally accepted standards for sustainability management and reporting, VANOC could demonstrate a systems-based approach throughout its seven-year lifecycle in a consistent and comparable way. Future Games Organizing Committees, such as for the London 2012

---

2. The International Organization for Standardization's 14000 family of standards: http://www.iso.org/iso/iso_14000_essentials (accessed 1 July 2010)

3. GRI's G3 Guidelines can be found at: http://www.globalreporting.org/ReportingFramework/G3Guidelines/ (accessed 1 July 2010)

4. SSET website: www.sustainable-sport.org (accessed 1 July 2010)

and Sochi 2014 Games, are already applying and adapting lessons learned by VANOC in their own plans for convening sustainable Games with positive legacies.

Environmental Stewardship and Impact Reduction

Given the Olympic Movement's experience with striving to convene green Games, VANOC aimed to go greener in two substantial ways. One was through the extensive application of Canadian green building standards for the new sport venues and the two Athlete Villages. The second was around managing the Games' overall carbon footprint.

Green building guidelines influenced siting, construction operations, materials and innovations associated with each sport facility and residential structure. In the end, VANOC was recognized by the Globe Foundation and World Green Building Council for the largest group of simultaneously constructed, single project, low environmental impact facilities in North America. The built structures incorporated practices and technologies that minimize environmental impacts: conserving biodiversity, energy and water; using low carbon and/or renewable energy; reducing waste and pollution; improving indoor light and air quality; and taking advantage of local resources, innovation and business. Each new built structure met at least the 'Silver' level criteria under the Leadership in Energy and Environmental Design (LEED) Canadian green building rating system.

Two examples of the eight new sport venues constructed for Vancouver 2010 that demonstrate green building include the Whistler Olympic Park and the Richmond Oval. The Whistler Olympic Park features the cross-country skiing, ski jumping and biathlon venues. The integrated site includes legacy trails for recreationists, a LEED certified day lodge and low footprint water and waste water treatment facilities. The Oval features pine beetle affected wood in the two hectare roof, rainwater and waste heat capture and reuse technologies in and around the building, as well as multi-purpose design for the venue ranging from a fitness centre, meeting and convening space, conversion capabilities for speed skating, hockey, basketball, adaptive basketball, and volleyball. In fact, each of the Vancouver 2010 newly built sport venues have environmental and multi-purpose attributes integrated in the design and venue use.

VANOC's approach to carbon management was informed by stakeholder input ranging from environmental NGOs, climate change specialists, the academic community and government representatives during the bid phase and throughout the 2010 Games lifecycle. With its carbon neutral Games target, a minimum 15 per cent across-the-board reduction in greenhouse gas emissions through clean energy sourcing and planning was established. In addition, VANOC applied its carbon management strategy over a seven-year period (rather than just the 17-day Olympic Winter Games period) and included pre-Games operations greenhouse gas emissions such as business travel, fleet emissions and emissions associated with venues and facilities managed by VANOC. It also included Games-time travel of athletes and officials and greenhouse gas emissions associated with the Olympic and Paralympic Torch Relay within the direct carbon footprint of the Vancouver 2010 Games. Carbon management included public tracking and reporting on direct Games-based emissions, as well as indirect emissions from Games-time travel by participants and spectators (an estimated total of 268,000 tonnes of carbon emissions after reductions). VANOC was the first Games Organizing Committee to secure a carbon offset sponsor (Offsetters). Together, Offsetters and the selected clean energy technology partners created an offset portfolio showcasing clean technologies key in transitioning to a low-carbon economy, and invited all Vancouver 2010 partners and spectators to participate in a voluntary program to offset emissions from their travel to the Games' region. The bulk of the offset projects featured locally-based innovative solutions that also provide job, business and technology development to the region.

Carbon-smart innovations, as well as strategies to reduce waste, were featured in pre-Games communications such as VANOC's website and on signage at venues and villages, in field-of-play public service announcements and videos, and at public speaking events at Games-time. Striving for a low-footprint Games also involved a long-term strategy called the *"Zero Waste Challenge."* Over the seven-year period, VANOC focused on initiatives to reduce waste at source, procuring recyclable materials and products where possible, and engaging suppliers, Games personnel and spectators in waste management awareness and education programs. Supplier workshops, contracting specifications, waste management plans, partnerships, signage, training, tracking and reporting were programming elements. Program highlights included the following: innovative solutions to managing wood waste on site in the outdoor mountain venues associated with site preparation; managing a comprehensive waste diversion program in VANOC's headquarters and Whistler offices; procuring recyclable and compostable dinner-ware for indoor and outdoor venues and the two Athlete Villages; working with large suppliers like HBC to reduce uniform apparel and furniture packaging; and targeting 85% waste diversion from landfill for waste generated at Games-time. VANOC achieved 76.8% Games-time waste diversion with strong tracking, reporting and assurance. Lessons learned focus on bin signage and support at waste collection stations as well as managing waste in load-in and tear-down phases, with suppliers and partners not only directly contracted by VANOC but also with those contracted by partner organizations like ceremonies and broadcaster providers.

Social Inclusion and Responsibility

For VANOC, advancing social inclusion meant broadening the notion of accessible Games to include not only people with physical disabilities but also inner-city residents and businesses, Aboriginal peoples and others who do not typically benefit from mega events. VANOC focused on joint-ventures and public-private partnerships that created job, training and business opportunities among its target communities and with its corporate sponsors, government partners, NGOs and social enterprises.

The Vancouver 2010 RONA Fabrication Shop was the result of a public, private and community partnership that established a place for trainees to learn carpentry, life skills and help produce the thousand props needed for the Games. Items ranged from ramps, ski racks, and simple furniture, to the stunning pine podiums for the athletes receiving medals and victory bouquets. Job trainees ranged from new immigrants to urban Aboriginal and inner city residents. The majority graduated with an initial certification in carpentry.

The victory bouquets provided to athletes were an example of how VANOC's Buy Smart Program could invite joint-venture partnerships and bring business benefits to enterprises, which in turn provided training and job opportunities for women with barriers to employment. The bouquets reflected Canada's West Coast flora and were arranged by women who had recovered from drug addiction, abuse or completed time in prison; all were seeking opportunities to build a new life with a new skill for future employment.

Finally, VANOC's asset donation program targeted identifying and selecting Vancouver 2010 related items that suited community needs locally and nationally. Items tagged as donation items ranged from mattresses to sport gear and office equipment. Recipient organizations were located not just in Vancouver and Whistler, but across the country, including First Nation communities in the far North.

Lessons learned focused on the benefits of establishing engagement and partnership opportunities in the early years of the Games lifecycle. This, together with a focus on a few early project wins like the RONA Fabrication shop, invited unprecedented collaboration, innovation and awareness of what is possible for socially inclusive Games.

Aboriginal Participation and Collaboration

VANOC and Canada signed a historic Protocol with the Four Host First Nations (FHFN), which marked the first time a Games Organizing Committee entered into such a partnership with indigenous peoples. This partnership was established to ensure that the First Nations, in whose traditional territories the Games were being held, were involved with planning, hosting and legacies. By the end of Vancouver 2010, the cumulative effort was deemed "the world's largest potlatch", an expression used to describe a festival or ceremony celebrating partnerships, collaboration, and hospitality together.

Highlights of the FHFN Protocol include the national poster program celebrating amateur First Nation athletes for schools and community centres across the country. The Aboriginal licensing and merchandising program profiled authentic art and generated royalties from the sale of products that, in turn, generated royalties for an enduring Aboriginal Youth legacy fund. During the event, an Aboriginal Pavilion was located in Vancouver's city centre and showcased Aboriginal cuisine, culture and entertainment. The Cultural Olympiad and Opening and Closing Ceremonies dazzled audiences with the breadth of Canadian culture and talent, including that of FHFN. One hundred Aboriginal youth from across Canada participated in the Opening Ceremonies of the Olympic Games, fostering understanding and cultural awareness through their Games-time experience with their peers.

Lessons learned have focused on the power of partnership, recognition and respect. The opportunities to participate in sport development, procurement, licensing and merchandizing, cultural programs and ceremonies generated a new pride, cultural identity and mechanisms for economic development for Aboriginal peoples in Canada.

Economic Benefits

VANOC aimed to convene the Vancouver 2010 project with a balanced budget. It also strived to create value from spending through the sustainable purchasing and ethical sourcing program, collectively called Buy Smart. VANOC was able to source many products and services in ways that respected environmental regulations, human rights, provided opportunities for social inclusion, and reduced waste and carbon emissions at the source. Compliance audits were applied to every factory of every official licensee that produced official merchandise. Information workshops were provided by government partners and VANOC to support entrepreneurs and business owners interested in becoming suppliers to VANOC. Inner-city and Aboriginal-focused spending was tracked and reported. Two case studies on VANOC's Buy Smart Program were published to the BuySmartBC.com website for those interested in supply chain management from a sustainability perspective.

The ingenuity of VANOC's government partners and sponsors, as well as VANOC itself, led to a total of 62 sustainability innovations. The Vancouver 2010 Sustainability Star program involved a jury-review process to recognize these creative innovations that demonstrated positive and measurable social, economic and environmental benefits. Many Vancouver 2010 rights-holders extended their corporate social responsibility initiatives to their specific Vancouver 2010 operations, products, services and programs. The collective effort became the source of pride among the employees of the organizations involved and the source of Games-time stories of "sustainability in action" by the media.

Lessons learned have focused on the power of a mega event supply chain. With simple yet integrated processes, licensees, suppliers and sponsors can make better decisions that generate better products and services that support enhanced overall Games performance and brand. Investment in building capacity through sponsorships and donations coupled with integrated operations planning led to $5.7 million in VANOC spending with inner-city business and organizations and $59 million in VANOC spending with Aboriginal businesses. Many of the sponsor and government partner innovations not only supported stronger sustainability performance at Games-time, but they have also led to enduring changes among government and sponsor day-to-day business and operational approaches.

Sport for Sustainable Living

VANOC focused on a number of ways to engage the public and stakeholders and to raise awareness and inspire action on sport, healthy living and lifestyle choices. By encouraging Vancouver 2010 participants, spectators and others to "Do your part", VANOC believed the Games-time sustainability performance and the spectator experience could be enhanced. Common themes and easy-to-understand messages focused on ways to reduce waste at source and recycle on the Vancouver 2010 event sites. Messages also focused on ways individuals could reduce greenhouse gas emissions by choosing public transit, walking or cycling. Videos and on-line web resources invited individuals to learn how to calculate and offset their own Games-time carbon footprint.

Athlete engagement with Offsetters, Coca-Cola and three non-profit organizations (Project Blue Sky, Clean Air Champions (CAC) and Earth Day Network) collaborated to engage climate change and sustainability savvy athletes as Torch Relay and Games-time role models and communicators. Athletes communicated sustainability messages (e.g., bike, walk, take transit; recycle; buy smart and offset) through media opportunities, web-based communications, field-of-play public service announcements, and interactive kiosks at the two Athlete Villages. The athlete ambassadors invited conversations with the Vancouver 2010 athletes on ways and means they could protect the environment. Over 300 pledges were recorded by athletes in both the Vancouver and Whistler Athlete Villages. The program expanded the profile of Project Blue Sky in British Columbia and CAC across Canada. The CAC continues to engage with sponsors like Coca-Cola to build on their experience and connect spectators with athletes and sustainable lifestyle choices. The Earth Day Network went on to expand its reach to the international public through athlete engagement as part of its 40th year anniversary for Earth Day on April 22, 2010.

As part of VANOC's original education program, a national website provided interactive modules and materials for students and teachers on the Olympic and Paralympic Movement, Cultural Olympiad and Sustainability, and was developed and used for over three years. During the Olympic Games, 25 high school students were selected to be street reporters capturing stories and impressions of spectators and visitors in the Vancouver 2010 venue precincts.

Two video contests were hosted for youth, including one for British Columbians in 2009 and one for Canadians in 2010. High school students were invited to produce "U-produce U-reduce" videos that raised awareness, inspired action and focused on creative ways to think about protecting the environmental and choosing more sustainable behaviours. Finalists had their videos profiled with the media, at a United Nations Environment Program education conference, a Games-time special event and on the Vancouver 2010 website.

Last but not least, VANOC's own workforce, comprised of over 1400 paid staff and more than 25,000 volunteers, received general orientation and job-specific training that included relevant sustainability messages and requirements. The awareness training and on-the-job practices helped organizers maintain the ethos for sustainability and improve Games-time waste and carbon performance.

Lessons learned have focused again on the power of partnerships and collaboration with government, business and non-government organizations. The ingenuity of youth when challenged with an opportunity to take action, communicate and express their passion was indeed inspiring. Athlete focused initiatives leading up to and during the Games were a powerful channel to gain attention on sustainable lifestyle choices and solutions to seemingly overwhelming problems. Early investment in sustainability awareness and education among VANOC's paid staff and volunteers created an organizational culture that supported better day-to-day decision-making and a brand of hospitality that enhanced the Games-time experience for athletes, spectators, the Olympic and Paralympic family, media and the viewers. Future mega-event hosts will continue to enjoy the increased benefits associated with communications technology, including social media, especially when combined with long-term community engagement that is fun, animated and easy to participate in.

Conclusion

In the end, success around striving to convene sustainable Games in 2010 will be judged in various ways. VANOC focused on establishing and maintaining an enduring commitment to sustainability throughout the seven year project. The collective effort to plan and host Games that were thoughtful about environmental, social and economic benefits, and conscious about ways to reduce costs and risks, led to an array of practical solutions. VANOC's commitment and organizational culture invited collaboration and opportunities to share ideas, inspire innovations and celebrate sustainable action. Given that Vancouver 2010 drew an audience in excess of 3.5 billion television viewers, the incentive was great. VANOC and its partners recognized there was an enormous opportunity to set a new benchmark for sustainable Olympic and Paralympic Games with lasting legacies. This ambition was a tall order, and one regarded by many as a podium finish.

Note: For more information see the Canadian Olympic Committee website for Vancouver 2010's five annual sustainability reports on www.olympic.ca.

Chapter 11
Vancouver Green Capital

Branding the Host City of the Olympic Games

Joseph Weiler and Patrick Weiler

Introduction

Six months before the Vancouver 2010 Olympic and Paralympic Winter Games (2010 Games), the Mayor of Vancouver, Gregor Robertson, in a speech to the Vancouver Board of Trade, launched an Olympic Games legacy economic development strategy under the business brand of 'Vancouver Green Capital'. The objective of this program was to accelerate the already impressive growth of sustainability practices within the City, to take strategic advantage of Vancouver's reputation as one of the most livable cities in the world, and to use the 2010 Games as a spotlight opportunity to attract investment in Vancouver's cutting edge green industrial sector in order to become a world leader in the fast growing green economy. This strategy is a critical element of a larger community objective of being recognized by 2020 as the 'Greenest City on Earth'.

These are lofty goals, but Vancouver City Hall, working with the leaders of the local green intelligentsia, ('the Green Action Team'), had previously developed a detailed Action Plan about how to become a 'green capital'. This coherent and focused green industrial development strategy is a significant departure from the pattern of host community planning efforts in earlier hallmark mega events, which typically are more focused on the construction and operation of the mega event rather than post event industrial strategy. In those cases where there were efforts at implementing a legacy economic strategy, that had almost exclusively been focused on post-event tourism.

While almost every city would like to be known as a 'green capital', in Vancouver this was more than a faint hope because of the city's long and admirable track record of achievements in the green world. As the birthplace to world renowned environmental NGOs such as Greenpeace, home of cutting edge renewable energy firms such as Ballard Power and Pulse Energy and the leader among North American cities in the reduction of greenhouse gas (GHG) emissions, Vancouver had well-earned green credibility to be a worthy, authentic holder of a green capital business brand. In addition, the 2010 Games provided the City with an unprecedented global media opportunity, in the Mayor's words 'to own green'; in September 2009 he outlined the steps about how Vancouver would climb this Green Mount Olympus. In a coordinated effort, working closely with the Vancouver Organizing Committee for the 2010 Olympic and Paralympic Winter Games (VANOC), regional municipal and provincial governments, 2010 Games sponsors, environmental NGOs, local research universities and leading green companies, the Host City set out to attract the financing and talent that would be a key to Vancouver's green capital future.

We will trace the steps taken by the City in the decades prior the 2010 Games to become world renowned as perhaps the most livable city on Earth. We will then describe how the 2010 Games project, in its various stages, built on the natural competitive advantages of Vancouver (ocean, mountains and climate), to develop world-leading environmental designs for 2010 Games venues and infrastructure. We will show how Vancouver and its neighbouring cities collaborated with senior government and synchronized their efforts at Games time in February 2010 to showcase innovative local green technology and supportive economic development public policy drivers in order to attract the kind of financial and human resource capital needed to become the gold standard of a regional green economy.

Vancouver's Green Credentials

(1) *Community planning*

Vancouver had always been blessed with gorgeous natural geographic endowments of the green confluence of mountains, ocean and temperate climate. However, it was the result of many decisions by community leaders in the two decades leading up to the 2010 Games that built on these natural endowments to create the social and environmental elements that make it such an attractive place to live. Vancouver City Hall consistently embraced environmentally friendly strategic community development planning policies, such as: the adoption of the recommendations flowing from the comprehensive Clouds of Change Report to Council of 1990; the City Plan in 1995; the Transportation Plan of 1997; the Cool Vancouver Task Force Recommendations of 2002[1]; a Comprehensive Sustainability Strategy in 2002; a Climate Change Action Plan in 2005; formal adoption by City Council in 2007 of long range climate protection targets such as reducing GHG emission by 33% from 2007 levels by 2020 and to make all new buildings in Vancouver carbon neutral by 2030; issuing an Eco Density Charter in 2008 that involved increasing density in the City by innovative policies in relation to laneway housing, secondary suite options, leadership in green building standards on City owned land; and so forth.

The City has also taken significant action to reduce emissions from the City-owned fleet, created a comprehensive recycling and composting program, cooperated though the Vancouver Agreement with senior government to capacity building of the Inner City through measures such as proactive labour force development initiatives and preferential procurement practices for Inner City businesses, as well as aggressive action to reduce homelessness in Inner City neighbourhoods. All of these community planning and design steps helped to guide the City towards embracing sustainability as an essential ingredient of the planning process that is embedded in its civic culture. On the climate action front, the net result of these policies and programs was that the City has exceeded Kyoto Protocol targets by reducing its GHG emissions by 6% under 1990 levels despite a 27% growth in its population and an 18% growth in employment,[2] the most impressive climate action performance of any major urban centre in North America during this period, and a status that is the source of great pride among its citizenry.

(2) *2010 Games Bid*

It was not until the City of Vancouver applied to host the 2010 Games that sustainability was adopted as a critical distinguishing feature of selling the City as a model urban centre to the outside world. The 2010 Games provided the opportunity for the City to align itself in its Bid with the International Olympic Committee's (IOC) amendments to the Olympic Charter in 1994 to embrace the protection of the Environment as the 'third pillar of Olympism' (along with Sport and Culture), and the more detailed description of this priority in 1999 by the IOC in its Agenda 21, which provided the framework for candidate cities to embrace environmental and social sustainability as critical elements of their proposed candidacy to host the Games.

---

1. City of Vancouver, Administrative Report, Acting Manager of Sustainability to Standing Committee on Planning and Environment on Greenest City 2020 Implementation Plan, (February 4th 2010). Available online at: http://vancouver.ca/ctyclerk/cclerk/20100204/documents/penv4.pdf (accessed October 2010).

2. Johnston, Sadhu. "City of Vancouver: Becoming the World's Greenest City by 2020", (May 28th 2010). Vancouver Sun EPIC Sustainable Living Expo, Vancouver Convention Centre, Vancouver.

The Vancouver/Whistler Bid Corporation was well aware that the accolades won by the Sydney organizers of the 2000 Olympic and Paralympic Games as hosting "the best Olympics ever"[3], were attributed in part to the innovations in environmental sustainability in areas such as solar power, waste management, water conservation and public transportation. Consequently, when the 2010 Bid Corporation submitted its Bid Book to the IOC in the Spring of 2003, a major theme of the Vancouver/Whistler Bid was its significant commitment to sustainability and inclusiveness that the proponents believed would set a new standard for future Games, and provide a significant distinctive feature and competitive advantage over bids from Austria and South Korea.

The Vancouver 2010 Bid Book singled out the objectives of creating green buildings, improving solid and liquid waste management, addressing air quality and greenhouse gas management, and protecting the natural and cultural heritage of Vancouver and the surrounding regions.[4] Notably, for several of these environmental objectives, the Bid specifically referenced the high standing of Vancouver on environmental issues, and the opportunity for the City to highlight excellence in design, planning and technology.[5] In outlining its objectives under its Environmental Key Point Action Plan, the Bid Book proposed that the Vancouver/Whistler Games would include: (1) "new buildings and infrastructure...(that) will be a showcase of the best in green building design and construction techniques..."; (2) "leading-edge solid waste management plans that provide the platform to pursue a zero solid waste management strategy during the Games"...; (3) "Air quality in Vancouver is considered to be among the best of any major metropolitan region in North American...Our goal is to move towards a zero net emissions Games that is climate neutral"; and (4) "The province of British Columbia (BC) has one of the most diverse and beautiful natural landscapes in the world...This rich natural heritage is a key element of what defines BC and its citizens".[6]

These green promises in the Bid Book indicated both the manner in which Vancouver/Whistler intended to host the 2010 Games, and also the intention to utilize the Olympic stage to showcase the two host cities' environmentally sustainable expertise, technologies and services wherever possible[7] with a particular emphasis on sustainable transportation, sustainable

---

3. Former IOC President Juan Antonio Samaranch declared the Sydney 2000 Games the "best ever" at the event's Closing Ceremonies. See: http://newscdn.bbc.net.uk/sport1/hi/in_depth/2001/olympic_votes/1418567.stm (accessed October 2010).

4. Vancouver Organizing Committee, The Bid Book Chapter 4: Environmental Protection and Meteorology, online: http://www.vancouver2010.com/dl/00/08/81/bidbook-theme4_66d-fL.pdf at page 56 (accessed October 2010).

5. *Ibid* at page 57.

6. *Ibid*.

7. *Ibid* at page 59.

energy management and sustainable Olympic Athletes Villages.[8] Sustainable transportation initiatives were to include limitations on spectator parking at venues, use of event tickets for public transportation use, the use of low and zero-emission technology vehicles, and the creation of hydrogen fueling infrastructure.[9] Initiatives aimed at sustainable energy management emphasized energy management practices in buildings, but also specifically referenced the plan to source green energy when possible from (2010 Games Sponsor) BC Hydro.[10] Finally, the two Athletes Villages were specifically highlighted as complexes that would be constructed with high levels of green building design element displaying efficient use of energy, water and resources. The Vancouver Athletes Village would also be the centre piece of a major urban renewal project that would transform a previously heavily industrialized and contaminated South False Creek Area of Vancouver into a model sustainable community, housing 16,000 people living within an easy walk of the financial and commercial heart of the City.[11]

Never before had a Games Bid attached such significance to environmental and social sustainability as its critical distinctive elements and comparative advantage over competing bids. Consequently, when the IOC awarded the 2010 Games to Vancouver in July 2003, the opportunity to create lasting economic and social legacies from the Games became part of the longer term agenda for the Games. But first, VANOC needed to make good on the promises to the IOC in the Bid Book to construct and stage the 2010 Games displaying all of the sustainability elements outlined therein. By autumn of 2009, as we will describe in the next section, this work by VANOC had been largely accomplished. What remained was how to leverage the successful 2010 Games experience into a longer term winning green industrial development strategy. In a later section we will outline how the public and private sectors in the host communities are working together through a program called Metro Vancouver Commerce to transform the host region into a global magnet that will attract sufficient green investment and talent to make Vancouver the Greenest City on Earth.

2010 Games Venues and Infrastructure

The record will show that the sustainability promises in the Bid Book were indeed kept by VANOC and the Host City of Vancouver. The most obvious area where this took place was with the design and construction of the venues. Originally, VANOC had targeted the U.S. Green Building Council's LEED (Leadership in Energy and Environmental Design) Silver certification for its venues, but subsequently exceeded these standards upon com-

8. *Ibid* at page 60-1.

9. *Ibid.*

10. *Ibid.*

11. *Ibid.*

pletion. For example, the Vancouver Olympic/Paralympic Centre (curling), the Killarney ice hockey practice facility owned by the Vancouver Parks Board, and VANOC offices headquarters are attracting LEED Gold certification. From an environmental technology architectural/engineering perspective, the most impressive Games achievement is the Vancouver Athletes Village. Through innovative systems such as a district water heating system using heat from sewage water, roof gardens, rainwater irrigation systems, housing density achieved without sacrificing public space, roof top street systems, etc., all buildings in the Athletes Village complex of residential and commercial units received either Gold or Platinum certification, and the overall neighbourhood received LEED Platinum certification[12] which Mayor Robertson was proud to applaud at Games-time as the 'Greenest Neighbourhood in the World'.[13]

The 2010 Games was also the catalyst for a public and private sector partnership to construct the long anticipated $900 million Vancouver Trade and Convention Centre West, a facility that was completed in 2009 and served as the International Broadcasting Centre (IBC) for the 2010 Games. This breathtakingly beautiful building is the first convention centre in the world to receive LEED Platinum certification. Most impressive is its six acre 'living roof', which is the largest non-industrial living roof in North America, with 400,000 indigenous plants and grasses, four beehives and a drainage and recovery system that collects and uses Vancouver's plentiful rainwater for irrigation during summer months.[14] In addition, the Centre utilizes sustainability-sensitive facility operations and event management guidelines by which nearly half of the building's waste is recycled, and eighty-five percent of the buildings waste is diverted from landfill.[15]

Transportation Management and Infrastructure

Event operations plans for a sustainable transportation system at Games-time are being turned into long-term strategies for the Greater Vancouver Region. Organizers were successful in reducing carbon emissions through the encouragement of public transit, the use of a low carbon emission fleet

12. For more information about the Vancouver Athletes Village see: http://vancouver.ca/olympicvillage/index.htm (accessed October 2010).

13. Mayor of Vancouver, Press Release, February 16, 2010, "Olympic Village greenest neighbourhood in the world" online: http://www.mayorofvancouver.ca/blog/?p=711 (accessed October 2010).

14. Vancouver Convention Centre, Sustainability Fact Sheet, online at: http://www.vancouverconventioncentre.com/wp-content/uploads/2009/03/c01793_mod-guide_green_ro.pdf (accessed October 2010).

15. Vancouver Convention Centre, Sustainable Event Guidelines, online at: http://www.vancouverconventioncentre.com/wp-content/uploads/2010/04/VancouverConvCtre_Sustainable_Event_Guidelines_FINAL.pdf (accessed October 2010).

by VANOC, and emphasis on walking and cycling as a means for transportation for the duration of the 2010 Games. Post-Games statistics of public transit usage have remained far above year on year comparisons for the same periods. A major contributor has been the opening of a the new light rail line (the Canada Line) linking Vancouver International Airport, the City of Richmond (home of the Olympic skating Oval) and downtown Vancouver.[16] While not strictly a 2010 Games project, this long-awaited public transit facility was able to attract the requisite public private partnership financing as a 2010 Games-related infrastructure project. Since completion, the Canada Line now offsets the equivalent of ten lanes of auto emissions traffic, as well as providing a quick connection from Richmond to downtown Vancouver. Although not a direct VANOC undertaking, the "hydrogen highway" from Vancouver to Whistler was specifically mentioned in the Bid Book.[17] The media and ridership exposure attracted by this project during the 2010 Games, particularly the use of hydrogen powered public bus transit at Whistler, has been a huge spotlight opportunity for this technology. This will provide momentum for the implementation of the agreement between the Premier Campbell of BC and Governor Schwarzenegger of California to build hydrogen fuelling stations ranging from Whistler to San Diego to promote this zero-emission form of vehicle transportation as a central feature of a Pacific Coast assault on carbon.[18]

Public Private Partnerships

2010 Games sponsor, working together with VANOC and its government partners through the 'Sponsor Sustainability Initiative', developed the 'Sustainability Star' program, including the use of a distinctive trademark that highlights sponsor-driven innovations in environmental and social sustainability practices. Examples of Sustainability Star winners include Coca-Cola's promotion of the organic plant soft drink bottle[19] and Teck Cominco's "Going for Gold" employee engagement program that rewarded

16. Translink, Canada Line Documents: Consultation on Preliminary Design Consultation Summary Report online at: http://www.translink.ca/-/media/Documents/ Ride%20Info/Canada%20Line/Public%20Consultation%20and%20Surv%20-Reports/Consultation%20Summary%20Report%20on%20Preliminary%20Design.-ashx, page 2 (accessed October 2010).

17. Vancouver Organizing Committee, The Bid Book Chapter 4: Environmental Protection and Meteorology, online at: http://www.vancouver2010.com/dl/oo/o8/8I/ bidbook-theme4_66d-fL.pdf , page 61 (accessed October 2010).

18. Canadian Broadcasting Corporation, "Schwarzenegger, Campbell formalize green agreement" May 31, 2007, online at: http://www.cbc.ca/canada/british-columbia/ story/2007/05/31/bc-green.html (accessed October 2010).

19. Coca-Cola Canada, Coca-Cola Canada Opens Happiness at the Vancouver 2010 Olympic Winter Games, (February 9th 2010), online at: http://cokenews.ca/2010/02/ coca-cola-canada-opens-happiness-at-the-vancouver-2010-olympic-winter-games/ (accessed October 2010).

employee participation in health and fitness activities, community sustainability programs and volunteering.[20] In the Blue Sky program, Olympic athletes promoted individual sustainable lifestyle choices, including use of active transportation options that promoted health and fitness while also reduced carbon footprint. These individual personal activities were logged and aggregated on a sponsor's website as an easily understood 2010 Games-related initiative that would reduce the overall carbon footprint of the Games. VANOC also formed a partnership with a 2010 Games sponsor, Offsetters, to track all 2010 Games-related emissions and to purchase necessary authentic offsets in order to fulfill the Bid Promise that the 2010 Games would be carbon neutral.[21]

Vancouver Green Capital

As noted earlier, for decades Vancouver has incorporated concepts of environmentalism and sustainability into its urban planning and development initiatives. However, the 2010 Games presented an opportunity to not only meet the sustainability standards set by the IOC, but to go further and leave lasting sustainability legacies for the City. Cutting-edge green sporting venues, the Athlete Villages and the Convention Centre, the expertise gained by the teams of architects, engineers and contractors involved in their creation, sustainable transportation infrastructure and carbon reduction practices, and the new partnering experience gained by government, private sector and NGOs working together are all lasting sustainable legacies of the 2010 Games. What added value could be achieved in the post-Games period if these systems were to operate in the longer term, and how could this expertise and momentum gained during the 12 years of the 2010 Games project (from bid to delivery) be translated into a post Games industrial development strategy? Leadership at Vancouver City Hall started to focus on this challenge a year before the 2010 Games by attracting the best minds available to map out Vancouver Green Capital plan.

The first step in this plan was the creation of the Greenest City Action Team (GCAT) comprised of "independent experts representing knowledge and interest across a range of the most pressing environment interests..." to determine "...what Vancouver needs to do to become the greenest city in the world by 2020."[22] GCAT included representatives from green tech-

---

20. Vancouver 2010, VANOC Launches Sustainability Star Program, March 26, 2009, online at: http://www.vancouver2010.com/olympic-news/n/news/vanoclaunches--%E2%80%98sustainability-star%E2%80%9D-awards-program-torecognize-partner-sustainability-innovations-in-economic--environmental-andsocial-initiatives-_65072qE.html (accessed October 2010).

21. Offsetters named Official Carbon Offsetter of the 2010 Winter Games, available at: http://www.offsetters.ca/content/offsetters-named-official-carbon-offsetter-2010--winter-games (accessed October 2010).

22. City of Vancouver, Greenest City 2020, online at: http://vancouver.ca/greenestcity/background.htm (accessed October 2010).

nology companies, politicians, lawyers, academics, environmentalist advocates, and VANOC.[23] The GCAT developed an initial report entitled "Greenest City: Quick Start Recommendations"[24] on April 27, 2009, with the intention of "...setting out a host of actions, all of which can be initiated and most of which can be completed in time for Vancouver's Olympic moment in February 2010." As noted in the report at page 3: "This Report rests on a single, critical assumption: there is no time to lose. Vancouver is already in the world's spotlight in anticipation of the 2010 Winter Games. That event will be an opportunity to promote the City to prospective residents and potential businesses as an international exemplar."[25] The GCAT provided a variety of recommendations on how Vancouver could become more sustainable in three broad subject areas: jobs and the economy, greener communities, and human health.

How could Vancouver utilize the media attention and goodwill attached to the 2010 Games to help attract the needed talent and financial muscle to build equity in its new business brand as a Green Capital? As previously noted, the hope was to use the publicity from the 2010 Games to launch and promote 'Vancouver Green Capital'. In order to do so, nine municipalities in Vancouver joined together to form Metro Vancouver Commerce (MVC). This initiative invested CA$700,000, along with CA$800,000 from the federal government's Ministry of Western Economic Diversification, in order to promote local businesses and attract new investment to the area, with the added attention Vancouver would be receiving during the 2010 Games.[26] MVC aimed at using the combination of the high living standards, business incentives, green know-how and other competitive advantages in their marketing strategy. MVC "strategically targeted international business which were considering investing or moving [to Vancouver]"[27] and was successful in hosting seventy-one companies to the Vancouver area in four days visit cycles during the 2010 Games. These visits were aimed at strategically connecting companies with prominent local business leaders, politicians and relevant economic development agencies

23.City of Vancouver, "Vancouver 2020 A Bright Green Future: An Action Plan for Becoming the World's Greenest City by 2020" online at: http://vancouver.ca/greenestcity/PDF/Vancouver2020-ABrightGreenFuture.pdf, page 2, Provides overview of GCAT members and their respective backgrounds. (accessed October 2010)

24.City of Vancouver, "Greenest City: Quick Start Recommendations", (27th April 2009). Available online at: http://vancouver.ca/greenestcity/PDF/greenestcity-quickstart.pdf (accessed October 2010).

25.Ibid, page 3.

26.The Province, "Vancouver mayor says $1.5-million Olympic boost pays off in jobs, investment." Frank Luba, (April 28th 2010). Available online at: http://metrovancouvercommerce.com/files/MVC_2010-04-28_Province.pdf (accessed October 2010).

27.Vancouver Sun, "Vancouver is back on track and fulfilling its potential" Gregor Robertson, (May 15th 2010). Available online at: http://www.canada.com/vancouversun/news/westcoastnews/story.html?id=49fbc7ed-4f80-49f3-bcaf-6ae20be584f9 (accessed October 2010).

in order to get a first hand look at the local business environment, and of course to enjoy with them the unique 2010 Games experience as valued guests of MVC.[28]

The focal point of the Vancouver Green Capital hosting strategy was the Vancouver House Pavilion situated in LiveCity Vancouver, one of the busiest sites at the 2010 Games. In this central venue, the public had a chance to see and hear about the changes and green economic strategy in Vancouver that the City was now pursuing aggressively. In addition, Vancouver House Pavilion was the locus of the private business development hosting program aimed at influential business leaders, including both global and domestic 2010 Games sponsors, as well as the crème of the Vancouver business community at private events coordinated through the Vancouver Economic Development Commission to encourage investment and build economic partnerships.[29] In particular, Vancouver House showcased business leaders in Vancouver's fast-growing green economy, who were already doing their part in making Vancouver a hot bed in business activity.[30]

While at this time of writing, it is obviously too early to accurately assess the effectiveness of the Vancouver Green Capital industrial development strategy since its launch in September 2009, but early returns seem promising. For a cost of only CA$1.5m incurred to date, contracts among foreign investors amounting to over CA$60m have been concluded with local companies in green initiatives within the first eight weeks after the 2010 Games, exceeding the original 18 month target for the program.[31] With the exception of the lucrative CA$27m partnership formed with the Abbotsford-based Cascade Aerospace and Lockheed Martin, the promised investments are all in the clean energy tech area.[32] For example, the North Vancouver-based Hydrogen Technology and Energy Corporation (HTEC) has agreed to a partnership with Air Liquide of France to build a CA$15m plant in North Vancouver that will take by-product hydrogen and turn it into fuel to service fuel-cell buses in Whistler, as well as local industrial needs and fuel-cell initiatives.[33] Other partnerships in the Region involve notable international green companies such as KC Cottrell, as well as companies from the

---

28. Globe and Mail, "Olympics generated $60-million worth of deals for Vancouver area." Stephanie Levitz, (April 29th 2010). online: http://metrovancouvercommerce.com/files/MVC_2010-04-28_GlobeAndMail.pdf (accessed October 2010).

29. Robertson, Gregor, City of Vancouver, "Vancouver House to Showcase City as Green Capital." (February 9th 2010). Available online at: http://www.mayorofvancouver.ca/blog/?p=675 (accessed October 2010).

30. Ibid

31. Globe and Mail, "Olympics generated $60-million worth of deals for Vancouver area."

32. Ibid

33. Vancouver Sun, "2010 Olympics Translate into Major Business Deals." Brian Morton, (April 29th 2010). Available online at: http://metrovancouvercommerce.com/files/MVC_2010-04-29_VanSun.pdf (accessed October 2010).

UK, Spain, the Netherlands, Germany and the US.[34] Several of the business leaders credited the energy in the City as being a major reason to invest in the area rather than elsewhere; meanwhile, other companies insisted that the 2010 Games provided a firm date to conclude deals that had been in the works for years.[35] However, the impact of the Green Capital strategy and MVC initiative will be measured over the next few years as the business relationships formed and/or nurtured over this period have more time to develop.

The important point here is that local government and business leaders have formed their own 'Olympic Team' and are collaborating under the Vancouver Green Capital business banner to aggressively pursue business opportunities in the clean tech energy sector, which is the fastest growing tech sector in British Columbia, and the leading target for new global energy investment. This has the early signs of becoming a text book example of how to leverage off the Games to create longer term economic development gains in an industrial sector of clean tech energy that so ideally aligns with the sustainability values and goals of the IOC's Agenda 21. The implementation of this strategy to date is also impressive, because of its astute media/communications program that has taken advantage the unique goodwill, profile and positive energy of the Games to attract both local and global attention to this ambitious, focused industrial strategy.

For the local audience, the Mayor of Vancouver launched Vancouver Green Capital as a 'business brand' at the Vancouver Board of Trade audience whose 8,000 member companies form the heart of the local business community. Using classic sports rhetoric, and shedding the prototypical image of a crusty civic bureaucrat, he issued a call to action, challenging every business to 'set the pace', to lead by example, to do its part to become more energy efficient, create less waste, make their City a better place to live for their employees and families. Rather than go it alone in competition with other regional municipalities, the City of Vancouver helped to create a Metro Vancouver Commerce shared effort to push the clean tech agenda offering to act as a salesman for the whole region in true Olympic Team spirit. When 2010 Games-time arrived, the regional municipalities operated a coordinated hosting program for targeted business leader guests.

In order to take advantage of the 15,000 media covering the 2010 Games, the Mayor rolled out a series of high profile announcements that validated Vancouver's credibility as an aspiring Green Capital. In early February 2010, Vancouver City Council formally adopted its own green capital program. This was followed by the announcement of the Vancouver Athlete Village being recognized as LEED Platinum, which the Mayor quickly dubbed as the "Greenest neighbourhood on Earth" and a prime example of Vancouver's status as a world leader in the built environment.

34.Ibid

35.Globe and Mail, "Olympics generated $60-million worth of deals for Vancouver area."

The presence of Pacific Coast carbon reduction political standard bearers Governor Schwarzenegger and Premier Campbell participating in the Olympic Torch Relay reinforced the image that the political leaders were working together on the environment. And finally, the joint announcement by Mayor Robertson and world famous entrepreneur Richard Branson of the 'Green Capital Global Challenge' during the first week of the 2010 Games set the stage for a benign competition among world urban centres to lead the fight against carbon emissions. Why announce this in Vancouver? Branson noted: "Vancouver has actually walked the talk -- or [in] this city should I say cycle the talk -- reducing greenhouse gas emissions to 1990 levels while the population has grown 30 per cent."[36] Since this point, ten cities have been selected for the Challenge with the winner being awarded at the 2012 Olympic and Paralympic Games in London (2012 Games). The fact that this competition would take place under a game clock running between the 2010 Games and the 2012 Games assured that the world media would likely follow the progress of these cities to climb to the top of the Green Mount Olympus. All these media friendly announcements ensured that Vancouver as a potential Green Capital would be at centre stage for the next few years, adding priceless profile to its green economy development agenda.

The most current example of the City of Vancouver building on the momentum gained promoting itself as a Green Capital from the 2010 Games is the presence of Vancouver Pavilion at the Shanghai World Expo. Located in the urban best practices area of the World Expo site, the Vancouver Pavilion promotes the use of wood products (of which British Columbia is a leading exporter) as a sustainable building material. Vancouver's exhibit also reinforces its status as a Green Capital by chronicling the thoughtfully planned redevelopment of the lands around False Creek in downtown Vancouver, lands that were the sites of major international events (Expo 1986 and the 2010 Games), thereby celebrating key legacies of redevelopment, including urban planning, architecture, transportation and community engagement. The Shanghai Expo 2010 thus provides a valuable platform for Vancouver to promote its new green business brand by demonstrating how it has established itself as a global hub that leads the new green industry with clean energy, mobility and green building projects.[37]

---

36. Vancouver Sun, "Branson launches civic carbon challenge in Vancouver" Scott Simpson, (February 18th 2010). Available online at:http://www.vancouversun.com/technology/Branson+launches+civic+carbon+challenge+Vancouver/2580046/story.html (accessed October 2010).

37. Vancouver Pavilion, EXPO 2010 Shanghai. Available online at: http://en.expo2010.cn/c/en_ubpa_tpl_279.htm (accessed October 2010).

Conclusion

Vancouver Green Capital is an important current example of how a Games Host City is attempting to translate the sustainability elements of this mega event into a post-Games focused industrial strategy. Taking advantage of the cutting edge 'green tech' sport venues and infrastructure put in place for the 2010 Games, the local government and business community are launched on a promising program to sell themselves as an ideal place to live and work for the increasingly mobile entrepreneurs, investors and talent in the green tech energy sector. The Vancouver based combination of technical expertise, collaborative public private partnership experience and media savvy leadership will be a formidable new Olympic Team to watch in the next few years as it competes in the Green Capital Challenge.

Chapter 12

The Olympic Movement as a Leader in Sustainability

David Stubbs

Introduction

This chapter looks at the role of sustainability as a contemporary interpretation of Olympic values, and illustrates how the Olympic Games (Games) can reflect and respond to societal trends, and themselves be drivers for positive change. This is discussed in terms of legacy planning and the role of key participants, notably athletes, broadcasters and sponsors.

The Games provide a unique platform for making sustainability relevant, engaging and fun. Simultaneously, the sustainability agenda provides the Olympic Movement with a renewed and coherent focus in its relations with society. Pierre de Coubertin, the founder of the modern Olympic Games, most likely did not use the word *sustainability* in his lifetime, but if he was with us today, I believe he would be a leading advocate for sustainability. His vision was steeped in positive values; he wanted to bring people together to celebrate achievement, but also to create a better future. This is essentially what is meant by *sustainability*: a process of positive and renewable change, which improves quality of life for people now and in the future. Implicit in this definition is the recognition that life is not static. Things change all the time – there is no steady state point of perfection. Nothing stands in total isolation from its surroundings or from society.

Sustainability is about people, and how we live and behave; it is not another term for environmentalism. Of course, within this concept there is a profound recognition of the need for responsible stewardship of the natural environment, which is a prerequisite for sustaining viable and healthy communities. But sustainability is a human concept, and as such, it has to be seen as something we do to balance present needs and aspirations with those of future generations – in short, ensuring long-term survival. There is a lot in today's society that is unsustainable: the exploitation of natural resources and depletion of the world's biodiversity; producing more waste than can be re-absorbed into natural systems; pollution of land, air and water; vast inequalities between rich and poor countries; consumption-driven lifestyles which are increasingly disconnected from the natural world; and, decreasing levels of activity and fitness.

The Olympic Movement is founded on a positive vision and ideals that project an optimistic view for society. The Olympic Movement has genuine global reach and influence, and thereby a leadership role to play in promoting this vision.

The Olympic paradox – a festival of consumption versus preaching sustainability

Many people believe that legacy is the real endpoint of promoting sustainability for the Games. Certainly the focus in Vancouver (2010 Games), London (2012 Games), Sochi (2014 Games) and Rio de Janiero (2016 Games) all promote the creation of a viable community benefit of new sporting infrastructure and a host of other socio-cultural, environmental and economic benefits. However, there is a paradox here.

Taken in isolation, the Games do not appear to be a sustainable activity. International travel, energy use, consumption, and waste happen as part of the Games event, just for a few weeks of sport. If a nation was serious about regenerating whole city quarters and revitalising rundown communities, would they start by setting out to host the Games? This is unlikely. However, consider the following; the Games bring a unique vision and an immoveable project deadline. These attributes unlock previously irreconcilable barriers to community objectives, such as funding and planning decisions. So, taken at a large scale, the relatively temporary diversion of resources to deliver the Games can be significantly outweighed by the long-term gains from achieving a sustainable legacy. The size and duration of those benefits depends on how well a host city marries the sometimes competing demands of delivering the Games and urban planning and regeneration.

The change-making agenda as a means of influence

Legacy has other important dimensions beyond the physical and social infrastructure left behind in a Games host city. The planning and staging of the Games can be excellent opportunities for creating new (and sometimes unlikely) partnerships and inspiring pro-environmental behaviour change. No other major event has such a lengthy and multi-faceted lead-up. The construction of new event venues and infrastructure and the four-year Cultural Olympiad provide a continual source of official and public interest, which if channelled effectively can be a driver for positive change. My experience is that people and organisations of all kinds want to be involved in or associated with the Games. While this can be tricky for brand managers, the effect on procurement is striking. The Games require vast quantities of products and services: construction and overlay materials, furniture, technology equipment and systems, clothing, merchandise, food, and of course people. In order to promote sustainable procurement, the London 2012 Organising Committee for the Olympic Games and Paralympic Games (LOCOG) has issued a Sustainable Sourcing Code, which in essence asks five basic questions of suppliers and licensees about their products:

- Where does it come from?
- Who made it?
- What is it made of?
- What is it wrapped in?
- What will happen to it afterwards?

These simple questions address ethical supply chain issues, local employment, environmental impact, recyclability and end of life reuse or disposal. Suppliers have responded by looking at their business practices to seek out more sustainable alternatives to delivering their product. This is driving companies to review their business practices, and many are finding increased competitive advantage through addressing sustainability. This is because Games' procurement is not happening in isolation. LOCOG has simply articulated and accelerated an existing trend in public and major corporate procurement. LOCOG is influencing change in different business sectors by bringing this trend to the Games.

People's behaviour is fundamental to moving towards sustainability. For example, sustainable living does not come from building an eco-development if the people who live there use it unsustainably. Sustainable living requires people to alter key lifestyle behaviours, such as consumption patterns and travel mode choice. These issues go well beyond the Games and are issues of public policy. However, the Games can accelerate changes that have already been set in motion within a host city. The Games can make people take notice through active measures to promote cultural diversity and inclusion, improved accessibility and local environmental quality, as well as educational and cultural projects. Moving towards sustainability can become relevant, engaging and fun; these are the stepping stones to making people do things more sustainably.

Key players: athletes, broadcasters, sponsors

A bit of stardust also helps. What makes the Games so special is of course sport, which requires athletes. The Games event draws over 15,000 Olympic and Paralympic athletes, who can collectively make a powerful army of advocates for healthier lifestyles. Their role as ambassadors for healthy living is critical, and they are an under-utilised resource in this respect.

Most people interact with the Games through TV. Games' broadcasters have the greatest reach of any Olympic Movement stakeholder. They are also a major component of the Games' infrastructure and have potentially significant impacts on the planning and fitting out of sport venues. If the major network broadcasters were to embrace sustainability like most other leading businesses are doing today, they could play an extremely important role in reducing direct event impacts, communicating this agenda and influencing vast audiences. The IOC's Olympic Broadcasting Services has the opportunity to play a leading role in this area.

All of the leading brands associated with the Games are active in the field of corporate social responsibility (CSR). Until recently, the two strands of sport sponsorship and CSR were rarely aligned; this is changing. Sponsors are increasingly taking an active role in the sustainability dimension of the events for which they hold marketing rights. The mutual association of sponsor brands and the Games requires all parties to be attentive to and proactive on sustainability – the reputational damage of one party failing to meet its responsibilities would impact severely on the other. This is a positive association which is received well by employees and customers, as well as the wider public.

Sustainability Partners

London 2012 has taken the emerging sustainability trend one step further with the creation of an additional marketing rights designation of 'Sustainability Partner'. This designation is limited to a maximum of six companies who have committed to working with the organising committee to implement and promote sustainability initiatives associated with the Games. The collective reach of these companies through their employees, customers and supply chains is considerable. Their focus on sustainability is a powerful message to convey to these large stakeholder groups. The added benefit of doing so is that while the specific Games-related sustainability initiatives may be temporary, the positive impacts on sponsors and their constituents can be long-lasting. Companies that have made the effort to integrate sustainability into their business model are not going to go back to old ways. The stimulus of supplying to the Games may have been the initial incentive but these are not one-off activities; they are business-wide changes. Examples of this type of change may be seen in packaging specifications, adoption of higher welfare levels in supply chains or certification to a standard.

The London 2012 Sustainability Partner programme is demonstrating that sustainability is now a key sales tool and revenue driver for a Games Organising Committee. It makes sponsors more likely to invest their brand in the Games and it adds a competitive edge to the procurement process of sponsors, suppliers and licensees. The same principles could apply to the IOC's Worldwide Marketing Partners (TOP sponsors), which would have the automatic advantage of providing a sustainability impetus for all future Games.

Impact of the Games

Sponsorship that engages sustainability is a truly win-win situation for sponsors and for rights holders, both commercially and in terms of brand reputation. It places sustainability as a core, strategic foundation of a Games Organising Committee, and with that incentive it is easier to put in place the necessary policies, processes and structures to embed sustainability practices across the organisation. It is only relatively recently that so called 'Green Games' initiatives were either something the host city authorities delivered, or were nice to have additions for Games organisers. Today the emphasis has shifted and sustainability in its full sense is integral to effective Games organisations. This is significant for the IOC and the Olympic Movement.

The IOC has set forward a path to reduce the size, cost and complexity of the Games. It has also established the Olympic Games Global Impact study to provide a long-term evaluation of the environmental, social and economic outcomes of hosting the Games on a city, region and country. Sustainability is the common thread through each of these initiatives. It is central to any contemporary interpretation of Olympic values and is essential for renewing the Olympic Movement's engagement with young people and societal values at large. It is not enough, however, simply to be a voice for sustainability; to be credible to new audiences the Olympic Movement has to deliver change too. During the 1990s the IOC adopted *Environment* as the third pillar of Olympism, along with related initiatives. While this was relevant at the time, environment and sustainability is a continually moving agenda, and these early efforts now need to be renewed and made relevant to today's society.

Conclusion

There is plenty of enthusiasm for sustainability in the field of sport; a new generation of event organisers, athletes and other specialists is increasingly attuned to the need for more sustainable event practices. There is a growing wealth of guidance and expertise available and in many countries there are political and regulatory imperatives that ensure a more positive direction.

The downside to this increased emphasis on sustainability in the sport sector is the clutter of information, tools and guidance of varying quality and consistency. What we need now is a common language that demystifies the complexities of the subject and is able to engage a broader audience.

There is an opportunity here – and arguably a responsibility – for the Olympic Movement and its partners to provide appropriate leadership and focus around sustainability. The added impetus of the sport world providing collective effort in this field could be influential and lead to meaningful and lasting change.

Chapter 13

The London 2012 Olympic and Paralympic Games

A Framework for Sustainable Development and Regeneration for Sport

Dan Epstein

Introduction

Sustainable development has become a ubiquitous term in the regeneration and development sectors in the United Kingdom (UK). Virtually every development now claims to be *sustainable*, but every project has a different definition of *sustainable development*, and many don't set objectives or targets against which a project's sustainability performance can be measured. What is needed is a meaningful and consistent framework for sustainable development, which covers the environmental, social and economic aspects of sustainability, against which individual projects can set project specific objectives and targets.

In the absence of clear guidelines and a framework for regeneration, the Olympic Delivery Authority (ODA), which is responsible for delivering the London 2012 Olympic Park, designed a bespoke framework, objectives and tools that reflect the nature, location and scale of the project. This chapter reviews the approach the ODA has taken to ensure the Olympic Park is a sustainable development.

Olympic principles and sustainability

The starting point for the London 2012 Olympic and Paralympic Games (2012 Games) Sustainable Development Strategy was the principles that have inspired the modern Olympic Movement. Pierre de Coubertin, who founded the modern Olympic Movement in 1894, saw the Olympic Games as a chance to bring the nations of the world together through sport to spread the ideals of tolerance, equality, fair play and peace. De Coubertin's Olympics aimed to promote sport, culture and education in order to nurture closer relationships between nations, enshrined in the Olympic Charter as *Fundamental Principles of Olympism*[1]. In 1994, the *Environment* was added as a third pillar of Olympism, along with Sport and Culture, through a revision of the Olympic Charter.

Setting new standards for sustainable development

London 2012[2] have responded to the Olympic values by setting out its intentions to be the most sustainable Games ever, seeking to set new standards, and create processes and tools that would influence future Olympic Games, regeneration projects, major sports venues and other events. The 2012 Games' vision is to "host an inspirational, safe and inclusive Olympic Games and Paralympic Games and leave a sustainable legacy for London and the UK". At the heart of this vision was London 2012's commitment to deliver a sustainable legacy. This is being achieved firstly by ensuring that the 2012 Games leaves behind a thriving new urban quarter for London, and secondly by setting exemplary sustainability performance requirements for the venues, Athletes Village, and utilities and infrastructure on the Olympic Park. The investment in the 2012 Games Olympic Park and Athletes Village is designed to leave an enriched physical and natural environment, enhance the economic and social well-being of communities in the Lower Lea Valley, encourage greater participation in sport in the UK and provide the infrastructure to support low carbon and healthier lifestyles.

The ODA set ambitious objectives for each of the three key strands of sustainability. It committed to be:

- The greenest Games ever; to create a high quality natural environment and establish new standards for sustainable design and construction.
- The most accessible and inclusive Games ever, and set new standards of inclusive design in sporting facilities, residential developments, transport

---

1. International Olympic Committee. *Olympic Charter*. October 2007.

2. London 2012 is made up of the publicly funded Olympic Delivery Authority (responsible for building the venues and infrastructure for the event) and the privately funded London Organising Committee of the Olympic Games and Paralympic Games (responsible for delivering the event).

projects and service delivery that would encompass the whole life experience of disabled people.
- A Games that supports economic development and provides significant improvements in education, skills and training, job opportunities and wider economic benefits.

What sets London 2012 apart?

Many Olympic and Paralympic Games (Games) host cities have sought to use the event as a catalyst for urban renewal and new development. London 2012 has adopted a similar approach, seeking to use the 2012 Games as a catalyst for regeneration of a highly depressed area of East London. Beyond this it has also adopted the most comprehensive set of social, economic and environmental objectives and targets of any Games host city.

Creating the Olympic Park and Athletes Village in the Lower Lea Valley, which is a core target growth area for London, has effectively brought forward plans for regeneration by 20 years or more. It has enabled the land to be assembled under the single biggest compulsory purchase order ever issued in the UK; it has funded the under-grounding of 52 pylons which blighted the site; it has provided funding for the first 2880 homes, the transport, highway and utility infrastructure for the full development; and, it has created the biggest new park in the UK.

The challenges posed by the determination to create a sustainable legacy should not be under-estimated. An Olympic Park has unique requirements: it will need to host 80 world Heads of State; over 17,000 athletes, coaches and other support staff, including some of the most high profile athletes in the world; 500,000 visitors a day; 40,000 journalists and the world's broadcasting media. This poses unprecedented logistical and security issues. Some of the challenges include: installing a security fence around the Olympic Park during the event and then opening up the site to the widest possible community after the Games as quickly as possible; creating venues that can hold much larger crowds during the Games than will ever be needed again; managing large crowd numbers over very short periods across pinch points like bridges and along major concourses; creating venues that are purpose built for elite athletes and high definition and 3D broadcasting during the Games and then for community use in legacy; and moving athletes, the Olympic Family and official media from the Olympic Park around a congested city to over 30 venues around London. These are huge challenges for which there are no perfect solutions; the ODA, the London Organising Committee for the Olympic Games and Paralympic Games (LOCOG) and the Olympic Park Legacy Company (OPLC) frequently found compromise solutions that would meet the needs of the event without undermining the ability of the Olympic Park to function successfully over the long term. Ultimately, the challenge is to minimise waste, maximise long term benefits from investment and deliver the 2012 Games in the most cost effective way possible.

In order to resolve the inevitable conflicts between the 2012 Games and Legacy requirements, every investment decision was required to demonstrate how it would contribute to a long term legacy. The driver for public investment was to invest once and invest wisely. To ensure balanced decisions were made, the ODA managed the delivery process on the Park, but LOCOG and the London Development Agency (LDA) (which assembled and owned the land on the site) were on the client team reviewing designs and ensuring their requirements were met. The OPLC was formed in 2009 specifically to assume the role of legacy owner from the LDA and to develop detailed legacy plans.

Projects needed for the 2012 Games but not justified for legacy were designed to be temporary, so that they could be removed either for reuse or to be recycled immediately after the 2012 Games, thereby avoiding the white elephant syndrome which has dogged other Games host cities. At the time of writing this chapter, the Olympic Stadium in Beijing, for example, has only been used for three events since the Beijing 2008 Olympic and Paralympic Games, although it is a major visitor attraction. The Athens stadium used for the 2004 Games remains empty.

The Olympic Stadium for the 2012 Games has been designed to be dismantled and turned into a 25,000 seat stadium in legacy, but also has built in flexibility and can be reduced to a 50,000 or 60,000 seat stadium if there is a demand for this in legacy. A better solution would have been to identify an end user for the Stadium before commissioning the project, in the same way the Manchester Commonwealth Games identified and worked with Manchester City Football Club. The Government Olympic Executive and the Greater London Authority worked hard to find an end user, but for commercial reasons were unable to secure a deal prior to Stadium design. As a result the stadium may require substantial additional investment depending on its end use. The transformation of the 2012 stadium will start immediately after the event, along with the wider transformation of the Olympic Park so that the OPLC can take ownership and open the Olympic Park to the public as quickly as possible.

Resource efficient infrastructure

Public investment in utilities and infrastructure is also designed to support a resource efficient, low carbon development that will help reduce carbon emissions from the Olympic Park legacy venues by 50%, and support low carbon lifestyles. Some examples of this are as follows:

- The Olympic Park energy centre includes a 110 MW Combined Cooling Heating and Power Plant (CCHP), a 3MW biomass heating system, and a 16km distribution network designed to serve all the Olympic Park legacy developments, helping to reduce the carbon footprint of the venues in the Park by 30% and the Athletes Village by even more.

- A non-potable water treatment system and distribution network has been installed with support from the private sector, to be used for toilet flushing, irrigation and other non-potable uses as part of a package of measures designed to reduce non-potable water demand on the Park by 40%.
- Extensive new and upgraded public transport facilities will leave East London as one of the best served public transport hubs in the UK. The Olympic Park will also be linked to extensive new cycle and pedestrian routes.
- At the heart of the development is the biggest new park created in London for over 100 years. It has been designed as a piece of green infrastructure that will enrich the biodiversity of the Lower Lea Valley, creating 45 hectares of ecological habitat. It will provide much needed open and accessible public space, flood mitigation for homes off and on the Park and green highways for fauna and human communities alike.
- The ODA, working with British Waterways, the Environment Agency and other partners, has cleaned up and improved access to eight kilometres of waterways and towpaths that cross the Park. Barges can now navigate from the River Thames to the Park for the first time in over 30 years.
- The Athletes Village will house 17,000 athletes and support staff during the Olympic Games and over 5,000 during the Paralympic Games, and will be converted into 2818 new homes in legacy under a range of tenures, including affordable homes, all built to the highest environmental standards. It will also provide social infrastructure including schools and health facilities.
- There is commitment to remove unnecessary assets after the 2012 Games, including road and concourse facilities, temporary bridges and temporary elements like Games-time seating in order to leave an unfettered site that is highly serviced and ready for legacy development.

Setting sustainability standards for design and construction

The ODA has sought to set new standards for sustainable design and construction. The ODA Sustainable Development Strategy has 12 headline objectives and a set of clear targets that have been embedded into all of the projects being delivered by the ODA[3]. The 12 objectives are as follows:

1. Carbon: To minimise the carbon emissions associated with the Olympic Park and venues.
2. Water: To optimise the opportunities for efficient water use, reuse and recycling.

---

3. Olympic Delivery Authority. *Sustainable Development Strategy*. (January 2007). Available at: http://www.london2012.com/publications/sustainable-development-strategy-full-version.php (accessed October 2010)

3. Waste: To optimise the reduction of waste though design and to maximise the reuse and recycling of materials arising during demolition, remediation and construction.
4. Materials: To identify, source, and use environmentally and socially responsible materials.
5. Biodiversity and ecology: To protect and enhance the biodiversity and ecology of the Lower Lea Valley and other venue locations.
6. Land, water, noise, and air: To optimise positive and minimise adverse impacts on land, water, noise and air quality.
7. Supporting communities: To create new, safe mixed-use public space, housing and facilities appropriate to the demographics and character of the Lower Lea Valley, adaptable to future climates.
8. Transport and mobility: To prioritise walking, cycling and the use of public transport to and within the Olympic Park and venues.
9. Access: To create a highly-accessible Olympic Park and venues by meeting the principles of inclusive design.
10. Employment and Business: To create new employment and business opportunities locally, regionally and nationally.
11. Health and well-being: To provide for healthy lifestyle opportunities during the construction of, and in the design of the Olympic Park and venues.
12. Inclusion: To involve, communicate, and consult effectively with stakeholders and the diverse communities surrounding the Olympic Park and venues.

Setting a sustainability strategy and targets for the Olympic Park was very challenging. There were no precedents to borrow from when deciding on the standards to adopt or tools and processes for measuring performance. The targets were designed to influence the wide range of projects being delivered, including sporting, broadcasting and media venues, structures, bridges and highways, the new housing development, parklands, utility projects and other facilities. The ODA, working with its delivery partner CLM, set up a number of Priority Theme teams to deliver these targets. Each of the Priority Themes established a technical and assurance team to ensure targets were embedded into the delivery process. The core targets were enshrined in the local planning conditions for the Olympic Park, which gave them a formal and binding status in law.

The targets formed part of the project business plan and design brief for each of the individual projects being delivered by the ODA. Each project was required to meet minimum and measurable performance standards. These targets formed part of the procurement process. It was left to the project teams and their design consultants to decide how to meet these targets most cost effectively.

An Environment and Sustainability Management System (ESMS) was developed, which set out targets, processes, procedures, tools and guidance notes for meeting, measuring and reporting against targets during the design and construction phase of the project. The ESMS was ISO 14001 accredited.

Contractors were required to employ a full time sustainability and environment manager to champion and oversee delivery on the ground. These managers were critical to the successful delivery of the sustainability targets, but they were most effective when they had the support of the contractor's Project Director and key staff, including procurement, commercial and operational Directors. Underpinning the management and delivery model was a high level commitment from the London 2012 Olympic Board and the ODA's own Board to deliver a sustainable Games. This commitment enjoyed high level support and resources to ensure it was implemented. The adoption of a 'legacy first' approach and a comprehensive suite of sustainability performance requirements lead to exemplary standards being achieved by the venues. One example is the 6000 seat Velodrome.

A case study: the Velodrome

The Velodrome is the most energy efficient venue on the Olympic Park. It is 30% more efficient than England's national building requirements. The building is compact, has high levels of thermal mass, is highly insulated and makes use of under-floor heating. The building is naturally ventilated and takes heat and hot water from the CCHP system which serves the Olympic Park. Extensive glazed areas in the roof have reduced the need for artificial lighting, which is provided by low energy fittings.

Potable water demand has been reduced from a baseline of 103 mega litres to 28 mega litres total usage including legacy, by a combination of rainwater harvesting and the provision of low water use sanitary fixtures. There is a 25m³ rainwater collection tank, which harvests rainwater from the western half of the Velodrome roof, and will meet approximately 50% of the buildings WC flushing requirement. The building will also take water from the Park-wide non-potable water network mentioned previously.

The building has been designed to minimise embodied carbon. The roof uses a cable net system, the largest in the UK, which uses 10 times less steel than a traditional steel truss roof. More than 10,000m² of timber from certified sustainable sources has been used on the Velodrome, both for cladding and in the support structure. The Velodrome track also uses timber from a certified sustainable source.

The most important lesson from this case study is the way the design team and contractor approached the sustainability brief. Sustainability sat alongside architectural quality and the functional brief as key elements which drove the design. The sustainability agenda was championed by the whole design team, which informed the form of the building, choice of materials, construction process and many other fundamental decisions.

Core challenges

Whilst the ODA established processes to ensure that the 2012 Games bid commitments were met, there were some targets that had to be modified. Through public consultation and in accordance with the GLA policy, the ODA established very challenging targets for carbon reduction and renewable energy production. A detailed strategy and plan was established that included installing a two megawatt wind turbine on the Olympic Park. During the course of the project it became apparent that wind turbines are more risky that first believed and the dangers posed by a blade, hub or mast failure meant that new standards for health and safety had to be established in urban areas. The consequence was that the turbine project was cancelled. Alternative onsite Park solutions have proved to be very difficult and expensive to deliver.

Targets for materials have also been very difficult to meet, partly because there is currently insufficient information about the carbon and environmental performance of many materials. Contractors tend to like to use materials and suppliers they have established relationships with and designers are often nervous about specifying innovative materials. At the same time, many of the big product and material suppliers are making significant investments to improve the environmental and social performance of their products. More consistent and better information is needed about the sustainability performance of materials, including independent verification. Innovation needs to be encouraged in an understandably risk averse industry.

Conclusion

London 2012 set out to deliver the most sustainable Olympic Games and Paralympic Games ever. The London 2012 Board set out a comprehensive approach to sustainability that influenced the choice of site, investment decisions, the design and construction of the Olympic Park, the staging of the Games and the long term legacy. A culture which promoted sustainability was established by the client, supported by investment in dedicated teams that were established to drive sustainability programmes and to provide technical support and assurance. There were no precedents for many of the standards that London 2012 set, and new tools and processes were developed which will influence future Games and regeneration projects more generally.

London 2012 worked very closely with a wide range of stakeholders to develop its standards. Value for money was an important driver of all development decisions, including the choice of sustainable technologies and interventions. The ODA invested heavily in large scale sustainable infrastructure, building flexible systems that could be upgraded over time as new technologies become available.

Overall, London 2012 has been successful in meeting its objectives and has many lessons to share with future Games host cities, other major sporting events and major regeneration projects. This was achieved by ensuring a clear sustainability framework and targets were established early in the development process, and by incorporating these policies and targets into formal planning conditions. The ODA has worked hard to find solutions to major challenges, such as with renewable energy and carbon reduction measures. More information about materials and products is required by industry to help drive sustainable procurement decisions.

Chapter 14
Sustainable Olympics – Assuring a Legacy

The Commission for a Sustainable London 2012

Shaun McCarthy

Introduction

It could be argued that hosting an Olympic Games is an inherently un-sustainable thing to do. Using thousands of flights, consuming vast quantities of power, disrupting communities and habitats and generating many tonnes of waste in the pursuit of entertaining people able to afford to attend or watch on television could be the definitive expression of what is wrong with our society. Placing entertainment above the needs of the planet and society is seen by some environmentalists and social justice campaigners as the root cause of the problem. On the other hand, optimists see the London 2012 Olympic and Paralympic Games (2012 Games) as an opportunity to change behaviour and to promote all that is best about our country as we attempt to stage "the most sustainable Games ever".

This chapter charts the history of the Commission for a Sustainable London 2012 (CSL), how the role of independent assurance developed, what we learned and why this approach may be essential to ensure truly sustainable projects in the future.

Early days

Having failed to secure the right to host the Olympic and Paralympic Games (Games) in 2000, when Manchester lost to Sydney, it was clear that the city of London would need to form the centrepiece of any future UK bid. West London was initially considered for likely sites, possibly using the new Wembley Stadium as a focus. However, a view started to be formed that the 2012 Games must do more than entertain; they should be used to change things and make a wider contribution to society. Attention then switched to the East. For readers not familiar with London, East London is not the London of Harrods, the Royal Opera House and St James's Park. The Boroughs of Hackney, Newham, Waltham Forest and Tower Hamlets are among the most deprived and diverse areas in Europe, with over 50% unemployment, some with over 60% non-native population, 60% residents under 16 years of age, high crime rates, poor housing, poor health and low educational attainment.

The principal objective for a sustainable 2012 Games was to act as a catalyst for redevelopment in East London. To flesh out the definitions behind the political aspiration, a sustainability manager was appointed as a full-time member of the bid team and advice was sought from the London Sustainable Development Commission (LSDC – an independent advisory group to the Mayor), and also NGOs WWF-UK and Bioregional Development Group. The bid team adopted the ten One Planet Living®[1] principles promoted by these environmental NGOs to shape the bid. This started to set aspirations to minimise the environmental impacts of the 2012 Games whilst taking maximum advantage of the opportunity to create a sustainable legacy. As the bid was developed, greater emphasis was placed on sustainability as the unique selling proposition for London. The challenge with this approach was overcoming the high incidence of "greenwash" used by corporations and governments alike at the time to sell their sustainability messages, and the relatively poor knowledge and definition of the subject matter itself. This gave rise to the idea of creating an independent commission to provide assurance over sustainability. Although this concept was established in the bid, very little detail was provided.

July 2005 was a bittersweet month for Londoners; the euphoria in Singapore as London was announced as the 2012 Games host city on the 6th of July was reflected by wild celebrations in Trafalgar Square and elsewhere. The very next day, the devastating suicide bombs on the London transport system will be forever etched in the memory of Londoners; these became known as the 7/7 bombings.

---

1. The ten One Planet Living principles provide a framework to enable a high quality of life within the productive capacity of the planet. See: http://www.oneplanetliving.org/index.html (accessed 1 September 2010)

Establishing the Commission

In common with most newly announced host cities, the hangovers brought a stark realisation that London now needed to deliver the largest peacetime exercise in the world, with more than 200 countries competing, over 7 million spectators and a large proportion of the world watching on TV. This is the biggest show on Earth, and it is coming to *your* town and *you* promised it would be sustainable! I am sure we have all woken up to promises we may regret in the morning, but this was a big one!

Immediately after the bid was won, it became necessary to create a working definition of *sustainability* for the new Organising Committee, and to understand how the independent Commission would be constituted. This necessitated various organisations working together, including the bid team, which was evolving into the London Organising Committee of the Olympic Games and Paralympic Games (LOCOG) and the newly formed Olympic Delivery Authority (ODA), who together make up London 2012, as well as the LSDC Olympic sub-group, which would eventually evolve into CSL. Working with the Government's Department for Culture, Media and Sport (DCMS) and the Greater London Authority (GLA), sustainability was defined as comprising five key themes: climate change, waste, biodiversity, healthy living and inclusion. Very shortly afterwards, the ODA developed a suite of objectives under 12 headings. Although the ODA's definitions have undoubtedly led to significant success in delivering sustainable outcomes, the various headings gave rise to some confusion in the early days, and with hindsight it may have been better to continue with the ten One Planet Living principles established in the bid.

Constituting an independent Commission proved to be problematic. Although LSDC was nominated to provide the assurance, it was not an ideal organisation to do so. Firstly, it was a strategic advisory body to the Mayor, not an assurance body; secondly, it belonged to the Mayor with no connection to central Government who were providing most of the funding for the 2012 Games venues and infrastructure. Using a body under the absolute control of the Mayor was not acceptable, so the new Commission would need to be funded by a consortium of organisations. Immediately after the bid, an Olympic Board was formed to act as a focal point for political leadership. This was co-chaired by the Mayor and the Minister for the Olympics, and also comprised the Chair of LOCOG and the Chair of the British Olympic Association (BOA). A decision was made to re-organise the LSDC sub-group into a new body (CSL). The Chair of CSL would report to the Chair of the Olympic Board and retain a position on the Executive Committee of LSDC, neatly circumnavigating the political and fiscal difficulties. This seems like an obvious solution, but in reality this was the result of months of negotiation and discussion between various bodies to achieve the right solution. The Chair of the UK Sustainable Development Commission at the time, Jonathon Porritt, was instrumental in helping to navigate these political waters.

CSL was the first body of its kind in the world, so there was no existing working model to follow. A unique partnership of PricewaterhouseCoopers and Forum for the Future was engaged to assist CSL in developing an assurance framework to describe how the CSL should be constituted and how it should operate. CSL comprises a part-time (50%) remunerated Chair, supported by a secretariat of three people, and is advised by voluntary Commissioners and Co-opted Experts with deep experience and knowledge of various aspects of sustainability. The Chair is accountable for the delivery of CSL's work programme and decides the number of Commissioners required and their areas of expertise. The Chair recommends appointments and dismissals to the Olympic Board. The secretariat is employed by the GLA, and they operate under the direction of the Chair. CSL operates under documented terms of reference with agreed protocols for appointment of Commissioners, public reporting and media relations.

The assurance framework requires a comprehensive annual review personally conducted by the Chair, and more detailed thematic reviews conducted by the secretariat and supported by Commissioners with relevant expertise. One member of the secretariat spends part of their time continuously monitoring performance and engaging with delivery bodies on day-to-day concerns. This is important to ensure relatively minor problems can be dealt with quickly and not escalated. Thematic reviews can be conducted around specific sustainability impacts such as carbon or skills and employment. They can also be related to a process such as procurement or design. CSL decided which thematic reviews should be carried out based on evidence from the annual review and continuous monitoring.

The figure 1. below describes CSL's assurance framework:

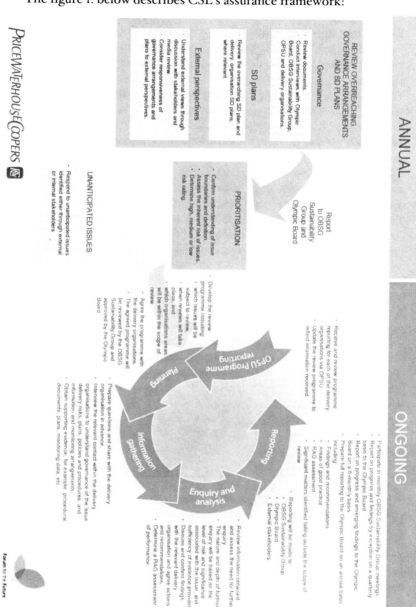

Establishing CSL in an effective manner was critical to the eventual success of the initiative. It is helpful to dwell on the lessons learned:

- **Endorsement** – the creation of an assurance body (CSL) was included in the 2012 Games bid. This was essential to close down any discussion on whether or not CSL should exist, and this moved the debate to how it should operate.
- **Political support** – support of the senior politicians was necessary to establish CSL's independence. Reporting directly to political leaders and not through officials is essential.
- **Leadership** – extensive consultation with the numerous bodies responsible for the 2012 Games was necessary, but the immoveable deadline required a balance between consultation and quick, decisive action to establish CSL at an early stage of the project.
- **Fear of the unknown** – establishing a brand new body with no reporting line through officials and the ability to report directly to the public understandably made officials nervous. This was addressed with strict protocols to ensure that the principle of "no surprises" was not compromised. The behaviour of CSL was of equal importance; balancing constructive engagement with the need to be independent was critical and relied heavily on the judgement of the Chair.
- **Credibility** – if CSL failed to be credible with stakeholders it would have descended rapidly into a bureaucratic waste of money. All stakeholders, particularly the major international NGOs, had to believe that CSL was authoritative and credibly independent. Once again, this proved to be a balancing act between assurance and campaigning. It was necessary to address stakeholders' positions responsibly without pedalling their agenda, whilst also acknowledging the achievements of the delivery bodies without being their advocates.

Dealing with the issues

Below is a summary of the major milestones in the CSL programme of work, including several formal London 2012 assurance reviews and commentary.

Governance and strategy

CSL's first annual review identified a number of London 2012 structural issues to be addressed. The two main London 2012 delivery bodies (LOCOG and the ODA) had appointed Heads of Sustainability staff positions, and made early attempts at developing sustainability objectives. The London 2012 Sustainability Group was established early on, and was made up of representatives of the delivery bodies and main Government bodies involved in delivering the 2012 Games. However, this was a co-ordination group and not a leadership group. Anticipating significant strategic issues to be dealt with, CSL recommended the appointment of a senior figure to lead the sustainability agenda. The Mayor's advisor for the Olympics was appointed to Chair the London 2012 Sustainability Group. This role reported directly to the Mayor and held a position on the Olympic Board Steering Group, which advised the Olympic Board. This proved to be a sound recommendation and response, enabling significant issues to be raised with senior executives and political leaders as the programme progressed.

Although the delivery bodies had established five key sustainability themes (carbon, waste, biodiversity, healthy living and inclusion), there was no comprehensive plan to support these themes. The recommendations in CSL's first report gave rise to the London 2012 Sustainability Plan, setting out the objectives in a more cohesive manner.

Carbon emissions were always going to be a significant issue for stakeholders, and CSL recommended that carbon should be treated as a strategic issue by London 2012. This resulted in a very comprehensive and groundbreaking carbon footprint exercise and a limited strategic approach being taken.

The first annual report also called for a more strategic approach to waste. We suggested that the London Development Agency (LDA) should be responsible for facilitating development of waste infrastructure in East London, using anaerobic digestion of organic waste that could produce biogas to supply the Olympic Park with energy. Despite worthy efforts of some of the people involved, this proved to be too difficult and never happened.

Hard times

Our second annual review had a picture of a salmon swimming up the river Tyne, and we nicknamed him "Geordie the salmon". This cover was meant to represent striving to deliver sustainability in the hard times of the recession. The London 2012 bid was won during an economic boom, but it was built during one of the worst recessions in living memory.

The most important finding of this report is that we saw no evidence of cost-cutting reducing the published sustainability standards. The presence of a then well-established Commission with independent relations with the media and the NGOs was a contributing factor. Nothing could be quietly brushed under the carpet. This was also a time when CSL started to show its teeth. This came with recommendations related to hydrofluorocarbons (HFCs) and the material polyvinyl chloride (PVC).

HFCs are gases used in refrigeration and air conditioning. They were developed as a replacement to chlorofluorocarbons (CFCs), the gases responsible for the hole in the ozone layer which have been banned. Ironically, HFCs caused problems of their own because they are greenhouse gases impacting climate change. The ODA did not develop objectives related to this issue but LOCOG did. Lacking guidance, the ODA's architects and engineers came up with a mixed solution with ammonia chillers in the main energy centre, but HFCs everywhere else. The ODA argued that it was too late to change and that the emissions were expected to be relatively small. For them the case to replace the chillers was not viable. This was not an acceptable argument to CSL, who took the matter up with the Olympic Board, advising them that they could be at risk of direct protest action if something was not done. This was a success, resulting in a new policy that presumed against HFCs unless their use could be demonstrated as the most sustainable solution. Subsequently it was determined that HFCs were the best solution for the Stadium, but not for the Aquatic Centre where the venue's huge chilling capacity was changed to ammonia.

The other major issue raised by CSL was PVC. This proved to be a very complex issue. Although technology has improved, the material is energy intensive to make and is hard to recycle. The presence of phthalates as a plasticizer is controversial, with some influential bodies claiming it is a cancer-causing substance, yet a claim hotly denied by the industry. Once again the ODA had no policy but LOCOG did. Following engagement with the Olympic Board and extensive consultation with NGOs, CSL recommended a ten-point generic specification for tensile plastic, a standard that had never been asked for or met anywhere in the world. This led the ODA to challenge the plastics industry through its procurement process, and an Italian company responded able to manufacture a phthalate-free product that complied with all the other technical requirements, including fire safety. This proved to be problematic for the Stadium roof and Basketball Arena, which failed the fire test and had to revert to a phthalate-based solution. The next venue was successful and the world had a new and safer product.

Carbon emissions

CSL's carbon review was instrumental, but its publication was delayed as a result of Government reluctance to publish the London 2012 carbon footprint. The process of developing a London 2012 carbon management plan could have been better if the following had materialised:
- Stronger leadership could have led to a strategic management plan for carbon, rather than commissioning a carbon footprinting exercise and then wondering what to do with the information for two years.
- The ODA could have acted sooner to set standards for embodied carbon impacts (the energy used to manufacture construction materials).
- LOCOG had some great initiatives but could have done more to set targets to reduce carbon emissions. At the time of writing, LOCOG have no

carbon target and have not targeted obvious things like logistics, where their partner has an excellent track record.

- Government needs to understand the lessons learned and make sure they are applied on future projects. As it stands at the moment, the good work done to date in carbon footprinting will be lost if it is not taken on and used on future construction projects.

May 2010 saw the cancellation of the ODA's wind turbine on the Olympic Park, and a very intensive period of negative publicity. CSL supported the ODA's decision, but insisted the ODA must honour their commitments to achieve 20% onsite renewable energy on the Olympic Park in legacy by other means. This was a real challenge to explain to a sceptical public.

Will it make a difference?

The most recent annual report at the time of writing this chapter starts to ask if London 2012 will actually make a difference to a sustainable world. This is a high quality problem because by this time there is a high degree of confidence in plans to deliver sustainable venues and the 2012 Games themselves.

The report explored the substance behind political promises to make the Olympic Park "a blueprint for sustainable living" and "a catalyst for waste management infrastructure in East London"[2]. The report also explored the recommendations of the carbon report in more detail and the need for the construction industry to learn new skills to support reduction of embodied emissions. There seemed to be very little substance behind these early

---

2. London 2012 Olympic Board, *London 2012 Sustainability Policy*, (June 2006). (updated November 2009).

Government promises and the Civil Service was paralysed by the imminent general election in May 2010 and the threat of savage cuts in public expenditure to recover the national debt caused by the recession in 2007/8.

CSL called for more to be done in this area and for Government to look for imaginative ways to take the agenda forward without the need for public funds. For example, it could use its own procurement power to signal the need for robust embodied carbon management and encouraging the construction sector to invest in the research and skills-development knowing they will be valued by public sector procurers in the future.

What a good Commission looks like

CSL is new and unique, so it is appropriate to reflect on the key success criteria. As previously stated, a lot of power and responsibility is vested in the Chair. Single point responsibility backed by a very well informed and challenging Commission has worked well. Chairing such a Commission is like walking a tightrope with sharks on one side and crocodiles on the other. The trick is to keep your balance at all times! Here are some tips to avoid the sharks and crocodiles:

- **Never go native** – it is absolutely necessary to have a constructive relationship with delivery bodies, but independence must be retained at all times. Never be part of a decision process and always make it clear when you are switching between "critical friend" and formal assurance.
- **Pro-active not reactive** – there are no second chances with a Games project. The Commission must take a forward view of the resources, plans and strategies and have the foresight to point out potential flaws.
- **Assurance not campaigning** – always remember that CSL is an assurance body and not a campaigning organisation. This is what separates it from the NGOs. Do not be tempted to pedal other peoples' agenda (or your own).
- **Be tough and courageous** – although campaigning should be avoided, being very challenging must come with the turf. If you do not challenge hard the NGOs will dismiss you as a waste of space, so you may as well pack in and go home.
- **Don't let them grind you down** – English officials are always very polite to you when they try to bully you into doing what they want you to do (different approaches may be adopted in other countries). Do not allow this to happen. A part-time Chair with an alternative income stream is ideal (provided there is no conflict). Be prepared to resign in a blaze of self-righteous publicity if necessary.

Chapter 15

A Tale of Two Villages

London, Vancouver and 'Sustainability'

Iain MacRury

Introduction

Olympic and Paralympic Games (Games) Athletes Villages are practical buildings fit for specific Games-time purposes, housing athletes, coaches, managers, and technicians, and are outfitted to accommodate the needs of both Olympic and Paralympic athletes. Villages are also emblematic objects: a 'human' platform for super-human feats and a terms-defining gesture within the legacy conversation. Ideally the Village concretises a joint aspiration from the International Olympic Committee (IOC) and the host city, part of an attempt to put the (global) Village back into the city; to open-up and leave behind a space that marks friendship[1], community and cosmopol-

---

1. The London Organising Committee of the Olympic Games and Paralympic Games (LOCOG) describes its Athletes Village as including an 'International Zone' where athletes can meet with friends and family. This is in the spirit of Olympian 'Friendship'. No doubt the security script around the Village will be limiting in many ways, which is a legacy on the Munich 1972 tragedy.

itan internationalism. The Athletes Village is an Olympic asset; part of the good of the Games.

Well before the Games begin, the unfolding processes of adaptation of the Village (physically and financially) for life after the event stands as a significant index; it is a sign pointing to something of the tone and substance of the host city's commitments to broader ideas of legacy. The Village seems initially to be the easiest piece of Games' furniture to inherit. It offers the host city an opportunity for a quick-win. Games organisers can make a practical contribution to legacy, while also forming a statement about relationships between the Games, the host city, the community and other stakeholders. As Spanish urbanist Francesca Munoz suggests, Games Villages point to "the history of ideas about how to develop the city, how to plan it and how to manage it" (Muñoz 1996).

The Athletes Village for the London 2012 Olympic Games and Paralympic Games, adjacent to the emerging Stratford itself, a large development. It is set in the end to yield in the region of 3000 homes. But it stands too as something more abstract; it is a test-bed for the developing working definition of a concept central to development planning up and down the Thames Gateway. That concept is *sustainability*. The final refinements to London's 2012 Games Village planning might be helpfully informed by a look at the Athletes Village in Vancouver, built for the 2010 Winter Games. Two years ahead of London in its 2010 Games preparations, Vancouver has shared some of the Games regeneration-development challenges associated with "legacy", facing economic conditions marked by the credit crunch and public spending cuts[2]. Vancouver organisers pitched the 2010 Games as the first 'sustainable' Games. High aspirations have been put to the test.

The British sporting imagery identifies the Olympic Movement squarely with *summer* events. Notwithstanding, Torvill and Dean in Sarajevo (1984), Eddie the Eagle in Calgary (1988) and Scottish Curlers in Salt Lake City (2002), the Winter Games have been a minority interest in the UK. Consequently, less attention is given to *winter* events, and to the achievements, stories and controversies surrounding Winter Games host cities. There are ostensibly good reasons for this summer-centrism. Winter Games host cities tend to be smaller than the cities that host Summer Games: thus Sochi not Moscow (2014 Games); Turin not Rome (2006 Games); Albertville not Paris (1992 Games). The component events, and there are far fewer of them than in the Summer Games, draw a smaller, less global audience. The mountains rather than the cityscape serve as frame, backdrop and focus for thinking about place-making and sustainable development. The budgets are smaller; the champions less familiar.

---

2. *The Economist* offers an assessment: "British Columbia's lumber industry has been hit by the housing bust in the United States. Unemployment has more than doubled since January 2008, to 8%; tax revenues are falling steeply. On September 1st [2009] the province's finance minister...forecast a C$2.8 billion ($2.5 billion) deficit in this fiscal year..." and ongoing problems leading to public spending cuts.

What insights can London, East London and the Thames Gateway take away from Vancouver? Telling comparisons are initially elusive. Vancouver is the model of a successful medium-sized city. Its growing population (est. 611,869) in its central locales is complemented by at least a further 2,000,000+ in the Greater Vancouver area. The metropolis is noted for successes in maintaining a vibrant residential core, integrated with and integrating the city's dynamic commercial life. It differs from East London (site of the London's 2012 Games Olympic Park) in size of course; but also in the degree to which, in Vancouver, gentrification and polarization – starkly evident for instance around London's Canary Wharf development – seem less pronounced. This, along with waterside living and spectacular scenery, contributes to the case made successfully for Vancouver as a supremely 'liveable' city[3]. At first blush then, it is tricky to see what connects East London and Vancouver.

In small details there *are* some neat London-Vancouver Games legacy links. One instance: the bleachers temporarily in use for the curling ice will be shipped to London for re-use during the 2012 Games. The 2010 Games curling venue, retro-fitted for easy conversion into an ice rink, swimming pool, library and nursery, will provide a refurbished community centre. In broader terms such projects point to London's and Vancouver's shared commitment to the rhetoric of legacy and sustainability. Vancouver seems wholly comfortable with 'legacy' discourse, engaged with IOC visioning, and alerted to the fallout from mixed Games experiences in the medium-term past: at the national level in Montreal 1976, and at regional-provincial level in British Columbia during the Calgary Games in 1988[4]. London is the first city to be awarded a Summer Games by an IOC which places Legacy squarely at the centre of its mission – so much so that the term has the quality (at times) of a mantra.

Between Vancouver and London: Testing "Sustainability"

Other links between the two Games host cities are more conceptual. In particular *sustainability* is playing a headline role in Vancouver's Games conversation, as it is in London. The front cover of the Organising Committee's (VANOC) sustainability self-monitoring papers offers a succinct definition: "For VANOC sustainability means managing the social, economic and environmental impacts and opportunities of our Games to produce lasting benefits, locally and globally" (VANOC 2008). The 2012 Games organisers

---

3. *The Economist's* liveability ranking system placed Vancouver at no. 1 of 140 world cities in 2010, with a score of 98 out of 100. See: http://www.economist.com/blogs/gulliver/2010/02/liveability_ranking

4. There has been some important thinking in serial bid city Toronto. Kidd, B. (1992). "The Toronto Olympic Commitment: towards a social contract for the Olympic Games."; *Olympika: The International Journal of Olympic Studies* 1 pp.154-167.

promise to create a 'blueprint for sustainable living' comes quickly to mind, as do more detailed Games sustainability commitments – subdivided to cover climate change, biodiversity, healthy living, inclusion and waste. Scrutiny will come in part from the Commission for a Sustainable London 2012, established by the 2012 Games organisers and government to "provide credible, independent assurance on the sustainability status of the London 2012 Games" (CSL 2007: 1).

'Sustainability' is not just an Olympic pre-occupation; it echoes in resolutions made by government bodies in the UK and in Canada. In the UK, the Thames Gateway London Partnership recently committed to seek "a balance between the drives for economic success, environmental protection and social equity" because "cohesive communities are forged when these are in harmony". The Canadian External Advisory Committee on Cities and Communities, EACCC2006, set down the following – part commitment, part rule of thumb:

> "Sustainability is most usefully regarded as a guiding principle, rather than a specific set of ideas applied in a single area such as environmental policy. The essence ...is to recognize that there are assets, costs and benefits not accounted for in market decisions and values. Sustainability looks to the public interest beyond narrow market decisions". (Holden, MacKenzie and Van Wynsberghe 2008)

Both cities have mobilised *sustainability* as a major narrative-term in legacy development. Indeed, the establishment of a working definition of sustainability in regional re-development is an important 'legacy' gain. The establishment and successful demonstration of this concept-in-action affords the means whereby 'intangible' legacies (celebratory affirmations of ethical commitments to ecology and social justice) might become translated into 'hard', 'tangible', 'lasting' gains – the promissory 'blueprint' made real. This, then, is one potential source of Thames Gateway Games legacy for the long term.

Hymn from a Village

Something else links London and Vancouver. Both cities planned their respective Athletes Villages with a mindset attuned to the world of accessible credit, growing land and property prices, and routine commitment to the idea of public-private financing: seemingly a best-of-both-worlds urban development paradigm. Both cities face delivering the Games and their legacy promises in credit crunch conditions, and with a protracted recession on the horizon. This puts massive pressure on public finances, with knock on pressures placed on the national- and local-political imagination. The public private formula is not delivering as planned.

Vancouver and London share something else. Both cites have long standing and developing problems with homelessness and affordable housing, with policy developments and house building failing to keep pace with need.

This is the major blot on Vancouver's copy book. It provides an uncomfortable contextualisation for elite-focussed assessments of liveability. Housing then is high on the agenda. This policy context brings additional energy to debates around the Villages and their legacy. The following Table 1 sets down some of the original dimensions and characteristics of the two Athletes Villages.

Vancouver Village: South East False Creek	London Village: Stratford, East London
Headline cost: CA\$996 million, which includes \$146 million in interest costs[5] or £560m[6]	**Headline cost:** £1,095 million
Financing plan: **Initially:** Property developer Millennium sought finance from a US Hedge Fund. An agreement was made, but the fund managers, having been hit by the crunch, eventually pulled out early in 2009.	**Financing plan:** **Initially:** Property developer Lend Lease planned to get financing from private investors. No deal was achieved. Public funds from the 2012 Games (contingency) budget were used to ensure continued work on the project while private finance was sought.
Now: A loan has been refinanced through a syndicate of Canadian banks. Vancouver city/public funding is guaranteeing the project costs for the Village (i.e. CA\$996 million)	**Now:** It was decided in the summer 2009 to place the Village in public ownership, with a portion of the Village sold to a social housing corporation. • £650 million of public investment • £268 million of funding for social housing
Games-time accommodation: 600 units for 2,730 athletes and officials and 350 Paralympians	**Games-time accommodation:** 2,818 units for 17,000 coaches and athletes
Indicative sale prices of private apartments post Games: The most expensive listing is more than CA\$1.5m for a penthouse, but the average prices are CA\$400,000 to CA\$700,000. The city is expecting to wait until the market improves as it seeks to maximize returns.	**Indicative sale prices of private apartments post Games:** Pricing structure currently unclear. 50% affordable housing will include various modes of ownership, shared ownership and rental.

---

5. Cernetig, Miro. The Vancouver Sun. *Olympic village $130 million over budget: audit* (6 October 2009) See http://www.vancouversun.com/business/Vancouver+Olympic+-Village+million+over+budget+report/2072466/story.html (accessed October 2010).

6. Exchange rate est: 1 CAD = 0.562217 GBP as at November 2009.

Legacy Housing:	Legacy housing:
First estimates: The development began with a commitment to a three way split: 1/3 affordable housing, 1/3 middle-income housing and 1/3 market housing. This was then revised down, following the financial difficulties in January-February 2009, with 80% allocated to market housing and 20% allocated to affordable housing.	**First estimates:** Approximately 4,000 homes and Games chiefs pledged that 30% would be affordable housing. This was then revised following the financial difficulties in 2008/09 to 2,818 homes with 50% affordable housing owned and managed by joint venture Triathlon Homes.
Indicative Environmental features	**Indicative Environmental features**
Meets highest levels of LEED (Leadership in Energy and Environmental Design) accreditation. A number of innovate green technologies around waste, water and energy management.	Aims to meet level four (beyond the EcoHomes 'excellent' rating) under the government's Code for Sustainable Homes, prior to legislation requiring this level of achievement.
Other amenities: a 45,000 square foot community centre, three child care centres, an elementary school, community garden, and public plaza[7]	**Other amenities:** A school, multi-use community facilities, and new infrastructure to connect the new communities with the Olympic Park[8]

The Vancouver Athletes Village suggests an impressive achievement. The waterfront apartment development looks stunning. The planning has opened up an important public space next to the water and the development communicates a sense of connectedness between the flows of the city and the waterside. A number of innovative green technologies are deployed across the complex, to harvest rainwater, to recover heat from sewers, and to enhance eco-education. The project stands as a flagship development in terms of environmental sustainability, qualifying for the highest level of accreditation under the U.S. Green Building Council's LEED (Leadership in Energy and Environmental Design) scheme.

In Vancouver, and notwithstanding the eye-opening eco-technologies and designer interiors of the impressively executed waterfront Village, the outcome seems to be, at best, mixed. In order to recoup the additional expenditures emerging from collapsed private finance arrangements this city has had to make some hard decisions about the housing mix in the Village. There have been strident calls for the city to ignore commitments to the 250 social housing units on the grounds that subsidising these (at est. CA$600,000 per unit) is not an economically efficient use of public funds. Housing, after all, could be built elsewhere, increasing the likelihood of

---

7. The City of Vancouver. Southeast False Creek & Olympic Village. Available at: http://vancouver.ca/olympicvillage/about.htm (accessed October 2010).

8. Information on London 2012's Athletes Village can be accessed online at: http://www.theathletesvillage.com/page/the-athletes-village (accessed October 2010).

higher market returns on the Village-legacy properties. Properties are marketed heavily on their Olympic-pedigree, with the offer of a chance to live in a legacy.

There have been protests linking the Games to the homelessness issue in Vancouver, with housing activists bring a "Poverty Olympics Torch Relay"[9] to protest. Press coverage has identified muddle, mismanagement and lost opportunities. The negative impacts on Games budget are likely to put other legacy projects at risk. The definition of *sustainability* – a vision that arguably looks to the public interest beyond narrow market decisions – has been challenged as market considerations have come to define one interpretation of the public interest. The Village seems unlikely to live up to the highest aspirations initially set out – for a sustainable, mixed community enjoying an environmentally well conceived housing development inspired by the 'glow' of Games legacy-success. The 'green' aspect of the development seems the only component of the sustainability vision to have survived uncompromised. Is this a feature of an Olympic fetish of 'green' sustainability – with harder, less glamorous, socio-economic sustainability issues deferred or avoided? Is there such a thing as a 'Green Elephant?'

The issue facing London then is how to maximise a return on the governmental investment while respecting commitments to a socially inclusive definition of *sustainable communities*. The London 2012 Athletes Village will encompass 11 blocks, composed of six to eight buildings each. Social housing will be allocated in buildings separate to the buildings assigned for private homes. There is already disquiet about the dynamics of this mix: a conflict between a marketing conception of Return on Investment and a Legacy conception of sustainability. There remains a good deal to settle, even while there are, as yet, no indications that published affordable housing promises in the Village will decrease. The credit crunch and consequential impacts on planning and financing the Village rocked, if not destroyed, Vancouver's ambitions for building a sustainability legacy. The public-private model has been found inadequate in this case.

If London can better resolve the problems facing Village sustainability in the immediate months, perhaps taking further heed of some of the complexities made manifest in Vancouver, then that would be progress. To more successfully address problems which seem to be remaining precariously unresolved in Vancouver is an Olympic challenge for London. If it can credibly meet that challenge, then London will have contributed a positive legacy, one with potentially good consequences up and down the Thames Gateway.

9.Poverty Olympics. Poverty Olympics Torch Relay: Shining a spotlight on BC. http://povertyolympics.ca/?page_id=87 (accessed October 2010).

References

Holden, M., J.MacKenzie, and R. Van Wynsberghe. (2008). 'Vancouver's promise of the world's first sustainable Olympic Games'. *Environment & Planning C: Government & Policy* Vol. 26 pp.882-905.

Kidd, B. (1992). "The Toronto Olympic Commitment: towards a social contract for the Olympic Games." *Olympika: The International Journal of Olympic Studies* 1:154-167.

Chapter 16

Green Britannia

Deconstructing 'Team Green Britain' and the London 2012 Olympic and Paralympic Games

Maxine Newlands

Introduction

London 2012[1] is pitching to host "the greenest Games" as part of its marketing and branding campaign[2]. They have said that sustainability is central to making the 30th Summer Olympic Games and Paralympic Games (2012

---

1. The London 2012 Games are run by two companies, one private and one public. The London Organising Committee of the Olympic Games and Paralympic Games (LOCOG) is the private sector company responsible for staging and hosting the 2012 Games. The Olympic Delivery Authority (ODA) is a publicly funded body who are responsible for building new venues and the infrastructure for the Games.

2. Olympic Delivery Authority Chief Executive, David Higgins, speaking at the launch of the ODA's Sustainability Strategy on 23 January 2007. For further information see *London 2012 - Sustainability strategy launched* available at: http://www.london2012.com/press/media-releases/2007/01/london-2012-sustainability-strategy-launched.php (accessed February 2010)

Games) "the greenest Games of the modern era",[3] and they are aiming to set the "highest standards in sustainability and legacy for other Games to follow"[4] (Weaver, 2007). However, less than two years out from the Games, the organisers (London 2012) have already been accused of failing to meet their targets to make the 2012 Games the "greenest Games in history" (Brierley, 2008). Increased flights[5] from the nearest airport (London City Airport),[6] proposals to lift the ban on night flights into London Heathrow, delays in releasing reports on carbon emissions and a row over an environmentally focused campaign by a major sponsor have all brought into question whether London 2012's green credentials are sound; these questions are all occurring even before the event begins. The problem is that any brand that makes sweeping declarations on the environment faces the challenge of either risking 'green fatigue' (De Bois, 2008) or accusations of misleading the public through greenwashing.

The British media have been less than flattering when reporting on claims that the 2012 Games will be the greenest Games in history. This response from journalists is similar to their reaction in Albertville at the 1992 Olympic Winter Games and in Sydney for the 2000 Olympic Games. British journalists have framed a series of financial miscalculations, escalating costs during a global economic downturn and the moving of venues[7] in negative terms, underpinned with accusations of greenwashing. Greenwashing can be defined as "public relations efforts to portray an organization, activity or product as environmentally friendly" (Beder, 2001); in reality it tends to mean "trying to cover up environmentally and/or socially damaging activities" (ibid). Environmental NGO Greenpeace have been critical of the

---

3. Ibid: Prime Minster, Tony Blair, speaking in 2007, at the same event as Higgins and Lord Coe.

4. Lord Sebastian Coe, speaking at the same event as Prime Minister Tony Blair and reported by Weaver in *The Guardian* newspaper at: http://www.guardian.co.uk/uk/2007/jan/23/greenpolitics.london.

5. In response to the UK having been awarded the 2012 Olympic and Paralympic Games in London, the CAA's Safety Regulation Group has set up the CAA Olympic and Paralympic Steering Group (COPSG). The primary purpose of the group is to ensure that a high standard of aviation safety continues to be maintained throughout the period leading up to, during and immediately following the 2012 Olympic and Paralympic Games. The steering group has acknowledged that flights will have to be increased up to and during the Games. see http://www.caa.co.uk/docs/33/ATSIN0159.pdf (accessed March 2010).

6. In July 2009, the London Borough of Newham, which is the local authority for London City Airport, approved an expansion of flight numbers from 80,000 to 120,000 a year. London City airport is six kilometres from the Olympic Park site. See http://www.londoncityairport.com/AboutUs/ViewRelease.aspx? id=1122 (accessed 12 January 2010).

7. Originally the ODA and LOCOG planned to build new venues on the Olympic Park site for Rhythmic Gymnastics and Badminton. These will now take place in a temporary venue at Wembley Arena alongside boxing, which has also moved from the Olympic Site to Wembley.

Olympic Movement over their less than green collaborative corporate partners, some of which hail from The Olympic Partner (TOP) programme run
by the International Olympic Committee (IOC)[8,9].

This chapter begins with an analysis of why the IOC, who previously had
little engagement with environmentalism, made the *Environment* the third
pillar of Olympism[10]. This work argues that in light of the Albertville 1992
Games and international pressure from the United Nations, there was a
need for transnational organisations to "respond to questions concerning
the relationship between their mega events and the impact they have upon
the natural world" (Cantelon and Letters, 2010: 419). The concept of an
Olympic Games and Paralympic Games (Games) as mega events can be seen
to contradict and contest environmental values; "while environmentalism is
based on the three R's – reduce, reuse and recycle – the Games are based on
the Big More: more spectators, more sales, more jobs, more tourism, more
growth, more infrastructure" (Hayes, 2008). The task for the IOC and host
cities is to try and bring these contradictions together. This challenge has
previously proved difficult for Games Organising Committees (OCOGs),
and continues to be a stumbling block for London 2012. This work con-
cludes with some observations from previous Games, and the implications
for the 2012 Games' challenge to be the greenest Games of the modern era.

Green Games

Environmentalism[11] and eco-centric plans have risen to prominence in the
Olympic Movement. Increasing concerns over the environmental impact of
a mega event, from the construction of venues and Athletes Villages to the
volume of spectators and media travelling to the Games, have pushed the

---

8. The International Olympic Committee: The Olympic Partner (TOP) Programme:
http://www.olympic.org/en/content/The-IOC/Sponsoring/Sponsorship/?Tab=1 (accessed August 2010)

9. Greenpeace contacted sponsors and suppliers prior to the Sydney 2000 Games and
Beijing 2008 Games, including Coca-Cola, Haier, Lenovo, McDonald's, Panasonic,
Samsung, and Yili, asking them to adopt climate friendly HFC-Free refrigeration
and air conditioning units instead of CFC units. They also asked the electronics
companies to use the Games as a way of showcasing greener electronic products
with less toxic substances. Greenpeace were disappointed when some sponsors
failed to fulfill their request. For more information see http://www.greenpeace.org/
raw/content/china/en/reports/sponsors.pdf (accessed October 2010)

10. The IOC Sport and Environment Commission. See: http://www.olympic.org/en/c-
ontent/The-IOC/Commissions/Sport-and-Environment-/ (accessed October 2010).

11. The IOC requires that bid cities submit 'environmental' plans, but is yet to use the
term 'sustainability'; however, the term 'sustainable development' is applied by the
IOC. The term 'sustainable development' was first used in the Bruntland Commission (1987). The Commission defined the concept of 'sustainable development'
as the "framework for the integration of environmental policies and development
strategies" (Torgerson, 1999:53). Thus for this chapter the author will use the term
'environmentalism'.

IOC to react. However, it was not until the Lillehammer Winter Games in 1994 that the IOC went from being "an organisation with no environmental policy to one with a policy fully integrated into its philosophy of Olympism" (Cantelon and Letters, 2010: 419-20). This chapter argues that the IOC shifted its position because of the disastrous Albertville 1992 Games, and international pressure from the United Nations following its resolution of Agenda 21 (1992).

The Albertville Games were held in southeast France in 1992, the same year as the Barcelona Summer Games. The Albertville 1992 Games were deemed by the international press and environmentalists as disastrous. Aside from the 11 venues spread across a wide geographical area, the majority of environmental damage came from the construction of new sporting venues and alpine courses, which often meant blasting or altering much of the natural environment. For example, the Nordic Skiing course required "specific undulation of [the] course, strict gradients, designated width track, and a minimum number of slopes" (Cantelon and Letters, 2010: 423), altering the natural landscape. Moreover, residents in La Plagne, host of the luge and bobsleigh competitions, wore gas masks to protect themselves against the "risk linked to the storage of the 40 tonnes of ammonia needed to freeze the bobsleigh [track]" (Terret, 2008:1916). Journalists reported the changes in unfavourable terms, and a series of eco-protests put environmentalism and the Games into the spotlight.

The IOC denied any environmental damage, dismissing the claim as "groundless accusations" and "virulent press campaigns" that were "pursued doggedly" (Winkler, 1993:87). The IOC and OCOG initially "appeared relatively unconcerned "by environmental questions during the Games preparation" (Terret, 2008:1916), which further exacerbated a "critical disjunction between the transnational ideology of Olympism and the pragmatic nature of IOC transnational operations" (Cantelon and Letters, 2010: 424). Slowly, the IOC realised they had to be seen to be doing something, but their lack of environmental awareness gave them little understanding in how to be "an effective and proactive environmental watchdog" (Cantelon and Letters, 2010: 425). Fortunately for the Olympic Movement, two options came their way which would help address the issue of environmentalism and detract away from the environmental conflict of the Albertville 1992 Games – these were the United Nations Conference on Environment and Development in 1992 (Earth Summit) and the Lillehammer Winter Games in 1994.

At the Seoul Games in 1988, the Norwegian Prime Minister, Gro Harlem Brundtland, presented Lillehammer's bid to host the 1994 Winter Games. The bid had a strong focus on environmentalism, placing central to their bid "a responsibility to the global balance of nature and an understanding of our role within it into the ideological foundation of the Olympic Movement" (Matheson, 1985:155 in Cantelon and Letters, 2010: 425). The bid was successful. Retrospectively, Lillehammer "was probably the best model of a large international sporting event organised on environmentally friendly principles" (Lenskyj, 1997:174). The Lillehammer 1994 Games also gave the IOC a platform from which they could prove their environmental credentials and bring them in-line with wider environmental politics and the impact of the Earth Summit.

The Earth Summit was significant, because it marked the turning point in green politics when the United Nations "adopt(ed) the first draft of the Earth Charter, a vision for an environmentally sustainable planet" (Cox, 2006:78). The Earth Charter put international pressure on large organisations to adopt an environmental position. At the Earth Summit, delegates passed a motion on Agenda 21[12] which "propelled and justified the term *sustainable development* into common currency" (Buckingham and Turner, 2008:50). Three years after the Earth Summit, the IOC "formally adopted an environmental position" (Toyne, 2009:232-3) by announcing after the Atlanta 1996 Games that "environment and sustainability would have to be part of any future bids" (Toyne, 2009:232). Since the validation of Agenda 21, the Sydney 2000, Vancouver 2010, and preparations for the London 2012 Games have included the wider social and economic inclusion of young and indigenous people into their sustainability programmes.[13] Indeed, the Sydney Organising Committee for the Olympic and Paralympic Games (SOCOG) acknowledged the significance of the 1994 Games in providing "waste management practices, use of biodegradable plates, and utensils, energy saving techniques, environmental specifications for suppliers of goods and services, and environmental legacy to the local community" (Otteson, 1998 in Lenskyj, 174).

Environmentalism is now a key term in Olympic discourse. Olympic values blend sports, culture and education, adding environmentalism across all three disciplines. The Games bidding process includes a requirement to address environmental impacts, which indicates the importance that the IOC places on environmentalism. In 1995, the IOC confirmed that "the environment joined sport and culture to make up the 'three pillars' of the Olympic Charter" (Toyne, 2009:233). However, the challenge comes in en-

---

12. The United Nation's Conference on Environment and Development (UNCED), the Earth Summit of 1992, was held in Rio de Janeiro, Brazil. The newly adopted Earth Charter put international pressure on large organisations to adopt an environmentally friendly position, in what came to be known as Agenda 21. Agenda 21 included the "importance of the involvement of women, children and young people, trade unions, and indigenous people" (Buckingham and Turner, 2008 p.50). For further information see: http://www.un.org/esa/dsd/agenda21/res_agenda21_00.shtml (accessed October 2010).

13. The Vancouver 2010 Organising Committee for the Olympic and Paralympic Winter Games (VANOC) built sustainability into their strategy by identifying the partnership between VANOC and the indigenous First Nation community. See: http://www.vancouver2010.com/more-2010-information/sustainability/discover-sustainability (accessed May 2010) In the Sydney 2000 Games the aboriginal community was included. See: http://www.sydneyolympicpark.com.au/education_and_learning/history/indigenous/aboriginal_timeline (accessed May 2010). Information on London 2012 can be found at: http://www.london2012.com/making-it-happen/sustainability/index.php (accessed May 2010).

suring claims of environmentalism are authentic. The IOC's decision to include *Environment* as the third pillar of the Olympic Movement was a clear indication of the commitment the IOC was willing to take in protecting the natural environment. The difficulty comes in producing truly sustainable Games. Since Lillehammer in 1994, host cities have attempted to put environmental protection central to their event planning; each host city has encountered problems, and London 2012 is no exception. Just under two years out from the London 2012 Games, early indications show how London's bold statement leaves OCOGs open to accusations of 'greenwashing'.

Greenwashing and the Games

The Sydney 2000 bid included a series of environmental principles[14], but neglected to discuss toxic waste on the site of the proposed Olympic Village. It was left to Greenpeace Australia to provide examples of the lack of research into the toxicity problems of Sydney. Both in Sydney 2000 and now for London 2012, organisers have been accused of greenwashing and the media have identified problems with both Games. The Olympic Park venues of Homebush Bay in Sydney and the Stratford site in East London are both formerly degraded, contaminated, and former landfill sites. They are similar in that both have a history of hazardous chemical waste being left to seep into the ground over time. Homebush Bay, to the west of Sydney, formerly housed a Union Carbide factory – manufacturers of the herbicide 'Agent Orange'. Homebush Bay had suffered "years of unregulated waste dumping ...it is the worst toxic waste dump in Australia, and the bay into which the waste leaches is so contaminated that fishing in it is banned" (Beder, 2002:247).

SOCOG was accused of manipulating the data for the purpose of public relations. After winning the bid to host the Games in Sydney in 1993, environmental groups began distancing themselves from the Games. Initially, Greenpeace and other key Australian environmentalists supported the Sydney 2000 bid. Yet, by 1995 the Australian Broadcast Corporation's (ABC) current affairs show 'Four Corners' (1995), featured Greenpeace "criticising" the cover up of the sites' toxic contamination (Beder, 2002:252). Two years later, a report (1995) by environmental group Green Games Watch 2000 (GGW) identified serious problems with the Sydney Olympic Delivery Authority's attempts at public participation and community consultation, and concluded that the process was "in danger of becoming ineffective, tokenistic and superficial" (Lenskyj, 2002:157). Greenpeace, the Australian Conservation Foundation and the New South Wales Nature

---

14. The Sydney Bid Committee stated the following goals: 1) Energy conservation and use of renewable energy sources, 2) Water conservation, 3) Waste avoidance and minimization, 4) Protecting human health with appropriate standards of air, water and soil quality, and 5) Protecting significant natural and cultural environments. (Lenskyj, 1998 p.176)

Conservation Council felt that the Australian government had misrepresented their support, claiming that "individuals affiliated with those organisations had joined the bid committee's environmental task force; the groups themselves emphatically denied their support" (Beder, 2002:250). Greenpeace continued to carry out direct action to highlight the level of dioxin contamination around Homebush Bay and the Olympic Park site up to Games time.

London emulated Sydney in its bid for the 2012 Games by making environmentalism central to their bid. Moreover, London's development plans have strong similarities with Sydney's. In East London, the land being transformed at Stratford for the London 2012 Olympic Park was previously owned by the London and Continental Railway Company. The London Development Agency (LDA) agreed to buy the land from London and Continental in November 2005 to "deliver the Olympics and the wider regeneration of Lower Lea Valley"[15]. The ground was contaminated from years of neglect and pollution. The LDA set aside a budget of £364 million "to remediate what ...was one of Europe's most heavily contaminated sites" (Jeory, 2010), compared to the estimated cost to clean up Homebush Bay of AUS$190 million (Beder, 2002:256). Despite the attempts to clean up the Stratford site, the press are less convinced London 2012 will be the 'greenest Games'.

The British press have accused London 2012 of greenwashing. *The Sunday Times*, *Sunday Express* and *Guardian* newspapers all questioned claims that London will host the greenest Games. *The Sunday Express* claimed that the ODA's reduction in environmental practices emerged around the depth of soil that was cleaned. *The Sunday Express's* headline, 'London 2012: Radioactive Waste? No problem, we've got a plastic sheet' (Jeroy, 2010) accused the ODA of camouflaging, not fixing, the contaminated soil in East London. The paper claimed "London 2012 chiefs have covered up land that is possibly contaminated with asbestos and radioactive materials with a huge, bright orange sheet ...while clean soil and debris have been placed above the sheet, anything below it is has to be considered hazardous unless proven otherwise" (ibid). The *Guardian* newspaper asks how the organisers are 'Going for Green' (Hayes, 2008) when "London was also the largest, the most costly and most complex of the credible bids for the 2012 Games" (ibid), and the *Sunday Times* newspaper felt the commitment to a 'low-carbon Olympics' was "proving tricky to honour...[as] the Games will still add 2m tonnes of carbon to the atmosphere" (Davis, 2009). The *London Evening Standard* newspaper accused London 2012 organisers of greenwashing,

---

15.*Commitment to Sustainable Regeneration: Olympic, Paralympic & Legacy Transformation Planning Applications for the Olympic Park*. Co-authored by the Olympic Delivery Authority and London Development Agency (February 2007). Document accessible at: http://www.london2012.com/documents/oda-planning/planning-applications/commitment-to-sustainable-regeneration.pdf (accessed March 2010)

in the delayed release of a report on carbon emissions connected to the site. The *Evening Standard* claimed "green campaigners have told the *Standard* that organisers have watered down their carbon emissions target to make it easier to hit the key objectives ...these include the massive emissions from spectators and media travelling to and from the Olympics ...campaigners say without these emissions the measuring exercise would be cosmetic greenwashing" (Brierley, 2008).

Environmentalism has been incorporated or co-opted into various discourses of politics and economic development; sport also comes under close scrutiny. The building and development of infrastructure to hold mega events, such as new venues, transport links, the Athletes Village and use of contaminated land leaves the OCOGs vulnerable to accusations of greenwashing and environmental mismanagement. However, accusations of greenwashing extend beyond new infrastructure and increased transport links. Environmentalism goes beyond the physical element of staging a global sporting event, through to the financial aspects of holding the Games.

Sponsorship, Environmentalism and Sports

I would like to suggest that the inclusion of the *Environment* as one of the three pillars of the Olympic Movement creates potential problems around sustainability and the practicalities of a Games event. Environmentalism and sustainability are increasingly crossing numerous social and economic boundaries. Energy companies, high street supermarkets, car manufacturers, airlines and so on are all using green rhetoric to promote their businesses. Sponsorship is central to generating income for the Games, but as such it is also open to accusations of greenwashing. Sponsorship generates an "income for corporate promotional activities" (MacRury, 2009:134) through television rights and partnership schemes. Potential sponsors can "buy into different kinds of relationships with the Olympic family in return for their financial input" (op. cit., 135). Sponsorship is crucial to the success of the Games, not only to support the "staging of the Olympic Games and operations of the Olympic Movement" (op. cit., 144), but also for future investment in the training and development of athletes. However, the Games offers two forms of official sponsors – global sponsors affiliated with the IOC administered through the TOP programme, and local/national sponsors affiliated with the OCOG. The IOC created its TOP programme in 1985, and it "offers world-wide sponsorship to Multinational Corporations that receive exclusive marketing rights as opportunities in their designated product category" (Cantelon and Letters, 2010: 421).

The Official Partners[16] for the London 2012 Games are BT, Adidas, British Airways, BP, BMW, Lloyds TSB and EDF[17].

Company	Industry
BT	Telecommunications
Adidas	Sportswear
British Airways	Airline
BP	Oil and Gas
BMW	Automotive
Lloyds TSB	Banking and Insurance
EDF	Utility Services

A quick glance at the list of official partners shows a diverse collection of national and international organisations aligning themselves with London 2012. A closer look reveals a questionable choice of sponsors in light of the key objectives for London 2012 to be the greenest Games to date. Today, many organisations feel that "to be perceived as environmentally aware tops the list of most firms' priorities in 2008" (De Bois, 2008), and this arguably includes many official partners of the London 2012 Games. The official partners of London 2012 include two energy corporations, BP and EDF, both of whom have poor environmental records.

In July 2000, BP re-branded with a slogan changing from British Petroleum to Beyond Petroleum. The new branding spoke of a rhetoric which presented the organisation as pro-environmental. Their advertisements co-opted the environmental movement through linguistic traits more commonly associated with environmental rhetoric. BP claimed that oil companies would "aid in the bettering of air quality" and be "looking after our future"[18]. Regardless of the discourse, Beder argues "BP's rhetoric is about social responsibility: profits count most... it will do all it can to ensure it can go on drilling for fossil fuels and expanding its markets for them" (2002:28). Paradoxically, BP's environmental record is questionable. Since 1989 BP have been at the centre of much of the world's major environmental oil disasters: the Exxon Valdes oil spill (1989), Prudhoe Bay field oil spill on Alaska's North Slope region (2006), a Texas oil refinery explosion killed 15 people and injured 170 others (2007), and the most recent death of 11

---

16. This list of Official Partners is as of August 15, 2010. See: http://www.london2012.com/about-us/the-people-delivering-the-games/international-and-uk-partners/index.php.

17. Energy De France (EDF) are a French owned energy company who supplies gas, nuclear power and electricity to the UK and France. The combination of EDF Energy and British Energy in 2009 forms one of the UK's largest energy companies (http://www.edfenergy.com/about-us/about-edf-energy/our-history.shtml, (accessed January 2010)

18. BP "Man on the street" advertisement campaign. See: http://www.bp.com/section-genericarticle.do?categoryId=9014509&contentId=7027666 (accessed October 2010)

workers when the Deepwater Horizon rig exploded (2010), and subsequent pollution in the Gulf of Mexico. BP's poor environmental record makes their 'Beyond Petroleum' campaign seem ill-conceived and means that "consumers may lose trust in their brands altogether" (De Bois, 2008). BP as a partner to London 2012 suggests that companies need to be transparent to "avoid the risk of public criticism of 'tokenism' and 'greenwashing'" (ibid). LOCOG needs to be transparent if they are to avoid any similar accusations; having already connected with BP as a Sustainability Partner has the potential for empty environmental rhetoric, which they have then repeated by aligning with EDF.

In July 2009, EDF launched their 'Green Britain Day' campaign as part of their association with the London 2012 Games. The campaign aims to show EDF's commitment "to reduce emissions by 60% by 2020" (Mitchell and Inkster, 2008). The idea behind the campaign was to "bolster its green credentials, with a heavyweight advertising campaign, majoring on its status as the 'sustainability' partner for the 2012 Olympics" (McCallister, 2009). The advertising campaign was carried over television, radio and print, backed by British Olympian James Cracknell and the former Olympics Minister Tessa Jowell. A television advert contained footage of the 1948 London Olympic Games. There are shots of the river Thames in a smoggy London, with steam boats and smoke rising over the city. The framing is black and white accompanied with a narrative equating the struggle of post-war Britain with contemporary struggles against climate change. The viewer is presented with a series of images ranging from the Royal Family, to a child in a doorway and a bombed London. The narrative then changes with a shot of a diver moving from black and white to colour, crowds from the London 1948 Games, and the announcement of London winning the right to host the 2012 Games, as the narrator tells us "London 2012 is our chance to lead the world in the fight against climate change"[19]. The final shot is of a green coloured Union flag. The same image of a green Union flag is used in newspaper and billboard campaigns. However, such a flag is already used to symbolise green energy by Ecotricity, which is an alternative energy company providing electricity from renewable resources (vis-à-vis wind and wave power) – it has been their logo since 2006.

The co-opting of an already established image opens EDF, and by-proxy LOCOG, to accusations of greenwashing and nepotism[20]. The Founder of Ecotricity, Dale Vince, has accused EDF of hijacking not just his company's logo, but also the British identity. His jingoistic claims questioned the role of nationalistic discourse in the advertisement campaign; "to most people, a green Union Jack represents something or someone green and British. And to most people, EDF are neither, being both nuclear and French" (Murray,

---

19. London 2012 - EDF Green Britain Day. See: http://www.youtube.com/watch?v=p-0G19R0k3UU (accessed January 2010)

20. The CEO of EDF is Andrew Brown, brother of former British Prime Minster, Gordon Brown.

2009a). EDF disputes claims of unpatriotic sentiment and of hijacking the logo, arguing that although they are owned by a French company they have a strong UK base. Further accusations of greenwashing target EDF's sister company, EDF Trading.

EDF Trading, based in London, brands itself as "one of the largest participants in the global coal market" (Pearce, 2009), importing into Europe over 30 million tonnes of coal per year, with multiple sources of supply worldwide. The combination of co-opting Ecotricity's logo and the expansion into global coal markets contradicts and questions EDF's rhetoric of environmentalism masked by the slogan 'Team Green Britain', or Team GB as it can also be read.

Sponsors are very important to the success of any Games. However, as the examples of BP and EDF indicate, there is a level of responsibility required by the OCOG to reaffirm their own values, as set out in their original bids, when choosing Official Partners. As the evidence shows, the choice of BP and EDF conflicts with the idea of setting the "highest standards in sustainability and legacy for other games to follow"[21] (Weaver, 2007), or even aspiring to achieve the "greenest Games to date". OCOGs need to be transparent in their choice of partners. Even the choice of an airline, car manufacturer or financial company raises questions concerning their suitability as partners. LOCOG and the ODA are, however, making concerted efforts to produce the London 2012 Games with an emphasis on environmentalism, in an attempt to keep within the three pillars of the Olympic Movement.

It's not easy being green

There are many positive environmental projects around the London 2012 Games. The seats used at the Vancouver 2010 Winter Games' Curling arena will be dismantled and re-used during the London 2012 Games. VANOC has shared their knowledge with the ODA and LOCOG to prevent repetition of problems they have encountered with the "Olympic regeneration-development challenges associated with 'legacy'" (MacRury, 2009 b:9). Another positive London 2012 initiative is the 2012 Olympic Stadium. The stadium has been constructed such that it can be dismantled, removing up to 55,000 seats after the London 2012 Games, leaving 25,000 permanent seats. The ODA has set a target of moving 50% of construction materials by rail or water transport, and the first of 4,000 semi-mature trees have been planted on the Olympic Park. A new lock was built to take construction material off the roads and onto the waterways, and "London is pioneering decentralized energy systems; the Olympic Park will be powered by a combined cooling, heating and power plant" (Hayes, 2009).

---

21. Lord Sebastian Coe speaking at the same event and reported by Weaver in The Guardian newspaper at: http://www.guardian.co.uk/uk/2007/jan/23/greenpolitics.london (accessed May 2010).

The challenges faced by LOCOG and the ODA in attempting to go for green can have a beneficial impact not just on the event itself, but can also accelerate the introduction of environmental considerations across public policy. The Games can thus work as a lever for "better environmental stewardship" (ibid). LOCOG and the ODA are not only competing with the British press and the logistical problems in creating sustainable London 2012 Games, but are also fighting against a less than favourable history of environmentalism and the Olympic Movement.

Conclusion

The IOC's decision to include the *Environment* as the third pillar of the Olympic Movement is arguably problematic. Mega events inevitably have an environmental impact. In light of the Albertville 1992 Games and international pressure from the United Nations, there was a need for transnational organisations like the IOC to embrace environmentalism. Yet, there are many factors to think about when making claims around environmentalism. For example, the OCOGs need to be cautious when choosing their Official Partners. Environmentalism and sustainable development includes the building of Games' venues and Athletes Villages, good transport links, the regeneration of disused and contaminated land and long-term economic investments, as well as sponsorship. What is clear is that the inclusion of Environment in the Olympic Charter indicates the importance of environmentalism and sport, and of trying to find the right solution to what is clearly a complex and multifaceted problem.

The inclusion of environmentalism and sustainability into any mega event is problematic. It can often be understood as an impediment to authentic sustainable practice. The co-opting of environmental rhetoric can be seen to mask greater problems or poor practice by large organisations. BP and EDF are two clear examples where their company rhetoric fails to match genuine concerns for the environment, only offering empty rhetoric in place of real discussion and opportunity to make a significant environmental change. To create an environmental Games, or even the greenest Games, is possible; but as the Albertville, Sydney and Athens Games have shown, a lack of transparency leaves any OCOG open to accusations of greenwashing. Future OCOGs need to ensure their choice of partners, design and planning engages with "increasingly savvy audiences ...to find a new kind of language and avoid the risk of green fatigue" (De Bois, 2008) and, most importantly, circumvent accusations of greenwashing.

References

Beder, S. (2001). 'Greenwash'. In: Barry, J. & Frankland, G. (eds.), *International Encyclopaedia of Environmental Politics*, London, Routledge.

Beder, S. (2002). Global Spin, The Corporate Assault on Environmentalism, Glasgow, Green Books.

Brierley, D. (2008). "London 2012 'not as green as advertised'", London Evening Standard, 5 August, available online at http://www.thisislondon.co.uk/standard-olympics/article-23526374-london-2012 (accessed 31 January 2010).

Buckingham, S. & Turner, M. (2008). Understanding Environmental Issues, London, Sage.

Cantelon, H. and Letters, M. (2000). The Making of the IOC environmental policy as the third dimension of the Olympic Movement, in Girginov, V. (ed) (2010) The Olympics: a critical reader, London, Routledge, 417-430.

Cox, R. (2006). Environmental Communication and the Public Sphere, California, Sage.

Davis-Holly, T (2009). 'London goes for gold at the low-carbon Olympics', Sunday Times Newspaper, November 29th, p12.

De Bois, M. (2008). "Environmental ads: greenwash or green communication?", Ad Map, December, 500, available online at www.warc.net

'EDF Trading at a Glance' on-line at: www.edftrading.com/EDF_Trading_At_a_glance_May_2010_2U8Wn.pdf. *(accessed May 2010)*

Hayes, G (2008). Going for Green: London aims to be the most sustainable Olympics ever in 2012, but there are a number of reasons why we should be sceptical, The Guardian Newspaper, 2nd July, accessed on-line at www.guardian.co.uk/environment/2008/jul/02/green-building.olympics2012 (Jan 2010)

Hill, G. (1996). Olympic Politics, Athens to Atlanta 1896-1996, Manchester, Manchester University Press.

Jeory, T. (2010). "London 2012: Radioactive waste? No problem, we've got plastic sheet...", Sunday Express, 14 February, available online at http://www.express.co.uk/posts/view/157972/London-2012-radioactive-waste-no-problem (accessed 14 February 2010).

Lenskyj, H. (1998). Green Games or Empty Promises? Environmental Issues and Sydney 2000, The International Centre for Olympic Studies, University of Western Ontario, London, Ontario, Canada, accessed at http://www.la84foundation.org/SportsLibrary/ISOR/ISOR1998a.pdf (retrieved Nov, 2009)

MacRury, I (2009). Sponsorship, advertising and the Olympic Games in Powell, et al, The Advertising Handbook. London, Routledge

MacCrury, I (2009b). A Tale of Two Villages: London, Vancouver and 'Sustainability', Renew, Regeneration in the Thames Gateway, Thames Gateway Partnership Newsletter, Winter 2009.

McCallister, T. (2009). "Energy companies fight for green crown", The Guardian, 9 July, available online at http://www.guardian.co.uk/business/2009/jul/09/edf-npower-british-gas-green-climate-change-row (accessed 21 November 2009).

Murray, J. (2009a). "Legal action casts shadow over EDF's Green Britain Day", Business Green, 10 July, available online at www.business-green.com/article/2245797

Murray, J. (2009b). "ASA gives thumbs up to EDF green ads, but Ecotricity row rumbles on", Business Green, 28 October, available online at www.businessgreen.com/article/ 2252138

Mitchell, W. & Inkster, C. (2008). "Lead with consumers benefit to get green participation and buy-in", Ad Map, December, 500, available online at www.warc.com (accessed 20 July 2009).

Pearce, F (2009). Are EDF trying to cut our use of energy? Surely, some mistake. The Guardian Newspaper, 2nd July, p5.

Terret, Thierry (2008). 'The Albertville Winter Olympics: Unexpected Legacies - Failed Expectations for Regional Economic Development', in International Journal of the History of Sport, 25: 14, 1903 — 1921

Torgerson, D (1999). The promise of green politics: Environmentalism and the public sphere. Durham, NC: Duke University Press

Toyne, P. (2009). "London 2012 – winning the Olympic 'green' medal". in: Poynter,G & MacRury, I. Olympic Cities: 2012 and the Remaking of London, Farnham, Ashgate, pp.231-243.

Weaver, M. (2007). "London 2012 organisers plan greenest games ever", The Guardian, 23 January, available online at http://www.guardian.co.uk/uk/2007/jan/23/greenpolitics.london

Winkler, A (1993). 'Reaping the Rewards', Olympic Review 305:86-7

Chapter 17

Is the Booming Sustainability of Olympic and Paralympic Games Here to Stay?

Environment-Based Procedures Versus Dubious Legacy

Arianne Carvalhedo Reis and Lamartine DaCosta

Introduction

The 2010 Olympic and Paralympic Winter Games in Vancouver, Canada (Vancouver 2010) made history for being the first 'sustainable' Olympic and Paralympic Games, from planning to execution. In contrast, previous Summer and Winter Games in the last two decades were presented as 'Green', with an emphasis on eco-efficiency rather than a more complex approach to sustainability, a concept which goes beyond structure-oriented environmental care. In this concern, the difference between the so-called *Green Games* and the *Sustainable Games* would rely on the rationale that 'sustainability' involves more than just environment friendly procedures, but would incorporate also social and economic well-being into its framework. The Green Games utilised technologies and practices that were aimed at reducing the environmental impacts of the mega event on the host cities/towns, within a discourse aligned with the protection of the local natural environment. The Vancouver 2010 'Sustainable Games', on the other hand, proposed to expand the 'green' programme and go "beyond the environmental impacts of the Games to include the social and economic dimensions of sustainability" (Vancouver 2010, 2010, n.p.).

A similar proposal is in place for the London 2012 Olympic and Paralympic Games (2012 Games). The 2012 Games organisers (London 2012)[1] claim that positive global impacts will accrue from the 2012 Games:

> "Sustainability underpins the entire London 2012 programme. By showing how changes in the way we build, live, play, work, do business and travel could help us to live happy and healthy lives, within the resources available to us, the 2012 Games will set an example for how sustainable events and urban planning take place around the world in future. As the most high-profile event in the world, the 2012 Games will provide an opportunity to show off the best that the host city and nation have to offer. This will be achieved in several ways: by pioneering new approaches to sustainability; changing people's behaviour through the power of sponsorship, media and communications; inspiring new standards of sustainability in the construction, events and hospitality sectors; influencing our supply chain to adopt more sustainable practices; and transferring our learning and knowledge."
>
> (London 2012, 2009, p. 5)

Taking into account this context, the present chapter will briefly analyse the paradigm shift in mega event bidding processes, particularly in the case of the Games, where environmentalist discourse increasingly is being used to legitimize successful proposals. This review is justified by the complexity involved in the implementation of sport projects that aggregate several distinct purposes (social development, tourism, an increase in job opportunities, etc.), particularly projects of the size and scope of mega-events such as the Games, but that at the same time claim to be sustainable. Additionally, this chapter will succinctly examine the sustainability proposal presented by the 2016 Rio de Janeiro Games Organising Committee (Rio 2016), with the aim of assessing the validity and continuity of what is now called the 'Sustainable Games'.

Environment, Sustainability and the Olympic Games

The environmental impacts of mega events are one of the newest concerns of event organizers, sponsors, environmentalists and citizens. The first impact study on the Olympic Games related to environmental issues dates from 1980, when the Games were staged in Lake Placid; but, it was only after the Games in Albertville and Lillehammer that this concept was included as a topic in the Olympic Movement (Chappelet, 2003). In 1994, the International Olympic Committee (IOC) elected to make the *Environment* one of its three pillars, demonstrating that attention was increasingly being paid to environmental issues.

---

1. London 2012 is comprised of the privately funded London Organising Committee of the Olympic and Paralympic Games (LOCOG) and the publicly funded Olympic Delivery Authority (ODA).

In order to fulfil the emerging demands not only of the IOC, but also of the society and consequently of the institutions which hold the rights of some mega events, bidding committees have increasingly recognised environmental issues and created projects for urban development and facilities construction that are aligned with principles of environmental care and protection. The 1994 Lillehammer Winter Games were successful in this matter by making consultative alliances with environmental organizations, and putting into practice a recycling project which recycled 70% of the total waste produced during the 1994 Games (TED, n.d.). The 2000 Games held in Sydney is also known for its environmental care and alliances with conservationists, being the first Games to have Greenpeace analyze and contribute to its 'green' proposal (Chappelet, 2008).

However, by associating its 'sustainability' language solely with environmental protection, the IOC for some years limited the contribution of the Games to the promotion of a more holistic approach to sustainable development. This narrow association can be seen in the Olympic Charter, where the only mention of sustainable development is found in Rule 2, Paragraph 13: "The IOC's role is: [...] to encourage and support a responsible concern for environmental issues, to promote sustainable development in sport and to require that the Olympic Games are held accordingly" (IOC, 2007, p. 15).[2] There, sustainable development is clearly associated with environmental issues, a position that reinforces the restricted vision of sustainability that dominated the discourse of Organizing Committees for the Games (OCOGs) that followed the inclusion of the third pillar of the Olympic Movement. In following the Olympic Charter, OCOGs attended to IOC requests for environmental protection, but other important issues for the development of sustainable societies and lives often were overlooked, with communities being displaced, big stadia underused and subsequently dismantled, social projects discontinued and the uneven distribution of benefits within host societies (Lenskyj, 2007).

The problem is, however, of greater complexity. As Holden, MacKenzie and VanWynsberghe (2008) argued recently, the sustainability jargon has been loosely used ever since the United Nations' Brundtland report coined the term 'sustainable development' (Bruntland, 1987), and what an OCOG might consider sustainable practice might not necessarily reflect the IOC's expectations of sustainability. This problem derives from the "frustratingly ambiguous, perilously contradictory, and/or eminently co-optable concept [that is sustainability] that damages more than it provides" (Holden, MacKenzie & VanWynsberghe, 2008, p. 884). Therefore, sustainable devel-

---

2. It is important to mention here that the use of the uni-dimensional concept of sustainability emerged during the 1992 UN Conference on the Environment, held in Rio de Janeiro, which focused mainly on the environmental aspect of sustainable development. This approach, according to DaCosta (2010), began gradually to embrace social and economic demands during the 2000s, creating the three-fold conception now more accepted for its mutual reinforcement of the different aspects of sustainability.

opment targets frequently have not been achieved, when the emphasis has been only on certain practices that reduce the impact of the Games on the host's natural environment.

It is for these reasons that Vancouver 2010 has been considered a turning point in Olympic history. For the first time, an OCOG has promised to deliver a Sustainable Games, without focusing only on environmental protection. As the *Impact of the Olympics on Community Coalition* report, from May 2007, states:

> "For the first time in history, these Commitments[3] include a pledge to ensure the benefits of the Olympics are available to all people, regardless of income or social position, and further, to ensure those most marginalized in society are not displaced or otherwise harmed by the Olympics." (IOCC, 2007, p. 4)

Although the report graded the performance of the 2012 Games Organising Committee (VANOC) as 'D'[4], it is important to highlight the effort made by VANOC and all its partners to build a participatory environment for the assessment of the impacts of the Games, in light of comprehensive sustainable development targets having been set. Environmental protection is only one among several social, cultural and economic targets. Although still subject to intense criticism, as were the ones presented by the Coalition, VANOC has the merit of putting into practice, or at least attempting to through its written commitments to the people of Vancouver, Whistler and Canada, for the first time a wide-encompassing sustainability framework for the organization of the Games.

London 2012 has followed this same pattern of focusing on a broader definition of sustainability for the 2012 Games, but also included new, pertinent points to its vision. VANOC's Sustainability Performance Objectives were centred around six themes, described as: accountability; environmental stewardship and impact reduction; social inclusion and responsibility; aboriginal participation and collaboration; economic benefits; and sport for sustainable living (Vancouver 2010, 2009). London 2012 focuses on five distinct themes: climate change; waste; biodiversity; inclusion; and, healthy living (London 2012, 2009). This shift in focus reflects current discussions about sustainability, which recognize a fourth pillar or "a 'quadruple bottom line' of environmental, social, economic and climate responsiveness" (UNWTO-UNEP-WMO, 2007, p. 2).

What seems clear from the recent experience of Vancouver 2010 and the current preparations for the 2012 Games is that the Olympic Movement, through the OCOGs, has moved to a new level of responsiveness to social, cultural, economic and environmental demands, as a consequence of

---

3. "Commitments contained in the Inner-City Inclusive Agreement, the Olympic Bid Book, and the Multi-Party Agreement ("Commitments"), which the organizers of the 2010 Winter and Paralympic Games undertook to ensure that Vancouver's inner-city residents, the environment, and all British Columbians benefit from the Games in Vancouver and Whistler." (IOCC, 2007, p. 4).

4. Referring to the grading system of 'A' to 'F', being 'A' excellent and 'F' fail.

the hosting of such mega events. The level of success in attaining the goal of hosting truly Sustainable Games is still to be assessed, but the Games have now reached the point where sustainability, even with all the ambiguities carried by this term, is paramount for the development of a successful bid. The question we pose now is; whether Brazil, and Rio de Janeiro more specifically, are prepared to take on, beyond rhetoric, what should be the newest legacy from the Games, which is the increased awareness that sustainable development must necessarily include social justice, heritage/cultural preservation, environment protection and economic redistribution.

The 2016 Rio de Janeiro Olympic and Paralympic Games and Sustainable Development

Although the terms 'sustainability' and 'sustainable development' are cited frequently throughout the 2016 Rio de Janeiro Bid Book, there are a few indications that suggest that these terms are being used loosely, allowing multiple interpretations (Rio 2016, 2009). The major problem may be due to the constant use of the experience of the 2007 Pan American Games as the starting point for the proposed 2016 Games. Although the Pan American Games technically were a success, they were far from being exemplars of sustainable practices, at any level.

The Pan American Games is one of the major multi-sporting competitions in the Americas. In 2007, 42 countries were represented, with over 5,500 athletes competing in more than 300 events. These Games were used to test Rio de Janeiro's ability to host a sport mega event that was similar in format to the Olympic Games, in order to present a stronger case to the IOC. The event was hosted with no major incidents[5] and did indeed pave the way for Rio de Janeiro to be selected as the host of the 2016 Games.

However, several problems were encountered during the 2007 Games with promises undelivered, particularly the ones related to the natural and social well-being of the city. According to Gaffney (2010), Rio de Janeiro's proposal for the Pan-American Games was based around 'Olympic constellations', or the complexes produced for the delivery of the 2007 Games. These 'constellations' "are the tangible, physical elements of the Olympic city including new and upgraded communications and transportation infrastructure, stadia, tourist amenities, cultural installations, environmental remediation projects, housing developments, and security apparatuses" (Gaffney, 2010, p. 8).

According to the Pan American Games Organising Committee, these 'constellations' would be the actual legacy of the Games, ones that would be enjoyed by the rich and by the poor. However, what resulted from the

---

5. Barros (2008, p. 578) lists a few examples of 'minor incidents' concerning the delivery of the Pan American Games, such as faults in some big screens, damage to some facilities due to strong winds, double booking/sale of seats in some events and change in competition schedules without prior announcement to the public.

Pan American Games was "an ambiguous social and urban legacy" (Gaffney, 2010, p. 18).

> "Rio did not deliver the promised transportation infrastructure, did not improve the housing situation for Rio's poor, did not open new sporting venues in order to develop a generation of Olympic athletes, and neglected promises of environmental remediation while contributing to the generalized opacity of mega-events. Tens of thousands of police prevented public violence in the city for a short period of time before conditions returned to 'normal'." (Gaffney, 2010, p. 18)

Some examples that prevented the Pan American Games from being able to be labelled as truly sustainable, and that need to be addressed if the 2016 Games is to follow on the sustainable trend initiated by Vancouver 2010, are: the exponential increase in the original budget used for the 2007 Games, due to successive delays in construction (684% in five years according to the Brazilian newspaper *Folha de São Paulo*, 7th March 2007); the displacement of low-income families (mostly *favelas* in and around construction sites for competition venues) (Benedicto, 2009); construction sites that were embargoed by popular lawsuits and were then abandoned without removal (Behnken & Godoy, 2009; Mascarenhas & Borges, 2009); construction of the Athletes' Village over marshland (Gaffney, 2010); and privatization of publicly-funded venues (Benedicto, 2009; Gaffney, 2010).

Overall, the operational success of the 2007 Pan American Games, which had strong support from the local population, contrasted with shadow costs and social impacts that were not visible to the direct observation of the general public. The issue of the legacy of the 2007 Games, as depicted by DaCosta (2008), became more a classification exercise developed by government and sport leaders than a responsible managerial process.

Although the proposal for the 2016 Games is much larger and more complex in nature than the Pan American Games, the latter was 'sold' to the public as an 'experiment' and as a draw card for securing the Olympic Games and, therefore, that facilities and projects would be re-utilised and improvements to facilities and infrastructure would make the city ready to host the 2016 Games. Hence, it is worrying for social researchers to envision a similar approach to the 2016 Games, as the Pan American Games were clearly not driven by sustainability concepts. In fact, this requirement was not included in the original commitment of the city of Rio de Janeiro to host the 2007 event.

Conversely, for the 2016 Games, Rio's proposal had a clear involvement with environmental issues, particularly through the selection of the location of venues, all of which are surrounded by spectacular nature. Rio de Janeiro has the largest urban forest in the world (Tijuca National Park), and is surrounded by rocky and bush-clad mountains rising from the coast line with world-renowned beaches. It is, therefore, the perfect landscape to sell and use to build an awareness of sustainability concepts. It is clear from the bid proposal that these features were indeed used as an important selling point:

"In Rio, nature is not just part of the city; it is the city itself. With Games venues strategically located to embrace nature, the beauty of Rio's physical environment will be clearly evident to all members of the Games Family." (Rio 2016, 2009, p. 87)

Using the management method of contrasting risks with opportunities, it is appropriate to raise the question: will this phenomenal tool for building sustainable development awareness, and most particularly environmental conservation/preservation, be used wisely and to the advantage of the city's population? Being so close to such a fragile environment, one of the last remnants of Atlantic Forest in the country and in the world, the 'spell can turn against the caster' and further pressure can be placed on this already stressed environment. With development proposals planned in areas such as Barra da Tijuca, a suburban area where wetlands are predominant, there is a high risk the 2016 Games will have a significant negative impact on the natural environment and, as a consequence, on the people of the city also.

Conclusions

The 2016 Games present a unique opportunity for Rio de Janeiro and Brazil to develop an increased awareness of more sustainable practices that contribute to a better quality of life for all segments of the population. However, the 2007 Pan American Games dubious legacies highlight the risks lurking behind the 2016 project. This tension demands a close follow up of the next steps of Rio 2016 preparation.

The ingenious decision made by Rio 2016 to place the 2016 Games in very close contact with the extraordinary natural environment of the city, as well as in some areas of low-income population, presents possibilities for the propagation of not only the third pillar of the Olympic Movement (the Environment), but also the new 'ideal' embraced by VANOC and London 2012 in organising the Games: to deliver Games that are sustainable in every aspect. In doing so, the 'legacy' discourse that legitimised the Pan American and the Olympic bids can move toward a 'sustainability' discourse (DaCosta, 2008), where fair distribution of benefits and losses can be achieved and where the population as a whole gains from the experience of hosting the Games that were created to promote peace between all people.

References

Barros, J.A.C. (2008) Gestão dos Jogos Pan-Americanos Rio 2007: Pontos fortes e fracos segundo o Programa de Observadores. In L.P. DaCosta, D. Corrêa, E. Rizzuti, B. Villano & A. Miragaya (Eds.), *Legados de megaeventos esportivos* (pp. 575-579). Brasília: Ministério do Esporte.

Behnken, L.M. & Godoy, A. (2009). O relacionamento entre as esferas pública e privada nos Jogos Pan-Americanos de 2007: Os casos da Marina da Glória e do Estádio de Remo da Lagoa. *Esporte e Sociedade, 4*(10), 1-36.

Benedicto, D.B.M. (2009). Desafiando o coro dos contentes: Vozes dissonantes no processo de implementação dos Jogos Pan-Americanos, Rio 2007. *Esporte e Sociedade, 4*(10), 1-29.

Bruntland, G. (Ed.) (1987). *Our common future: The World Commission on Environment and Development.* Oxford: Oxford University Press.

Chappelet, J.-L. (2003). The legacy of the Olympic Winter Games: An overview. In M. Moragas, C. Kennett, C. & N. Puig (Eds.), *The legacy of the Olympic Games: 1984 – 2000* (pp. 54-66). Lausanne: International Olympic Committee.

Chappelet, J.-L. (2008) Olympic environmental concerns as a legacy of the Winter Games. *International Journal of the History of Sport, 25*(14), 1884-1902.

DaCosta, L.P. (2008) Modelo 3D para gestão do planejamento e re-planejamento de legados de megaeventos esportivos. In L.P. DaCosta, D. Corrêa, E. Rizzuti, B. Villano & A. Miragaya (Eds.), *Legados de megaeventos esportivos* (pp. 239-248). Brasília: Ministério do Esporte.

DaCosta, L.P. (2010 in print) Estudos de viabilidade ambiental, social e econômica para otimizar espaços de cultura, esporte e lazer: Contexto atual e perspectivas futuras. In A.C. Bramante (Ed.), *Fazendo mudanças: Estudos de viabilidade econômica, social e ambiental.* Brasília: SESI DN.

Gaffney, C. (2010). Mega-events and socio-spatial dynamics in Rio de Janeiro, 1919-2016. *Journal of Latin American Geography, 9*(1), 7-29.

Holden, M., MacKenzie, J. & VanWynsberghe, R. (2008). Vancouver's promise of the world's first sustainable Olympic Games. *Environment and Planning C: Government and Policy, 26*, 882-905.

Impact of the Olympics on Community Coalition (2007). Olympic oversight interim report card 2010 Olympic Games. Retrieved from http://iocc.ca/documents/2007-05-07_OlympicReportCard.pdf

International Olympic Committee (2007). Olympic Charter. Retrieved from http://www.olympic.org/Documents/olympic_charter_en.pdf

Lenskyj, H. (2007). The best Olympics ever?: Social impacts of Sydney 2000. Albany, NY: State University of New York Press.

London 2012 (2009). Towards a one planet: Sustainability plan (2nd ed.). Retrieved from http://www.london2012.com/documents/locog-publications/london-2012-sustainability-plan.pdf

Mascarenhas, G. & Borges, F.C.S. (2009). Entre o empreendedorismo urbano e a gestão democrática da cidade: dilemas e impactos do Pan-2007 na Marina da Glória. *Esporte e Sociedade,* 4(10), 1-26.

Rio 2016 (2009). Candidature file for Rio de Janeiro to host the 2016 Olympic and Paralympic Games. Retrieved from http://www.rio2016.org.br/sumarioexecutivo/default_en.asp

Trade and Environment Database (n.d.). *Lillehammer Olympic Games.* Retrieved from http://www.american.edu/TED/lille.htm

UNWTO-UNEP-WMO (2007). *Davos declaration: Climate change and tourism – responding to global challenges.* World Tourism Organization – United Nations Environment Programme – World Meteorological Organization. Retrieved from http://www.unwto.org/pdf/pr071046.pdf

Vancouver 2010 (2009). Vancouver 2010 Sustainability Report 2008-2009. Retrieved from http://www.vancouver2010.com/dl/00/27/14/sustainabilityreport08-09_44d-ZN.pdf

Vancouver 2010 (2010). 12 Ways VANOC Built Sustainability into the Games. Retrieved from http://www.vancouver2010.com/more-2010-information/sustainability/discover-sustainability/

Chapter 18

Bidding Cities and Sustainable Legacies

A Member of the Chicago 2016 Bid Team Reflects on Lessons Learned

Robert Accarino

Introduction

On April 4th 2007, a crowd gathered at a sports venue in Chicago, and listened with excitement and relief as Peter Ueberroth, Chairman of the United States Olympic Committee (USOC), named Chicago to represent the United States in the race to host the 2016 Olympic and Paralympic Games. However, little did we know that disappointment would be our final destination when, on October 2nd 2009, Jacques Rogge announced that Chicago's bid to host the 2016 Games had ended.

Being a member of a bid team is a humbling and exciting experience. I must emphasize here the notion of *team*. The Chicago 2016 bid team consisted of Games experts, fans of the Olympic Movement, people like me who were seconded because of a particular set of skills or expertise, volunteers, and people who simply wanted to create a positive legacy for Chicago.

I was able to utilize my planning and organizational skills, and experience in recognizing environmental trends to develop the bid's *Blue Green Games* environmental plan. However, this was something that could only have been done through the efforts of a strong team. At Chicago 2016, we took a team oriented approach, and I had the privilege of leading a very talented team with great support from many organizations throughout the City of Chicago. Like all functions within the bid, the environment function was supported by an Environmental Advisory Council. The Council, chaired by Frank Clark, Chairman and Chief Executive Officer of the local utility ComEd, consisted of people from business, government, and local non-governmental environmental organizations. The Chicago 2016 environmental staff were organized around the issues that we needed to address within the plan. Mary O'Toole, Alexandra Yeung, Jade Paul, and Cindy Farr developed the carbon, water, resources and conservation, and policy portions, respectively, of the plan. They were supported by working teams or advisors who were experts in a particular field or represented a particular group of stakeholders. Throughout the planning period, we were supported by a team of talented individuals who helped with specific tasks, including Steve Moylan of Abbott Laboratories, John Schmitz and Gina Wammock of CH2M Hill, Mary Gade, Marla Westerhold, Nick Guana, Sarah Heckert, Kathleen Allanson, and David Lowy.

Bid Timeline

Working on a Games bid has been described as sprinting through an entire marathon. Just like a marathon runner develops a race plan and then meticulously executes their plan during the race, one of the keys to finishing a race to become a Games Host City is to develop a plan and then to execute against the plan, understanding that detours will occur and you will have to react appropriately.

The race to host the 2016 Games began officially on April 4th 2007, when Chicago was awarded the right to represent the United States as the country's sole applicant to the International Olympic Committee (IOC). The IOC application process for becoming a Host City is very proscribed and marked by a number of significant milestones, but it is fundamentally split into two phases – the Candidature Acceptance Procedure and the Candidate City phases. During the first phase, "Applicant Cities" are required to answer an IOC questionnaire, one which is mainly technical in nature and includes a section on environmental conditions and impact. Each Applicant City is asked to describe current environmental conditions, provide an assessment of the environmental impact of hosting the Games, and submit information regarding any impact studies that were completed for the proposed venues.

Chicago's Applicant City file was due on January 4th 2008. Based on that submission we were selected on June 4th 2008 to become a Candidate City and advance into the next phase. During this phase, we submitted our Candidature file, also called a Bid Book, on 12th 2009. The bid book is divided into 17 themes or chapters, one being Environment and Meteorology. It is this chapter in which a Candidate City describes how they will plan and operate Games that respect the environment and provide for a positive environmental legacy.

Although meeting the requirements prescribed through the formal process milestones are critical for success, there exist many sanctioned but less formal opportunities to learn what past Host Cities have accomplished, and also about the expectations of individual IOC members and others associated with the international sports community. For Chicago 2016, these opportunities were invaluable in providing information about the substance and pace of Games environmental and sustainability trends. This was critical for our planning as we hoped to build on these trends in order to provide momentum about how large scale sporting events could become more sustainable. For example, in October 2007, by participating in the 7th World Conference on Sport and the Environment in Beijing, we were able to learn about programs and initiatives that the Games Host Cities of Beijing, London and Vancouver were implementing and use that information to improve our planning.

Chicago 2016 Bid City Timeline

April 4, 2007	Chicago selected to represent the United States in its bid to host the 2016 Games
May 16, 2007	IOC bid process for the Games of the XXXI Olympiad launched
January 14, 2008	Applicant file submitted to the IOC
February 12, 2009	Candidature file submitted to the IOC
April 4 - 7, 2009	IOC Evaluation Commission visit to Chicago 2016
August 2 - 3, 2009	First formal presentation to the IOC membership
October 2, 2009	IOC vote for the host city of the XXXI Olympiad

The Chicago 2016 Bid and Environmental Sustainability

Developing our proposed plans for the 2016 Games required the Chicago 2016 environment team to reach out and learn from the experiences of many others. We examined the expectations of the IOC and looked to learn from the experience of previous Games Host Cities. We spoke with experts in the field of sustainability and sport, and to local community members, whose support was critical to a comprehensive plan that would meet local expectations. In order to develop a robust plan, we had to understand all stakeholder expectations and IOC requirements.

The International Olympic Committee and Sustainability

The IOC communicates Games bid requirements in many ways, including published guideline documents and technical manuals. The Technical Manual on Olympic Games Impact provides an explanation about how to incorporate sustainable development principles in Games planning and execution. As described in the Manual, sustainable development is considered a key part of an Olympic Games.

> "Sustainable Development is one of the underpinning principles of the Olympic Movement"

> "Encompassing the three key areas of environment, social/culture and economic, it is an integral part of Olympic Games planning, management and its subsequent legacy."

> "Responsibility towards and respect of the sustainable development guiding principles by the Host City, the Organizing Committee and its partners is therefore very important to the successful staging of an Olympic Games. With long-term strategic planning, community planning and receptiveness from all parties, the multitude of opportunities offered by hosting the Olympic Games can be optimised (sic) in order to respond, not only to the requirements to stage the Games, but also to the needs and expectations of the Host City's current and future generations."[1]

Sustainable development can be used as a bridge between the operational Games-time needs and expectations of the Host City, allowing the Organizing Committee to maximize the value of the opportunities that arise from hosting the Games. This should be done with a view that starts at the beginning of the process and end well past the time period of the Games.

Lessons from Previous Games Host Cities

We examined the results of previous Games Host Cities to understand what they accomplished and the challenges they encountered. The Games hosted by both Lillehammer and Sydney, by our analysis, were two of the most successful Games measured by what they planned to accomplish versus what they accomplished. However, each Host City that we examined was able to achieve some positive sustainability-oriented changes, whether they were energy or water efficiency measures, increased recycling rates, or greenhouse gas reductions. But, some host cities fell extremely short of achieving sustainability goals that were promised, and we did not want to fall into the trap of over promising and underperforming.

Through our research, we uncovered several opportunities for Chicago 2016 to not only inform our planning but to establish our credibility. We decided to utilize a greater degree of transparency and public participation in our planning than what we perceived was done in with previous Games bids. We involved our bid leadership to communicate our environmental goals and engaged in public projects designed to have immediate positive impact. In addition, strict adherence to IOC standards, policies and protocols was our demonstration that we respected the rules and would abide by them. All of this was important, as it began to establish Chicago 2016 as a faithful partner for what we hoped would be a long relationship.

---

1. International Olympic Committee, (2007). Technical Manual on Olympic Games Impact, 4.

The Blue Green Games Plan

It was apparent from the start that we were chasing after multiple object-ives; first and foremost, we had to win the right to host the 2016 Games. The environment plan attempted to support the answer to a question which was on the minds of IOC members: "Why Chicago?" We also had to maintain a high level of local public support and interest, and satisfy the desires of many constituencies including government, environmental organizations, residents of the City of Chicago, and Chicago 2016 supporters. As time passed and local stakeholders became more engaged, it was increasingly im-portant that the environment plan address their concerns and expectations. Local stakeholders expected that our plan advance local environmental ef-forts. It had to support the green agenda of the City of Chicago, work in concert with the Chicago Climate Action Plan, provide a catalyzing effect for improved environmental performance of the City of Chicago and re-gion, and foster increased economic activity. The plan had to become a catalyst for positive change both within and outside the local community. Stakeholders expected that we would build bridges to the world, extending the City of Chicago's reputation internationally as a green city, and expand-ing opportunities for greater involvement by other cities in sport and envir-onmental initiatives.

We decided that hosting the 2016 Games in Chicago provided an oppor-tunity to highlight how a large-scale sporting event could be located within an urban environment and operated in a way that was consistent with envir-onmental protection standards, and also provided a catalyst effect for con-tinuing co-existence between the urban and natural environments. It was our belief that this could be the greatest non-sport related legacy of the Games in Chicago.

Through our planning and stakeholder involvement, we developed the concept of the Blue Green Games. Our use of the colors blue and green paid homage to the location of Chicago and to the natural resources that all ath-letes need for competition. Blue represented clean air and water and Chica-go's proximity to Lake Michigan, and green represented the historic park-lands in the Chicago area and how the 2016 Games would be operated in an environmentally sustainable manner. The theme of the Blue Green Games was woven throughout the entire bid. For example, many venue locations were within one of the great parks in Chicago. Through the Blue Green Games plan we would utilize the Games to focus a spotlight on the interac-tion between nature and the parks and residents of the City of Chicago.

The Blue Green Games environment plan was designed to achieve the following primary goals: to provide athletes with the conditions necessary to achieve their best performances; to ensure a positive impact on Chicago from hosting the 2016 Games; and to leave a lasting legacy of sport and sus-tainability. In addition to those goals, we established four related objectives: 1. to advance the IOC's sustainability work - by this, we intended to improve socio-economic conditions, provide for conservation and management of resources from a sustainable development perspective, and strengthen the

role of major groups such as athletes or citizens of the City of Chicago;
2. focus global attention on the critical importance of clean air and water;
3. to provide a compelling environmental model for future Games Organizing Committees; and, 4. to promote responsible, affordable solutions that enhance the sustainability of sport operations.

Through the Blue Green Games plan, the Chicago 2016 Organizing Committee would achieve the goals described in the bid book through the following five core programs.

1. **Climate Cool** – Through this program, the 2016 Games would result in a low carbon Games. Climate Cool included strategies for minimizing, accounting for and offsetting greenhouse gas emissions associated with the Games. Chicago 2016 provided in the Candidature File a comprehensive estimate of carbon emissions associated with the proposed plan, one of the first Candidate Cities to do so.

2. **Water Positive** – A Water-Friendly Games - While Chicago is blessed with proximity to the fifth largest freshwater lake in the world, Lake Michigan, access to clean water is a critical issue for millions around the world. Through the Blue Green Games plan, Chicago 2016 was committed to increasing global access to potable water and using the Games as an opportunity to educate spectators, visitors and athletes about water conservation and sustainability.

3. **Resource Conserving** – Reducing the amount of waste begins with responsible sourcing. Through the Resource Conserving plan, the Organizing Committee would focus on responsible and local sourcing of materials, resource conservation and recycling, and reuse of materials whether for their original applications or different purposes.

4. **Habitat Friendly** – An overarching goal of the Blue Green Games was to provide the city and its inhabitants with an enhanced natural environment that would last for generations to come, and to involve more citizens in conservation programs.

5. **Legacy Sustainable** – The Blue Green Games plan established a sustainable environmental legacy on multiple levels. If implemented as planned, Legacy Sustainable would have resulted in permanent benefits for Chicago and the world. Some of these included: permanent greenhouse gas emissions reductions, the creation of green roofs, enhanced natural habitats, development of new waste minimization technology and increased water access for developing countries. The most creative program would have seen tens of thousands of temporary seats from the stadium being removed at the end of the Games and utilized as seats in wheelchairs. These would have been donated to those in need, providing a lasting legacy and reusing materials that would normally have been salvaged after the Games.

Each of these programs were designed to attract attention to the bid, provide proof of capability to the IOC, respond to stakeholder concerns, support and integrate into the overall bid plan, and advance the intersection of sport and environment in a responsible manner.

Key Learning

I learned many valuable things during more than two years spent working on Chicago's bid to win the right to host the 2016 Games. Below are some of my lessons learned, which may provide value to others who travel down a similar path.

1. **Teamwork** – Creating a successful plan takes a team of talented, dedicated experts that have the ability to engage and motivate the community and local leaders. Team members need to work collaboratively, handle a wide variety of tasks, but most importantly, be able to work under pressure. It seems that every week carried a new challenge and deadline; team members needed to be able to work in an unstructured, sometimes stressful environment, but still get the job done.

2. **Maintaining Interest and Enthusiasm** – To some local environmental stakeholders, the prospect of holding the Games in their backyard was very threatening. People generally will not want to hear that your plans are just preliminary and subject to community input once you win the right to host the Games. They want to be involved from the very beginning, whether they understand the expectations of the IOC and the bid process or not. Therefore, it was critical to educate the community about the selection process, and gather strong community support by having a mechanism for stakeholders to become involved from the beginning. Although there are many ways to gain community support, one way is to create community benefits through the planning process. For example, Chicago 2016 did this by creating a program that was managed by others for the benefit of the community. The 21st Century Green Centers program was co-created by Chicago 2016, the City of Chicago and The Climate Group, and managed by The Climate Group.

3. **Create a Vision Early in the Process** – Creating an environmental vision for a bid in the early stages is critical, as it can act as a guidepost for plan development. We developed the Blue Green Games plan as a way to communicate our balanced emphasis on climate, water and habitat issues.

4. **Find the Environmental Sweet Spot** – The environmental plan should reduce impact but also be cost effective by helping to reduce overall costs. This does not imply that meeting environmental expectations will not cost money. It is to say that cost savings should also accrue from a thorough program. For example, we were able to find technologies that

would not only reduce the carbon footprint of the Games but also reduce venue construction and operating costs. This provides a great legacy.

5. **Don't Over Promise** – During a bid, there is a tendency to make promises that could overly burden the Organizing Committee. Since the bid phase is a competition, there needs to be a balance between creativity and developing the best program possible, and simply proposing a solid program that serves the needs of stakeholders, athletes, sponsors and the IOC family.

Pulling It All Together

Working as part of a Games bid team is a truly rewarding experience. It is an opportunity to apply career knowledge in order to create green venues, the best conditions for athletic competition, educate millions of people about how to be more sensitive to environmental needs, and to influence future generations through legacy environmental programs. On hearing those words from the IOC President, "and the next city to host the Games is .....", the work just begins.

Chapter 19
Coca-Cola, Sustainability and the Olympic Games

Vincent Gaillard and Katherine Symonds

Introduction

Anyone who visited the Vancouver 2010 Olympic and Paralympic Winter Games (2010 Games) had the opportunity to buy a bottle of Coca-Cola or water packaged in a plastic bottle partly made from plant materials, served to them by a person wearing clothing made from fabric manufactured from up to 100 recycled bottles. It would have been chilled in an HCF-free cooler, having been delivered to the venue in a hybrid truck. Once finished, the empty bottle could be placed in one of hundreds of Coca-Cola recycling bins placed inside the venues. That visitor could also rest assured in the knowledge that carbon emissions that Coca-Cola's presence at the Games created were offset.

This chapter will explain why we at Coca-Cola take sustainability seriously, and why we see major international sporting occasions as the ideal place to talk about it with our consumers, customers, employees and stakeholders. It will share the journey that Coca-Cola has taken to get where it is today, and indicate the path that it plans to travel next. Above all, this piece aims to explore ways to fully tap into the potential that global events have to offer, and hopes to encourage others to do the same.

Coca-Cola and Sustainability

Where big consumer brands are concerned, nothing is more important to the health of the business than trust. The equity of the Coca-Cola brand – and its recognition by billions of people around the world – conditions the health of the Coca-Cola business. Yet, it is intangible by nature, fragile, and largely dependent on the reputation we have forged, and the way in which our products 'connect' with millions of people every day. For the product and the company to remain relevant, honesty and transparency are of the utmost importance, together with an unequivocal demonstration of good corporate citizenship and social responsibility.

That is why, over the last decade, we have devised and refined an articulation of what Coca-Cola stands for – our "Live Positively" commitments – which include goals, metrics and principles for a broad range of sustainability issues. This includes: our work in developing beverage benefits; supporting active healthy living programmes; building sustainable communities; improving environmental programmes for our operations; and creating a safe, inclusive work environment for our associates. It is a modern expression of our company's heritage of caring about our people and our planet, and is embedded in the DNA of how we operate.

Coca-Cola and Global Sporting Events

Coca-Cola's sponsorship of global sporting events continues to play an important role in our sustainability journey. While all recent Olympic Games and FIFA World Cups™ have provided the stage to showcase sustainability initiatives being implemented in our core business, we will focus here on our Olympic Games experience.

Coca-Cola has supported the Olympic Games since 1928. We are the longest continuous corporate partner of the Olympic Movement, and the Olympic Games is our most important and valuable "marketing asset". We believe Coca-Cola and the Olympic Movement are natural partners; both have global recognition and reach, with a presence in over 200 countries. We share the same values of optimism, are committed to supporting youth participation and work hard to bring people and countries together. More pragmatically, we see our Olympic Games sponsorship as a powerful leadership statement and a fantastic opportunity to create connections with our consumers, customers, employees and stakeholders around the world through their passion for sport. At Coca-Cola, we are immensely proud of our reputation for being a responsible partner of the Olympic Movement. Our partnership supports the Olympic Games financially, helping them to grow (the major portion of our sponsorship money is used to develop sports around the world) and also helps to promote the wider goals of international friendship, inspiring youth and protecting the environment.

Sustainability at the Olympic Games

The Olympic Movement is based on a positive vision of how the world could be, and projects an optimistic view for society. This commitment to creating a better future has, naturally, come to embrace sustainability.

In 1992, the Rio Earth Summit defined the basic principles and definitions of *sustainable development*. Later that decade, the International Olympic Committee (IOC) published a document aimed at encouraging all of its members to participate actively in sustainable development, presenting fundamental concepts and the actions to be undertaken to achieve this objective. This document, title the *Olympic Movement's Agenda 21: Sport for Sustainable Development*[1], acknowledged the diversity and fragility of our planet. It also recognised the inherent synergies between the Olympic and global sustainability agendas, and the powerful role sport can play in contributing towards the harmonious development of man to ensure the wellbeing of people and the planet.

So, the stage for sustainable development at the Olympic Games was formally set, and Coca-Cola's Olympic Games leadership logically extended to embrace this new point of view. While the world was becoming increasingly aware of the need to protect our environment, and Coca-Cola was developing its own internal sustainability processes and goals, we committed to leverage our Olympic Games sponsorship to not only showcase the best-in-class initiatives which were being implemented in our business, but to leverage the power of our brands and our marketing know-how and engage in a series of initiatives designed to change behaviour. Our journey started right around the 'Games of the new millennium' in Sydney.

Sydney 2000

The Sydney 2000 Olympic and Paralympic Games (Sydney 2000) was arguably the first Games when the environment and sustainable development were high on the agenda of many stakeholders. Public awareness of sustainability issues meant there was heightened sensitivity to the environmental impact of such a large scale event. It is therefore appropriate that this was the Games where Coca-Cola made its first significant Olympic Games sustainability commitment to the international community, initiated by a ground-breaking relationship between Coca-Cola and Greenpeace. It marked the beginning of an important journey for us and, we believe, for the Olympic Movement and all its corporate partners as well.

---

1. International Olympic Committee, the *Olympic Movement's Agenda 21: Sport for Sustainable Development*, adopted June 1999. See: http://multimedia.olympic.org/pdf/en_report_300.pdf (accessed October 2010).

Salt Lake 2002, Athens 2004, Torino 2006

The majority of Coca-Cola's endeavors following Sydney 2000 were focused on energy reduction and climate protection, such as HCF-free[2] technologies for our cooling equipment, low-emissions vehicles and various recycling and waste management initiatives. A notable initiative took place at the Athens 2004 Olympic Games, when Coca-Cola co-founded Refrigerants Naturally – together with the United Nations Environment Programme (UNEP), Greenpeace and McDonald's – to find alternatives to HCF refrigeration. By 2006, Coca-Cola was exclusively using HCF-free coolers at global events. In parallel we were pursuing a global roll-out of such technologies, eventually leading to a commitment to procure only HCF-free coolers for the entire Coca-Cola System (by which we mean the Coca-Cola Company and our bottlers) worldwide by 2015. The role that the Olympic Games played in accelerating this change should not be underestimated.

Beijing 2008

For the Olympic and Paralympic Games (Beijing 2008), we developed a more comprehensive sustainability plan, focused around the theme of environmental stewardship. All our coolers were HCF-free, cutting greenhouse gas emissions from our sponsorship by approximately 4,000 metric tons. Our efforts were rewarded by Greenpeace, who presented Coca-Cola with the first 'Green Medal' of Beijing 2008.

It was during this year that Coca-Cola established a global partnership with WWF, aimed at conserving seven major water sources around the world – including China's Yangzi River. It therefore felt appropriate to make water stewardship a key theme of our Beijing 2008 Games time preparations. In 2005, we launched an environmental education campaign designed to empower students and their families to save water, called the "Save a Barrel of Water" campaign. By 2008 it had reached 500,000 students in Beijing and all 14 Olympic co-host cities in China. We built on this work by investing $1m in creating a unique public-private partnership to improve water resource management in communities throughout China. To bring our focus on water to life for visitors to Beijing 2008, we introduced Coca-Cola Drops of Hope Olympic pins, donating a share of the proceeds to the programme.

Beijing 2008 also saw our first scaled efforts to use the Olympic Games to promote recycling. We supported the Beijing 2008 Organising Committee in establishing a recycling process for all PET bottles, and used our assets – staff uniforms, beverage displays, and bins – to encourage visitors to

---

2.HFC gas is commonly used as a refrigerant but has a very high global warming potential if it leaks. HFC stands for hydrofluorocarbon. Ironically, it was introduced to replace ozone-depleting CFC gases.

recycle. For the first time, we used recycled plastic (rPET) in our staff uniforms to show that waste can have a second life when recycled.

We recognised local environmental champions across China and around the world by rewarding them with an opportunity to carry the Olympic Flame during the Olympic Torch Relay. We also celebrated athletes who made a commitment to care for the environment as part of our Village Green concept inside the Athletes Village, which marked the beginning of an ambitious Athlete Engagement program designed to raise environmental awareness and change behaviour.

Vancouver 2010

The introduction to this chapter provides a sense of the depth of our commitment to recycling in Vancouver, driven by a determination to deliver a 'zero waste, zero carbon' sponsor activation programme. A proportion of the plastic waste collected in Vancouver during the 2010 Games (Vancouver 2010) was recycled into warm clothing for a shelter in downtown Vancouver.

Building on the start we had made in Beijing, we also sought to engage athletes on sustainability through an interactive pledging mechanism inside the Athletes Village. Over 300 athletes made environmental commitments to change their behaviour.

So far, we have primarily dealt with the environmental aspect of sustainable development, but encouraging people to lead active, healthy lives is another core pillar of Coca-Cola's sustainability strategy. The Olympic and Paralympic Games are an extraordinary celebration of sport which see the best athletes in the world compete against each other. As well as acting as an inspiration for the world's elite, we know that the Games have the power to inspire all of us to get active, and we are eager to harness that to encourage people to make positive behaviour change.

The 2010 Games saw the creation of Coca-Cola's Sogo Active initiative, a national program that awarded over 1,000 torchbearer spots in the 2010 Olympic Torch Relay to teenagers who demonstrated a commitment to adopting an active lifestyle. The $5 million, five-year initiative was delivered in partnership with ParticipACTION and various experts across the country.

Preparing for London 2012

Looking ahead, we know the profile of sustainability during the London 2012 Olympic and Paralympic Games will be high, likely generating unprecedented amounts of media coverage. This is largely as a result of three drivers: first, a greater public awareness of the urgency to protect our planet, particularly among UK citizens; second, a natural tendency for each Olympic host country to want to do better than the previous host; and third, the strong leadership that has been shown by the UK Government, the Greater London Authority and the London 2012 Organising Committee (LOCOG) in viewing sustainability as a priority consideration for the Games.

For Coca-Cola, this unique context is the perfect background against which to showcase the work that we have done to create a responsible business in the United Kingdom. When the spotlight falls on London, we will be ready with our most sustainable sponsorship activation to date.

Our first priority is to get the basics right. This means ensuring all our delivery vehicles are highly efficient and that the coolers we bring into Olympic and Paralympic venues are HCF-free. It means working with our suppliers to ensure all merchandise we plan to sell, or uniforms our staff will wear, are made from recycled materials. It also means putting processes in place to monitor and reduce our carbon emissions, and taking steps to manage the entire project according to BS 8901, a new British Standards specification for sustainable event management.

In addition, we want to work in partnership with others to maximise the impact of our efforts. We have been active participants in LOCOG's Food Advisory Group, devising minimum sustainability standards for all food and drink consumed during the London 2012 event. We are also in dialogue with a number of other sponsors to see how we might collaborate, and several strong ideas are emerging.

However, like LOCOG, we recognise that the positive impact of the Games can be multiplied many times if we succeed in engaging consumers and inspiring them to think and behave differently. The Coca-Cola System in the UK has been investing for several years in promoting recycling, and London 2012 is an ideal time for us to engage people with this campaign. We are supporting LOCOG to ensure it is easy for visitors to recycle, by working in partnership with them to create clear iconography for the recycling bins, and using our various assets to encourage people to recycle – such as messages on staff uniforms, the coolers, umbrellas and tables in food and drink concessions.

In addition, we will seek to raise awareness of the value and importance of recycling, devoting a space within the London 2012 Olympic Park entirely to exploring recycling in an engaging, fun and family-friendly way. Coca-Cola's large fixed structure 'Showcase' will be open to all visitors to the Olympic Park, at no additional cost.

We hope all of this activity will encourage people to think differently about recycling when they go home again, leading to a change in their behaviour, and hopefully, an increase in national recycling rates.

Building on our success with promoting active living in Vancouver, we will also use London 2012 to encourage people to embrace sport. Coca-Cola's Schweppes Abbey Well is the Official Water of London 2012. We launched a campaign around this brand to encourage people to go swimming and have already succeeded in getting thousands of people into their local pool, while supporting a swimming charity at the same time.

We have also formed a significant relationship with StreetGames, a national charity which gives young people in disadvantaged communities access to a wide range of sports and activities. We will use our sponsorship of London 2012 to raise the profile of this charity's important work, and to give participants once-in-a-lifetime opportunities to see London 2012 up-close.

Having taken successful steps to educate and engage athletes in Beijing and Vancouver, we are now exploring how to develop that idea for London, reaching out to them in advance of the Games, and then empowering these highly influential young people to be spokespeople for sustainability back in their own communities after the Games. At Games-time, we will have a programme of activity designed to educate athletes about sustainability in a compelling, interactive way. We aspire to get athletes pledging to adopt certain environmentally positive behaviours (such as recycling) while at the London 2012 event and once they return home.

Measuring Success

Coca-Cola will measure and monitor the carbon footprint associated with our London 2012 activities, which will include consideration of the long term benefits of delivering a sustainable sponsorship of London 2012. We can quantify these in two ways: the carbon saving attributable to investments made for the London 2012 event, and the positive impact of inspiring pro-environmental behaviour change. The former is relatively straightforward to calculate; we can measure the long term carbon benefit of actions like procuring HCF-free coolers or low-emission vehicles for the London 2012, and then use them to retire old stock after the event. The impact of changing people's behaviour is far harder to quantify, but potentially far more significant over time.

Of course, another measure of success from Coca-Cola's activities associated with London 2012 will be positive changes in how the general public perceive the company and our brands. We hope our concentrated efforts will be widely acknowledged and well-received, and rewarded by continued custom.

Looking Ahead

We want to ensure that our experience of London 2012 serves as a benchmark and, indeed, a springboard, for how Coca-Cola approaches future Olympic Games. With Sochi 2014 and Rio 2016 right around the corner, we – alongside the entire Olympic Movement – must consider how we will raise the bar further and ensure the continuity of our efforts in a context where challenges will be numerous.

A major paradigm shift is needed; the Olympic Games can be a major contributor to sustainable development and must no longer be viewed as just a "festival of consumption" which simply destroys habitat and biodiversity, consumes energy and creates waste. If the single most important challenge of sustainable development is changing people's behaviour, a global event of the magnitude and reach of the Olympic Games undoubtedly has a major role to play. Yet, while we believe the Olympic Games in London will have a significant, positive impact on sustainable development, it remains to be seen if LOCOG will fully tap into its potential. In particular, the extent to which the Olympic athletes and the Olympic broadcasting network will be utilised to drive messaging and awareness remains unknown. The opportunity seems extraordinary but will require a significant political will and collaboration between the relevant stakeholders.

As for Coca-Cola, we will need to continue to raise the bar at each successive Olympic Games, in the face of new challenges and a more complex agenda. Despite "greening" our operations, their environmental impact remains too great if the initiatives put in place do not trigger a significant shift in behaviour change. We have a unique leadership role to play here considering our long-standing association with the Olympic Movement, our global presence, and the reach of our brands. Hence, our focus will increasingly be on tapping into assets that can offer scale and widespread impact. For instance, engaging athletes as spokespeople, empowering them to reach a broader audience before, during and after the Games to raise awareness among the general public is a major opportunity which we have only just started to explore.

Hosting the Olympic Games is a massive undertaking and responsibility and we are determined, as a company and as individuals, to support future host countries to make the Olympic Movement ever more sustainable. Collectively, we have not yet exhausted the opportunities for connecting the practice of sport, amateur and professional and also exciting, with the fight against climate change and the promotion of active living.

The Olympic and Paralympic Games have global reach and impact and continuing to harness that power as a force for good is important and exciting – and in all of our interests.

Chapter 20
Sport and Wellness – A Lifetime Journey

Tony Majakas

Introduction

At Technogym, our mission is to offer innovative and engaging solutions to help people achieve personal Wellness, by educating them on the benefits of movement and a healthy lifestyle. That which guides us and unites us is a belief in Wellness as a social responsibility and by inspiring as many people as possible to take up engaging physical activity, exercise or sport, we can actively protect their health. Today, the Technogym Vision 2012 is a culmination of 27 years of a Wellness Journey based on innovation, design and sustainability.

Technogym is an exclusive Olympic Partner - Supplier of the summer Olympic and Paralympic Games since Sydney 2000 through to London 2012. Technogym's Founder and President Nerio Alessandri is a Wellness Designer, and his background in engineering and design saw the birth of Technogym from his home garage and the foundation of the company on 20th October 1983. Technogym's approach to Corporate Social Responsibility led to it becoming one of the first companies in Italy to be externally audited as an SA8000 Company, and adopting the Social Accountability certification in 2008[1].

Healthy People, Healthy Planet

London 2012 has made a commitment to become the first Sustainable Olympic and Paralympic Games ever, based on the concept of *Towards a One Planet Olympics*[2]. London 2012's sustainability policy and strategy is based on five themes: climate change, waste, biodiversity, inclusion and healthy living. Technogym's recently launched campaign 'Healthy People, Healthy Planet' shares its sustainability story and vision with London 2012. Technogym's new Wellness Village is an embodiment of this approach in real, sustainable terms – a company trying to *walk the talk* today and for a sustainable future. Our aim is to create a global reference point for the Wellness Lifestyle, where people and employees can enjoy a Wellness experience. For Technogym, this is the reason why we have adopted environmental practices in our core business strategy. In our approach, people's health goes hand in hand with the health of the planet. We therefore must first think of 'Healthy People' living in a 'Healthy Planet'; without personal health as a base, sustainability does not help people live a quality of life and it does not address a major epidemic of modern societies – physical inactivity. Sport can play a pivotal role in helping to tackle the epidemic of physical inactivity, and thus in turn plays a pivotal role in promoting a sustainable planet.

Technogym's Sustainable Design story has developed organically over more than 25 years in the Italian town of Gambettola. From the beginning the company employed its own team of sports medical scientists. These are the human science engineers who help define safe and innovative movement science solutions. The designers, engineers, stylists, and the multi-disciplinary teams work together in a human touch design approach – again a core foundation of sustainable design. Linking the internal movement science team with universities, scientists and inventors across the world has allowed us to test new methodologies of sports science in the development of new products. Technogym has also worked closely with many top sports teams as a part of learning what will be required in the future for elite and everyday performance. We believe that elite sports performance techniques and training methods can filter down to the general population.

---

1. SA8000 is a voluntary international standard for socially responsible employment practices, created by Social Accountability International. SA8000 seeks to ensure ethical sourcing of goods and services, including basic human rights of all workers in the supply chain.

2. London 2012 Candidate City (2005) *Towards a One Planet Olympics – Achieving the first sustainable Olympic and Paralympic Games*. Available online at: http://www.bioregional.com/what-we-do/our-work/one-planet-2012/ (accessed November 2010).

Sport and Health

The role of sport and physical activity in creating a sustainable planet is most importantly to impact health. As we face the challenge of aging societies people living longer, however at what cost and covered by whom; to the even more disconcerting growth in childhood obesity and the long term impacts on future generations sport has the opportunity to position itself as a new Health Supporter in society.

It is clear that future governments will place greater emphasis on self-responsibility for health from an individual and family prospective. This is driven by simple economics and the need to control spiralling health care costs. Companies will also be involved in this new style management of health. If we spend so many hours a day at work, the corporate environment will need to play a positive role in the management of the health of employees. Sport is a great way to engage large numbers of people to have fun and work out together – creating teamwork and respect of others. If companies fail to address the health of their employees, corporate and personal health-care insurance costs will only increase. In this sense, forward-thinking companies can design new sustainable offices and spaces for employees.

Technogym's Nerio Alessandri had a Wellness Vision that was to be challenged at the very heart of the company – its own headquarters. One of the perks of working in Technogym's headquarters is the fact that staff have a flexible working lunch time – two hours is available so that they can visit the Wellness Centre or take up other activities during the extended lunch break. This approach is a fundamental part of our vision, and has been recognised through awards such as naming Technogym as *Fortune Magazine's* 'A Great Place to Work'. Our approach is to encourage people to lead healthier, sportier lives. Employees now train indoors and outdoors for marathons, cycling events, triathlons and the annual beach tennis and volleyball tournaments.

Technogym Village – A Dream is Born

The Technogym Village project started in 1992, when the company first began talks with a local Council. The Technogym Village proposal was a completely different prospect based on sustainable development in the local community. It is part of a bigger sustainable development project – the Wellness Valley – a haven of wellbeing offering a wealth of experiences to improve people's overall quality of life. Sustainability is viewed at a community level, fostering relations within the local area, its institutions and its schools. As a place of research and innovation, it promotes local growth, helping drive sustainable development. The appointment of Antonio Citterio and Partners studio – a global benchmark of excellence in the design and realisation of innovative projects – together with the appointment of

Marie Engineering, part of the Fiat Group, ensured that the local community was to enjoy an investment of many millions of euros for the local economy.

Technogym Village is now an asset for all our staff, their families, local residents, institutions and all who share our mission. It is a cultural centre, think-tank and production centre, where all who enter can enjoy a comprehensive Wellness experience.

Sustainability in the Technogym Village

This project had to ensure certain principles were respected. The sustainability of Wellness had five key pillars: Naturalness (materials); Eco-Sustainability; Natural Light; Energy Saving and Nature's Shapes.

Naturalness: Our references were shapes present in nature and the project strives to integrate buildings with the surrounding natural environment, seeking a balance between the nature and an industrial production location. The Technogym Village is a production centre, but also a centre of creativity, wellness, work and life, promoting a newly found relationship between humans and the environment: thus Wellness becomes an expression of nature. Naturalness is also the source of inspiration for the choice of building materials, such as wood. It is also pursued through the use of glass walls, whose transparency enables those inside the building to enjoy the outside area and natural light. Naturalness also helps us to define Nature's Shapes, which we will review later.

Eco-Sustainability: Eco-sustainability is a pattern of resource use that aims to meet the needs of the present without compromising the ability of future generations to meet their own needs. Sustainable development – which can be broken into three constituent parts: environmental sustainability, economic sustainability and socio-cultural/political sustainability – has been combined in the Technogym Village project. All of the buildings that make up Technogym Village are positioned in such a way as to allow them to make the most of the environmental principles of eco-sustainability, drawing on concepts of bio-architecture and green buildings. Being in this region of the Mediterranean, the north-facing building is designed to exploit natural heat transfer mechanisms, ensuring a working environment that is cool in the summer and warm in the winter. Large, automatic-opening glass panels below the roof use re-circulated air to lower the temperature inside the building through the early afternoons, even in mid-summer, without the need for cumbersome air conditioning units. Eco-sustainability also means re-utilisation of resources. Every cubic metre of soil is re-utilised to create natural barriers that stretch some 800 metres parallel to the motorway, and this provides a natural soundproof buffering of the motorway traffic.

Natural Light: Light is an essential element for a good quality of life. By choosing to follow the sun's path from sunrise to sunset, we have worked hard to ensure an excellent work environment in terms of natural light and quality of light. The industrial building faces north to make the most of the bright white light of early morning which floods the building through the large glass windows, without any unwanted reflections. The glass façade of the Headquarters, which house the Technogym offices, faces south to benefit from the afternoon sun, bathing it in a warm, stimulating light. Overhead, like a huge natural umbrella, the wood and aluminium roof shields the base of the building, protecting below from reflections and ensuring greater efficiency in the workplace.

Energy Conservation: Technogym Village has endeavoured to maximise self-sufficient energy systems. A large solar cell system built into the roof of the building helps make the building self-sufficient in terms of electricity. Combined with low energy light bulbs and constant brightness adjustment in line with external ambient light, this allows the building to guarantee maximum reductions in energy consumption.

Nature's Shapes: Naturalness has been a source of inspiration for the choice of the building materials, and natural shapes are reflected in the design. As if snuggled in a cradle, Technogym Village is entirely surrounded by a lush natural environment, whose soft, undulating shapes blend seamlessly with the architecture of the buildings. The beautiful wave shape of the roof is the distinguishing element between Technogym Village and the surroundings. Each wave is eighty metres long and reproduces the natural morphology of the land. The wave design is also symbolic of the natural waves of the nearby Adriatic Sea working in harmony with land and sea in the local community and environment. The wave shapes extend for 800 metres. The waves help collect rainwater to be reused during the production process – a natural process of harvesting.

Experiencing Wellness Spaces: Technogym Village is at heart an industrial plant, a business Headquarters and a Wellness Forum, which represents the heart of the community. The Wellness Forum houses an innovative medical-science research centre, classrooms and lecture areas, and a Wellness Centre allowing us to express a holistic mind-body approach to design, choice of materials and atmosphere. The Wellness Forum has direct access to the production areas to allow Research and Development (R&D) teams to interact directly with products in the production area – this integrated approach brings design in real-time from concept to production, from the virtual design world to the real physical world of products, to ensure a seamless process of design and innovation. Technogym Village is a place where we are trying to obtain the right balance between work, health and leisure time. It is designed to deliver a complete work and life experience. The actual working environment becomes a part of the product, as it fosters a holistic experience in those who work there through greater creativity and teamwork with a precise mission to spread the Wellness culture.

Our employees have become role models in a lifestyle project that we carry forward together on a daily basis. As previously mentioned the two hour flexible lunch break allows staff to participate in sports and exercise both inside and outside the Wellness Centre in the local community. A Wellness workplace encourages both mental and physical development and teamwork to face the challenges of the modern world.

London 2012 – Inspiring Lasting Change

As discussed earlier, the London 2012 bid team committed to creating the first sustainable Olympic and Paralympic Games – using the power of the Games to inspire lasting change[3]. This sustainability challenge is programme wide, including in the London 2012 training venues, the Olympic Village Gym and International Media Centre. Technogym is an Official Supplier to the London 2012 Olympic and Paralympic Games, and aim to support sustainable Games. One example is our approach to Inclusion, which is a London 2012 sustainability theme. By listening to the needs of the London 2012 organisers to be the most integrated between the Olympic Games and the Paralympic Games, we have adopted an approach through the R&D of products which drives us to deliver the Technogym Inclusive Line. Our range of IFI Stage 2[4] strength and cardio products will allow people of all abilities to train at the same time – whether in a wheel-chair or with another type of disability. Our slogan "Masterpieces are made up of small details" drives our teams to understand how to make design simpler for people of all abilities – ask someone in a wheel-chair why it's great to be able to adjust machines at a height of 84 cm or watch disabled children playing on Kinesis One and seeing their smiles as they feel their muscles working, and you will understand inspirational sustainable design of Technogym IFI products.

On-going discussions with LOCOG (London 2012 Organising Committee for the Olympic and Paralympic Games), the British Olympic Association and Paralympics GB allows us to create a new mix of products for London 2012 and use this platform to create sustainable legacy projects based on the learning from the event. At London 2012, we will have participants from across the world. In order to make athletes feel at home the Village Gym we can embrace new technologies like Visio Web – a digital platform that allows the athlete to change language on screens, allows them to access their Facebook pages and play their own music on the cardio machine via their iPod. Technology in the Gym – the origin of the name Technogym – now can be seen in the vision of our President: sustainable, innovative, technologically advanced design available for all.

---

3. London 2012 Vision, see: http://www.london2012.com/get-involved/jobs/why-work-for-london-2012.php (accessed November 2010).

4. The Inclusive Fitness Initiative (IFI) is a programme supporting the fitness industry to become more inclusive, catering for the needs of disabled and non-disabled people, raising physical activity participation levels. The IFI manages an accreditation scheme. For more information see: www.inclusivefitness.org (accessed November 2010).

The International Olympic Committee promotes the Olympic Games as 'Celebration of Humanity' – we at Technogym are looking forward to making London 2012 a 'Celebration of Human Energy'! By embracing the cleanest form of energy – Human Energy – we can make London 2012 truly the most sustainable Games ever. We can help position Sport as a partner for Health and Wellness, and continue our lifetime journey – the Sustainability of Sport and Wellness.

Chapter 21

Fostering Pro–Environmental Behavior Through Sport

Jill Savery

Introduction

Sport events have the potential to be primary forces that drive sustainable development and catalyze lasting change in a host city, host nation, and around the world. Sport event organizing committees are increasingly coming to this realization, and are beginning to consider sustainability when preparing for and hosting major sports events such as the Olympic Games. However, to date their approaches have been largely ineffective at reaching the much larger prize of engaging the sports event audience and fostering the adoption of pro-environmental behavior.

In this chapter I will provide a framework for developing an effective strategy to foster pro-environmental behavior through sport, after highlighting theories of learning and behavior. I will make the case for using sport events to promote sustainable behaviors through the lens of the Olympic Games for illustration, as this event and the Olympic Movement are arguably the most demonstrative examples. However, the framework presented can apply to any sport event. It is important to note that the notion of *sustainability* implies the holistic social, economic and environmental dimensions; this chapter concentrates on environmental aspects in particular, but the principles discussed would apply to all areas of sustainability.

The Olympic Games

The first modern Olympic Games were held in 1896; in just over a century it has become the largest international event on the planet, uniquely cutting across cultural and national boundaries. The Olympic Games provides a source of inspiration to billions of people around the globe. For example the 2008 Olympic Games held in Beijing drew the largest ever television audience for an Olympic Games at 4.7 billion viewers – this was 70% of the world's population![1] Nearly 11,000 athletes competed in Beijing from 204 countries. Hundreds of thousands of people witnessed the event in person, 70,000 volunteers were mobilized, and over 24,000 accredited media personnel from 159 countries were reporting from the event.[2] These figures are staggering, and illustrate the potential reach the Olympic Games can extend to organizing committees and host nations who seek to capitalize on activities aimed at fostering pro-environmental behavior.

Fostering Pro-Environmental Behavior

Human actions have had an enormous impact on the environment. In many circumstances, these impacts have been harmful, and have led to polluted air, water, and land, including associated negative impacts on human health. Collectively, our actions have led to environmental degradation, including global climate change. If we are to alter the current global trajectory of natural resource consumption, waste generation, greenhouse gas emissions, and pollution in our environment, we must address not only the built environment, but the behaviors of individuals.

We are now demanding more from the environment than it can deliver; Earth Overshoot Day happens earlier each year as we extract more resources and emit more waste than the Earth can replenish or absorb.[3] Al-

---

1. The Nielson Company. Press Release issued 5 September 2008. Hong Kong. Available at: http://blog.nielsen.com/nielsenwire/wp-content/uploads/2008/09/press_release3.pdf (accessed September 2010).

2. International Olympic Committee. Beijing 2008. http://www.olympic.org/en/content/Olympic-Games/All-Past-Olympic-Games/Summer/Beijing-2008-summer-olympics/ (accessed September 2010).

3. 'Earth Overshoot Day' is a term coined by the New Economics Foundation (UK) to describe the day in a calendar year when human demand from the natural world exceeds the planet's ability to supply this demand. From this day to the end of the calendar year, humans meet their demand by depleting natural resources and adding greenhouse gas emissions in the atmosphere. In 2010, Earth Overshoot Day was August 21st. See Global Footprint Network, World Footprint at: http://www.footprintnetwork.org/en/index.php/GFN/page/world_footprint/ (accessed September 2010).

though our current environmental challenges seem daunting, we can foster alternative pro-environmental behaviors that can reduce negative environmental impacts. The Olympic Games can be an important catalyst in achieving these objectives, not only through such innovations as green technology and sustainable venue design, but by providing a worldwide stage to promote sustainable, pro-environmental behaviors.

The term *pro-environmental behavior* is used herein to describe "consciously seek[ing] to minimize the negative impact of one's actions on the natural and built world."[4] Many important advances have been made in describing factors that contribute to how people learn, as well as theories about why people engage in environmentally friendly behavior. In spite of these discoveries, we are left with the reality that learning and behavior are complex processes that do not lend themselves to one framework.[5] Early on, it was thought that environmental knowledge would eventually lead to pro-environmental behavior. It would follow, then, that by educating an audience on a particular environmental issue, they would in turn become concerned about this issue, and this concern would translate into changed behavior.[6] However, this simple linear progression between education, attitude and behavior does not typically hold true; the link between attitude and behavior is complex, and many researchers have determined multiple factors that influence behavior.[7]

Theories of Behavior and Learning

Highlighted below are several theories of behavior and learning, which are presented in order to then suggest principles that can be applied to Olympic Games-related education and awareness strategies aimed at fostering pro-environmental behavior.

Behavior theory seeks to determine factors that drive our behavior or actions. Hines, Hungerford and Tomera (1986) produced a *Model of Responsible Environmental Behavior*, whereby they found that the factors influencing pro-environmental behavior are: knowledge of issues, knowledge of action strategies, locus of control, attitudes, verbal commitment, and individual sense of responsibility. They found that the simple progression between knowledge, intentions and behavior "are weak at best."[8] Rajecki (1982) sug-

---

4.Kollmuss, A. and J. Agyeman. 2002. "Mind the Gap: Why Do People Act Environmentally and What Are the Barriers to Pro-environmental Behavior?" Environmental Education Research 8(3):239–260.

5.Ibid.

6.Ibid.

7.Hines, J.M., H.R. Hungerford and A.N. Tomera. 1986-87. "Analysis and synthesis of research on responsible pro-environmental behavior: a meta-analysis." The Journal of Environmental Education, 18(2): 1-8.

8.Ibid.

gests that "direct experiences have a stronger influence on people's behavior than indirect experiences."[9] Kollmuss and Agyeman (2002), Engleson and Yockers (1994), and others have concluded that while each framework developed contributes to our understanding of what drives behavior, there is no single framework that provides the absolute answer, and we have yet to truly crack the code of what causes pro-environmental behavior.

Constructivist learning theory is based on the notion that learning is accomplished when learners interact with their physical and social environments.[10] Observations, activities, and direct experiences all contribute to knowledge; learners mix past experiences with new observations to construct knowledge.[11] Also important to the theory of learning is the "sociocultural" perspective. In this framework, learning takes place in collaboration with others, and is "a process of becoming enculturated into a community of learners."[12] By conversing and experiencing situations with others, one learns through construction in their particular social and cultural situation. Learning itself still occurs within the mind of the individual, but is influenced by and dependent on social interactions with community members.

Free-choice learning is that which allows the learner to "exercise a large degree of choice and control over the what, when and why of learning."[13] Free-choice learning describes voluntary choices in terms of what and where one seeks learning, as well as whether the experience is individual or with others.[14] This methodology stands apart from learning typically done in schools where the learner does not have choice, and teachers must follow prescribed curriculum.

Kellert (1996) describes the difference between cognitive and affective education, and advocates combining both into values education. Cognitive learning provides facts and concepts, where affective learning involves emotional development and fosters a positive connection between humans and their natural environment. He states: "A knowledgeable and ethically responsible citizenry, environmentally literate and morally concerned, will be

---

9. Kollmuss, A. and J. Agyeman. 2002. "Mind the Gap: Why Do People Act Environmentally and What Are the Barriers to Pro-environmental Behavior?" Environmental Education Research 8(3):239–260.

10. Engelson, D. and D. Yockers. 1994. "A Guide to Curriculum Planning in Environmental Education." Madison: Wisconsin Department of Public Instruction. Pp. 52–81.

11. Hein, G. E. 1995. "The Constructivist Museum." Journal for Education in Museums 16:21–23.

12. Ibid, siting Rogoff and Lave, 1984; Wenger, 1998; Wenger *et al.*, 2002.

13. Falk, J. H. 2005. "Free-Choice Environmental Learning: Framing the Discussion." Environmental Education Research 11(3): 265–280.

14. Ibid.

an indispensable ingredient in securing and restoring the integrity and health of the biosphere."[15]

Community Based Social Marketing (CBSM) draws on principles of commercial and social marketing, communications strategies, and behavioral theory to guide behavior change among a target audience.[16] Rather than selling products, social marketing aims to change behavior for social good. CBSM seeks to remove barriers to and increase the benefits of new behaviors by engaging people at the individual level. The process for developing CBSM programs includes: defining the target behavior, identifying the target audience, identifying barriers and benefits to the desired behavior among the target audience, creating appropriate campaigns to encourage the desired behavior, pilot testing the campaign, implementation, and monitoring and evaluation. Environmental psychologist Doug McKenzie-Mohr, PhD, is a pioneer and leading practitioner in CBSM. Recognizing that a sustainable society requires sustainable behaviors, he outlines an approach to achieve behavior change through CBSM. Tools are used to encourage behavior change, such as making a commitment, prompts, altering social norms, communication and incentives.[17]

Developing an Engagement Strategy

Fostering environmental stewardship during all stages of the Olympic Games event (preparation, staging and legacy) requires a holistic and sophisticated strategy aimed at reaching multiple constituent groups. These groups include, but are not limited to: athletes, spectators, the media, government, the events industry, suppliers, sponsors, local residents near event venues, and a vast number of event television viewers. Drawing from learning and behavior theory, environmental education, as well as principles of social marketing, a comprehensive strategy can be designed around the Olympic Games to encourage people to adopt pro-environmental behaviors in their daily lives. Collectively, this shift can lead to more efficient use of resources, less pollution, and better care for our natural environment. Tailored correctly, thoughtful awareness campaigns can capitalize on this situation to capture the attention of multiple event constituent groups.

The Olympic Games experience, whether viewed on television or experienced first hand, is not a typical or recurring event in an event spectator's or event participant's life. Therefore, it will have a great personal impact, and will likely be remembered long into the future. Taking advantage of this op-

---

15. Kellert, S. (1996). The Value of Life: Biological Diversity and Human Society. Washington, DC: Island Press/Shearwater Books. Prologue and Chapter 3.

16. McKenzie-Mohr, D. (Fall, 2007). Fostering sustainable behavior: An introduction to community-based social marketing (3rd Edition). Gabriola Island, B.C.: New Society.

17. McKenzie-Mohr, D. *Quick Reference: Community Based Social Marketing*. See: http://www.cbsm.com/Reports/CBSM.pdf

portunity to capture the attention of millions, and even billions, of people has tremendous advantages.

The next section provides a series of guiding principles based on theories of learning and behavior change to be considered when developing a strategy for fostering pro-environmental behavior leading up to, during and after the Olympic Games. While not all of the ideas will be appropriate for each phase of an event nor for each constituent group, important lessons should be drawn from commercial marketing, social marketing, environmental education, and behavior theory.

Guiding Principles

- People will construct knowledge based on their previous experiences; therefore, strategies that build on these experiences will more likely lead to increasing environmental knowledge, which is a precursor for behavior change. The learning experiences established in Olympic Games programs should be configured within the context of constituents' particular lives. While this will be difficult to do precisely for each and every one of the millions of constituents at the event, audience segmentation can ease this process.

- Think about the types of people going to various places at the event and what might trigger a response in them. For example, what types of people tend to watch the triathlon event at the Olympic Games? If this information is not known, simple surveys can be conducted of audience members at Olympic Games test events or other triathlon events to determine whether these spectators have common interests or experiences. Maximize the opportunity to use these commonalities to deliver relevant information at the event that will promote awareness objectives.

- People learn through a variety of means. Some prefer visual aids, others prefer to read material, and some prefer to hear information. Learning may require multiple forms of transmission, so it is important to offer a variety of forms of education to suit multiple audiences. Through empirical research, psychologists tell us that 75% of what people know is gleaned through sight, 13% through hearing, 6% through touch, 3% through taste, and 3% through smell. Interestingly, this means that 88% of what we know is from seeing and hearing.[18] It is important to keep these discoveries in mind when creating a variety of learning choices, because visual and auditory methods may prove to be more successful than other means for particular issues.

- Social learning environments enable collaborative learning. Offer opportunities for constituents to learn together. Many people attend Olympic Games with friends or relatives. These personal relationships can enhance the learning experience by allowing for conversations and discussion of issues at hand. By way of example, museums and zoos tend to

---

18.Iozzi, L. (1989). "Environmental Education and the Affective Domain" Journal of Environmental Education 20(3):3–9; 20(4): 6–13.

foster such collaborative learning environments, whereby visitors view exhibits with other people and have the opportunity to discuss their reactions to presented material.

- Thoughtful consideration must always be given to social and cultural differences that will be present at the Olympic Games, which is a unique international event attracting a worldwide audience. At any given venue, for example, nations from around the world will be represented in the spectator population. The cultural and social differences between and within nations should be considered when creating awareness campaigns and educational experiences in order to have the desired impact, especially in any campaign that seeks to reach multiple social and cultural constituents. On the most basic level, material might need to be developed in multiple languages.

- Opportunities should be offered for constituents to be directly exposed to environmental challenges. Kiosks or experiential exhibits can be placed at various locations near or in Olympic Games' venues that allow constituents to interact with environmental issues. For example, kiosks can be woven into a venue to provide interactive displays and real-time monitoring to allow spectators to view challenges in the built environment, such as energy consumption, water use, or choice of venue building materials.

- Cognitive learning should be incorporated with affective learning in order to foster behavior change. Facts and figures alone do not lend themselves to changes in personal lifestyles. Social pressures and norms, emotional ties, and moral and ethical development should be included in campaigns. There may be multiple means for addressing the affective component to education at the Olympics Games, such as through storytelling, community group discussion, or through simply incorporating appropriate probing questions into messaging that will draw on emotional connections.

- The use of guilt as a strategy to promote environmental awareness is *not* a successful approach, so strategies should *avoid* this tactic.[19]

A Strategic Framework

In order to facilitate the development of a holistic strategy to foster pro-environmental behavior, a matrix can be developed highlighting the constituent groups associated with the Olympic Games, as well as various communications tools and strategies that can be used to target specific audiences. A matrix allows the user to easily reference activities that are suited to reach a particular constituency. The matrix maps constituent groups with strategies, while also considering the timeframe to initiate activities (before, during or after the event). These particulars should be addressed dur-

---

19. McKenzie-Mohr, D. "Promoting Sustainable Behaviour: An Introduction to Community Based Social Marketing." Journal of Social Issues. London: Blackwell. 2000.

ing initial strategy sessions for an overall environmental stewardship program plan. Research will be necessary to understand constituent groups, behaviors, barriers to desired behaviors, and the best outreach mechanism to reach the target audience based on the habits of these groups. A matrix can be used as an organizational tool when developing a targeted and comprehensive plan.

If the target audience for pro-environmental behavior change is young people between the ages of 10-12, for example, one means to reach this group is through school curriculum. However, this curriculum would need to be incorporated into an overarching strategy that also involves teachers, who must be taught how and when to use the developed materials in their coursework. This may involve a series of workshops for curriculum development as well as teacher training once materials are designed. In fact, teachers should be part of the entire curriculum development process. Pilot testing and evaluation are critical components as well, with teachers providing feedback. So in this example the target audience is youth, and one of the many means to reach youth is through school curriculum, which will also involve teachers. Of course, this would fit within a holistic strategy designed to reach youth that would incorporate many more activities and means of communication – curriculum is just one avenue.

A matrix may not list all of the possible environmental issues that can be addressed related to social marketing at the event. Each tool could communicate a specific environmental issue. For example, a public service announcement could focus on conserving water or energy resources in the home which could be aired on large screens at competition venues. In this way, a particular constituent group would be targeted (spectators at a specific sport venue), with a targeted message (resource conservation in the home). As well, kiosks could be added at the venue site that would provide direct exposure to information and interactive displays that would enhance the messaging used in the public service announcements. Brochures could also be developed for spectators if research concluded that this is an effective means to reach the target audience. Comprehensive planning will reveal tools and strategies that can be combined when targeting specific constituents. Once a target audience is selected, an inclusive process of assessment will reveal sustainable behaviors to encourage. It may also be possible to identify a group of behaviors that fit appropriately well together, and then use communications tools to reach the target audience.

It may not be possible or appropriate to implement the various activities listed in the matrix due to resource or other constraints; however, it is important that strategic planning efforts acknowledge the various activities and constituents. It is also important that these activities relate to the organizing committee's sustainability objectives. Later prioritization and a phased approach will allow for flexibility as well as maximum impact. Some of the tools have the potential of reaching a wide audience, such as videos or television commercials containing an environmental message. It might be prudent to develop these tools first if research uncovers that these reach the maximum number of constituents.

Conclusion

The ability of the Olympic Games to reach the world gives it an inimitable character; it can be a catalyst to spur environmental awareness and pro-environmental behavior. This unique moment in time has a legacy effect, and I would argue that no other event allows for substantive transformation on this grand scale. Fostering pro-environmental behavior before, during and after an Olympic Games can cause a ripple effect throughout the world, supporting a change in the way people lead their lives with respect to the environment.

The Olympic Games is marked by the notion of bringing forth human-kind's highest ethics and ideals. As an Olympian myself I have learned the invaluable lessons of Olympism; fair play, equality, excellence, respect and promoting a healthy environment. I have seen the ideals associated with Olympism drive people to accomplish outstanding feats in the face of adversity. I would like to see this ethic move people to protect our environment and promote sustainable living. This chapter has put forth a framework to promote pro-environmental behavior at the Olympic Games, based theories of learning and behavior, environmental education and social marketing. The Olympic Games provides us with an opportune venue for such action, using the power behind the Olympic rings to unite billions of people across the planet.

Part IV
General Themes on Sustainability and Sport

Chapter 22
The Polar Bear Rules

How International Sport Events Can Address Climate Change

Julius de Heer and Denis Bochatay

Introduction

Following decades of increasingly alarming scientific reports, climate change has become the major global environmental issue, thus eclipsing almost every other environmental subject. Politicians and the public are slowly but surely realizing the contribution of human activities to this phenomenon, and the necessity to act by reducing greenhouse gas emissions (GHGs). Actions are gradually being taken in every domain, and sport is no exception.

Sport event organizers have long been attentive to the environmental impacts associated with their events. Initially, their focus was mainly on local issues such as waste management. However, climate change has progressively become the central issue in terms of major sport event related environmental efforts. Herein we will describe how climate change mitigation at sport events has evolved from the pioneering activities of the 1990s through to present-day. We also identify the flaws present in the assessment and mitigation methods currently used by sport event organizers, and propose seven rules (Polar Bear Rules) aimed at assisting organizers in addressing these insufficiencies.

Pioneering Campaigns

Actions regarding climate change were first taken at major sport events in the late 1990s, which is also the same time as the adoption of the Kyoto Protocol (1997). The first successful Olympic Games campaign related to climate change was led by Greenpeace in the lead up to the Olympic and Paralympic Games held in Sydney in the year 2000. The campaign was aimed at the official event beverage company that planned to use refrigerators running on hydrofluorocarbon gas (HFCs), whose global warming potential is 1000 to 12000 times higher than the GHG carbon dioxide (CO_2), according to the type in use (Source: IPCC). The campaign was successful; Coca-Cola, a major International Olympic Committee (IOC) sponsor, changed not only the beverage company's policy for the Olympic Games held in Sydney in 2000, but their global policy as well. Indeed, at the Beijing Olympic Games held eight years later, all of Coca-Cola's refrigerators, coolers and vending machines used for the event were climate friendly. It was estimated that 4500 tonnes of CO_2-eq[1] would thus be saved (equivalent to the annual GHG emissions of over 430 Europeans[2]).

The Olympic Games organizers in Sydney undertook measures focused on reducing impacts associated with climate change, such as in the form of renewable energy, including the construction of major solar power facilities on the venues used for the event.

After the Olympic Games in Sydney, methodologies such as Life Cycle Assessment (LCA) developed, allowing sport event organizers to estimate GHG emissions. Sectors that were most damaging in terms of GHGs emitted could be identified, and associated measures developed to reduce sectoral emissions.

However, each Olympic Games Organizing Committee (OCOG) then began calculating GHGs associated with their event in their own way, without strictly respecting the emerging scientific principles. In some cases,

---

1. "GHGs differ in their warming influence on the global climate system due to their different radiative properties and lifetimes in the atmosphere. These warming influences may be expressed through a common metric based on the radiative forcing of CO_2. Equivalent CO_2 emission is a standard and useful metric for comparing emissions of different GHGs but does not imply the same climate change responses." (IPCC, 2007: Climate Change 2007: Synthesis Report. Contribution of Working Groups I, II and III to the Fourth Assessment Report of the Intergovernmental Panel on Climate Change [Core Writing Team, Pachauri, R.K and Reisinger, A. (eds.)]. IPCC, Geneva, Switzerland, 104 pp.)

2. Value as of 2006. Source: European Environment Agency (2008), *Greenhouse gas emission trends and projections in Europe 2008. Tracking progress towards Kyoto targets.*

event sectors were omitted, such as international transport, infrastructure or indirect emissions. Consequently, achieving 'carbon neutral' events through GHG emission reduction and compensation programs has become a very subjective exercise, with various methodologies and assumptions used at different events.

Comparison of Applied Methodologies

GHG emissions assessment

LCA evaluates the environmental impacts of a given product or service from cradle to grave, including its manufacture, its use and its final destruction. The tools and methodology for LCAs are now defined by international standards (e.g., Organization for International Standards: ISO 14040). In particular, an LCA must have a clear definition of its goal and scope, and the LCA system boundaries must be clearly established. With regard to a sport event, the LCA system boundaries shall at least define which participants are taken into account, the activities included, the geographical boundaries and time period. For example, excluding emissions caused by event spectators or emissions generated in the preparation of the event by the OCOG is fully inconsistent with LCA principles.

The following table represents the system boundaries of a selection of major sport and non-sport events whose organizers estimated the event GHG emissions.

Table 1: System boundaries of a selection of major events

Event	Emissions (tons CO_2-eq)	Emissions from Transport	Activities Included	Time Period	Geographic Boundaries	Participants Included
UN Summit -Johannes-burg 2002	290,000	95%	All	During Conference	All transport, to and from Johannesburg	Delegates
Winter Olympic Games - Salt Lake City 2002	180,000	33%	No accommodation, no construction of venues	Event and pre-Games test events	Additional direct emissions only, mainly USA flights*	Only spectators, not the Olympic Family
IAAF World Champion-ships - Helsinki 2005	36,000	97%	Temporary construction only	Event	Direct emissions only	All

Event	Emissions (tons CO_2-eq)	Emissions from Transport	Activities Included	Time Period	Geographic Boundaries	Participants Included
Winter Olympic Games - Torino 2006	119,000	29%	No constru- ction	Event	Direct emissions only	Only Olympic Family and Organizing Committee, no spectators
FIFA World Cup - Germany 2006	92,000	77%	All	Event	Within Germany only	All
Rugby World Cup - France 2007	570,000	84%	All	Event and preparation period	Direct and indirect emissions	All

* Only 20% of spectators came in charter flights, the other 80% were not accounted for

All included
Major restrictions

Table 1 displays highly different conceptions of an event's system boundaries, in terms of activities, time period and geographic borders. Of those listed, the Rugby World Cup 2007 in France is the more complete analysis; it includes each activity directly or indirectly linked to the event, all participants (teams, media and journalists, officials, working staff and spectators in France, Wales and Scotland), direct and indirect GHG emissions, and a consistent time period including the preparation, event and the post-event phases (dissolution).

Other analyses listed have been much less inclusive. The Olympic and Paralympic Winter Games in Salt Lake City (2002) and Torino (2006) minimized the impact of air transport by only counting spectators on extra flights added to the network due to the event (Salt Lake City) or by omitting the emissions of air transport generated by spectators (Torino). As emissions of air transport for similar events is responsible for 70 – 90 % of the total emissions (see table 1), these omissions result in a highly underestimated global assessment of GHG.

Most of the analyses above only included the event period and did not take into account the emissions generated during the event preparation phase. In the case of the Olympic Games, the preparation phase lasts seven years, and the bid phase can last up to four years. The event itself lasts only seventeen days (twelve additional days if including the Paralympic Games).

Large events such as the Olympic Games can draw television audience of more than 4 billion viewers[3]; no event has included the GHG emissions generated by an event audience watching from television. A fully consistent LCA, or at least an event environmental action plan, *could* take this into account (e.g., through awareness advertising).

Offsetting GHG emissions

International events generate a significant amount of GHGs; by there very nature, these events require transport of goods and people. In order for an event to be considered 'low carbon', 'carbon neutral' or 'zero carbon', OCOGs can offset their unavoidable GHG emissions. They can buy carbon certificates, or finance offsetting projects directly or through a specialized NGO or company.

Table 2 lists the compensation measures used for the events in Table 1.

Table 2: Compensation measures for events listed in Table 1

Event	Emissions tons CO_2-eq	Offsetting - tons CO_2-eq	Time period	Cost/ ton CO_2-eq	Projects in the host country	Projects abroad	Tree planting
UN Summit – Johannesburg 2002	290,000	48,000 (17%)	After the Summit	$8.3 USD	16 projects for $5 million (USD), $350,000 million (USD) collected		
Winter Olympic Games - Salt Lake City 2002	180,000	745,000 (413%)	Certificates	Donated	Sponsoring: O2 Blue certificates from Cleaner and Greener Program (78.6%)		Tree-cology Program (5.3%)
IAAF World championships - Helsinki 2005	36,000	Nothing planned					

3. The 2008 Beijing Olympics drew 4.7 billion viewers. See Nielsonwire 5 September 2008: http://blog.nielsen.com/nielsenwire/media_entertainment/beijing-olympics-draw-largest-ever-global-tv-audience/ (accessed October 2010).

Event	Emissions tons CO_2-eq	Offsetting -tons CO_2-eq	Time period	Cost/ ton CO_2-eq	Projects in the host country	Projects abroad	Tree planting
Winter Olympic Games - Torino 2006	121,000	69,600 (58%)	Carbon credits covering 4 years	€72	5 projects financed by the region (€5 million), Pinerolo		UNEP Plant for the Planet in Kenya (905 trees in 4 years)
FIFA World Cup – Germany 2006	91,700	100,000 (109%)	10 years in India, 3 years in South Africa	€12		3 projects, €1.2 million: Citrus fruit farm & biogas in South Africa, and India	
Rugby World Cup – France 2007	570,000	Still not impleme- nted	10 years in South Pacific			Integrated biogas and waste project	

Emissions offsetting practices for events are diverse. Offset project type, quality and location (taking place in the host countries or abroad) of projects vary, which results in large variation in the costs per ton of CO_2. Offsetting emissions abroad can be motivated by economic reasons as project costs can be lower; however, there is an argument to be made for investing in project offsets that reduce emissions in the event host country.

The question of time period is also applied differently by event organizers; how long can the emissions credit of the offset project be attributed to the event? For example, it takes five to eight years to achieve a carbon goal with a project of replacing light bulbs with energy saving light bulbs, before they need to be replaced. For a project of reforestation, the carbon goal is achieved when the growing forest (soaking up carbon) becomes a mature forest, which occurs up to 100 years after trees are planted. Furthermore, there is no guarantee about the effective working period of offset projects, as technical equipment can break after a couple of years without being repaired, or a forest can be cut or burned down for other purposes. Event organizers have no direct control over offset projects implemented in foreign countries.

The Polar Bear Rules

Climate change and associated impacts are real, and this reality is evolving faster than scientists predicted. For example, arctic sea ice has been melting rapidly since 1950 due to global warming. Models predict between 10% and 50% of additional decline of the area covered with sea ice. These figures rise to 50% to 100% during the summer, according to the World Conservation Union (IUCN). These circumstances negatively affect the population size of polar bears, due to the reduction of its area of occupancy and a decrease in its habitat quality. The predicted decline of the population of polar bears stands at 30% within 45 years, and has led the IUCN to upgrade the polar bear to a *Vulnerable Species* on its *Red list of Threatened Species* in 2006[4].

Scientists are clear that we must reduce GHG emissions quickly in order to avoid dangerous climate changes[5]; *later* will be *too late* to act for polar bears as well as for winter sports. The climate change impacts of major events, reduction measures applied and offset strategies employed vary significantly. Therefore, we suggest that major sport and non-sport events apply the following *Polar Bear Rules* in order to reduce, mitigate and compensate for event GHG emissions.

Polar Bear Rule 1: Think globally

- GHG emissions (or carbon footprints) should be calculated globally and comprehensively, following rigorous and widely accepted standards for LCAs.
- All type of sources (direct and indirect), all activities (including construction activities) and participant and spectator impacts related to all phases of sport events should be included (preparation staging and post-event), without geographical restrictions.

Comments

Climate Change is one of the biggest challenges for humanity. It is not credible to limit the event organizing committee's responsibility to only a portion of the emissions. Carbon reduction and compensation is critical.

---

4. IUCN (2010). IUCN Red List of Threatened Species. Version 2010.3. <www.iucn-redlist.org>. Downloaded on 18 October 2010.

5. IPCC (2007): *Climate Change 2007: Synthesis Report. Contribution of Working Groups I, II and III to the Fourth Assessment Report of the Intergovernmental Panel on Climate Change* [Core Writing Team, Pachauri, R.K and Reisinger, A. (eds.)]. IPCC, Geneva, Switzerland, p.104.

Polar Bear Rule 2: Do the job yourself

- Priority should be placed on staging a low carbon event. Everything should be done to reduce the carbon footprint of the event itself.
- Only the GHG emissions that cannot be reasonably reduced should be offset (to be carbon neutral).
- GHG emissions should be estimated during the event bid phase, because actions can be planned more efficiently if done early.

Comments

Offsetting GHG emissions is easier than reducing GHG emissions, which is probably why most event organizers start with this type of action. However, as climate change has become the major environmental problem in the world, we need new, ambitious and creative energy efficient solutions to reduce emissions at the source.

Polar Bear Rule 3: Compensate where you live

- Off-setting carbon emissions should be done in the place where the emissions are generated.

Comments

Sport events will generate direct GHG emissions in the host city and country. Reducing carbon emissions locally will also tend to reduce other types of local air pollutant emissions associated with burning fossil fuels. However, all international sport events attract a major share of participants and spectators from around the world, who typically travel by airplane. These carbon emissions can be offset abroad.

Polar Bear Rule 4: Offset your emissions now

- Carbon emissions generated during a sport event should be offset before (during the preparation of the event) or during the year of the event itself, not in the future.

Comments

As inertia is important in climate change and as scientists' models have often underestimated the consequences of climate change (for example the speed of arctic ice cap melting[6]), offsetting carbon must be done as soon as possible. If that is not possible, event organizers should communicate honestly with stakeholders and the public that the event will be 'climate neutral' only after a certain number of years in the future.

6.Stroeve, J., Holland, M.M., Meier, W., Scambos, T., & Serreze, M. (2007). Arctic sea ice decline: Faster than forecast, *Geophys. Res. Lett.*, 34, L09501, doi:10.1029/2007GL029703.

Polar Bear Rule 5: Plan for the future

- Actions (GHG emissions reduction or offsetting) that leave a lasting legacy and have positive impacts on sustainable development should be prioritized.

Comments

Many actions that reduce carbon emissions leave positive effects after the event itself (e.g., newly installed renewable energy systems). Offsetting projects in developing countries can have far reaching and positive environmental, social and economic impacts. Some actions are useful during the event itself, but will not leave a lasting legacy, as using energy efficient heating or cooling systems for temporary structures or overlay. Their efficiency should be evaluated.

Polar Bear Rule 6: Get help

- Implementing an effective carbon management plan requires the cooperation of all parties involved in an event, such as the sports world, event organizers, government, sponsors, spectators, and the television audience.

Comments

Many effective carbon reduction measures have been implemented by sponsors and even TV viewers, at nearly no cost for the event organizers themselves. For example, Salt Lake City 2002 used the Leonardo Academy's Cleaner and Greener® program[7] to encourage TV viewers to save energy at home, and to donate their emissions reduction to Salt Lake City 2002. Event organizers should put up the framework and set the goals, and then they should mobilize all of the actors.

Polar Bear Rule 7: Transfer of knowledge

- The transfer of knowledge from one event to another via post-event evaluations and reports is very important.

Comments

As the area of GHG emission reductions and offsetting is still relatively new and challenging, we need to collect good examples of carbon reduction practices and new technology. Major companies acting as sport sponsors can help put forward new environmentally friendly technologies.

7.Leonardo Academy's Cleaner and Greener® program. See: http://www.leonardoacademy.org/index.php/about/history/emissions-history (accessed October 2010).

Conclusion

Sport events in general, and high level mega sport events in particular, need excellent environmental conditions for athletes to compete without being hazardous to human health. Therefore, major events must show the way in their own interest, and cannot be inconsistent in their environmental action plan. With that goal in mind, the ever-growing audience of major sport events and sport stars represents a wonderful springboard that cannot be missed by international federations, event organizers and sport sponsors.

Chapter 23

Using a Major Sports Event to Deliver a Sustainable Social Legacy of Lasting Positive Change

Beth Nicholls

Introduction

What does a sustainable event legacy feel like?

If an event bid was a person, the technical bid would be her bones, the branding and marketing strategy would be her skin, the campaign strategy would be her brain and the communications strategy would be her voice. A genuine legacy strategy would not be the makeup she puts on to make herself look better, as the last thing she does before she goes out. Rather, it would be her beating heart, which gives her personality, makes her communications authentic and sends oxygen to her (campaign) brain. It would drive her passion, hold her values and guide her in making responsible and just decisions.

A sustainable event legacy is not an add-on that starts when the event takes place, it is a vital and fundamental part of any serious event bid, and should be part of the event planning from day one. A 'sustainable legacy' of a sport event is defined herein as: *the lasting, positive change created through and catalysed by the bidding for, planning and hosting of a sport event.* Through an swering a series of questions, this chapter gives particular attention to the social elements of a major event legacy, and how event bidders can craft a proposition that benefits them, their stakeholders and wider society.

An event legacy: who cares?

'Sustainability of sport', by its very definition, looks to the ability of a given sport to be sustained. Most major sports events showcase elite sport by their very nature. Elite sport is sustained by the money generated by elite events and professional clubs (broadcast, sponsorship, ticketing, merchandise, etc.), by the grassroots game (developing and nurturing the inspirational stars and talent pool of the future), and often also the supporters of the sport at the elite level. Major event rights holders who also govern the grassroots game have a vested interest in using the event to boost interest and participation in the game at grassroots level. Most serious bidders' objectives will boil down to delivering a technical bid that meets or exceeds the rights holder's requirements and securing the necessary number of votes to win the right to host an event. The primary objective of the subsequently established event Local Organising Committee (LOC), as an event management company, is to deliver the event flawlessly (i.e., an inspiring competition in a safe environment, on time and within budget). There will also be many other stakeholders, often including government, who will have different objectives for the event, ranging from nation branding, to creating or strengthening an event industry, from boosting the economy or regenerating an area to promoting sports participation. It is crucial to map these out early on, and if you are the bidder or LOC, to be clear about which are strategically important to you.

In reality, any major event will have an impact, and it will leave some kind of legacy regardless of whether or not the LOC plans it or tries to make it happen. However, it is possible for the LOC to influence whether that impact and legacy is negative or positive, and the degree to which it is far-reaching and deep-rooted. This can be strengthened or weakened by the promises made during the bid.

Without a vision, planning, partnership-building and appropriate resources, it is unlikely that the impact and legacy outcome will achieve the desired legacy ambition. In such a case it is likely that the legacy delivery performance will then be measured against other people's expectations about what it should have been – and it is unlikely that all of these expectations will be met. Therefore, the crucial questions to be asked in the very beginning are:

- What impact do we want to have?
- Why is it important?
- How much effort (time, energy, resources) are we prepared to put in to ensure that it happens?
- Who can help us make it happen?

The bid team and subsequent LOC need to determine and communicate their legacy intentions and put in place a delivery strategy. In order to do this, it is crucial to work with stakeholders and a variety of industry experts from the bid stage to understand the landscape and where the event could have the greatest impact. This enables the development of a shared vision and commitment, building on what already exists in the community. It also facilitates resource development to enable delivery, strengthening of established relationships and fostering new partnerships.

For example, in the case of sport development, it is usually necessary to strengthen sport development structures, increase the workforce, attract further investment and expand opportunities ahead of time, so when people are inspired to take up sport as a result of a sport event, there is somewhere for them to go to get involved. This also allows for sport to piggyback on the long build up to the event to encourage people into sport.

One of the motivations for planning for a legacy from the event bid stage may be that it is appealing to the rights holder, and may influence their decision on who is awarded the right to host the event. This is perfectly legitimate, but in such a case it is important that the shared vision and legacy offering is aligned to the mission and goals of the rights holder. A bid must show the rights holder how it is going to make them look good, feel good and do more good, on an appropriate scale with relevant geographical reach. However, to be authentic and make a real difference, it must do this without compromising the integrity of the plans or relevance to the community and beneficiaries located where the sport event takes place.

Why is planning for a sustainable social legacy imperative for all major sport events?

A major sport event has a number of potential costs to society, including use of public money, disruption to local communities and environmental impacts. There is, therefore, a strong argument for balancing these costs with clear benefits to society; a sustainable social legacy can be one of these benefits. One thing that is often overlooked in event legacy discussions is that if the bid is successful, the LOC subsequently established will usually be a powerful company with significant turnover, a large staff, a complex supply chain, a commercially attractive brand and a valuable communications platform. The LOC is uniquely placed to demonstrate socially responsible business practices and influence those of others, and to influence public opinion. Legacy can capitalise on this, forming a key part of the LOC's corporate social responsibility (CSR) strategy along with other key areas such as responsible and transparent governance, and responsible infrastructure development.

There are also specific legacy benefits for each stakeholder group, including the following:

For the bid team:
- Legacy can form a crucial part of the technical bid if aligned with the rights holder's mission and values. It is increasingly becoming a minimum requirement for event bidders, but it is still possible to make it a differentiator if it is done in an ambitious and creative but genuine way; and,
- The legacy commitments increase the perceived and actual value of the event to local communities, government and other key stakeholders and wider society from which it requires support for the bid, and upon which it may put considerable financial and other burdens.

For the LOC:
- Some would argue that with the right to host a sport event comes a responsibility and moral obligation for the LOC to wield its considerable influence in the most positive way it can, for the benefit of society;
- A strong legacy plan and CSR strategy can and should form a key part of the LOC's risk management strategy, as it can help mitigate both reputational and financial risks. Indeed, not having a strong legacy plan and CSR strategy can itself form a key risk for an LOC, as it is an area attracting increasing attention from media, lobby groups and local communities;
- The legacy can provide a commercial opportunity where it adds value to the event sponsorship proposition, offering commercial partners exciting and innovative ways to activate their sponsorship; and,
- The legacy can be crucial for stakeholder engagement, offering a tangible channel for involvement and influence over the impact of the event in an area where stakeholders' expertise can be welcomed.

For the rights holder (e.g., International Federation that awards host status):
- A tangible legacy can increase the perceived value of the event property and encourage more bids and investment in the future, helping sustain the event itself;
- A targeted sport development legacy can be a major catalyst to increased participation in sport at the grassroots level;
- A legacy plan which is aligned with the rights holder's own mission and values can further or complement the rights holder's own CSR strategy;
- An LOC with a strong CSR strategy is likely to reflect well on the rights holder, and form a key part of the rights holder's own risk management strategy; and,
- A long term vision can enable the growth of a cumulative legacy which expands with subsequent events, building on the work of previous event hosts, with the rights holder being the constant in the equation basking in reflected glory.

226

For the government (national or local):
- Depending on the nature of the legacy, it can contribute towards achieving multiple policy objectives; and,
- The legacy can help justify funding the event with public money if societal benefits can be clearly demonstrated.

For the national sport federation:
- A major event brings national and international attention to the federation's sport, and is a key opportunity to inspire new participants and motivate existing players; and,
- There are increasing opportunities for national federations to work with event sponsors to develop the grassroots sport on the back of the event.

For society and local communities:
- The event itself can provide new jobs and offer opportunities for individuals to develop new skills over a number of years leading up to the event (e.g., compare irregular event time volunteering to regular grassroots sport volunteering as part of a sport development legacy);
- A community-focused legacy can help strengthen the communities it supports, for example by contributing to social cohesion, reducing crime and improving an intangible sense of community pride;
- Depending on the focus, an event legacy can help tackle social issues affecting local communities and individuals (e.g. health, discrimination, education, and crime), either by using the event as a platform to mobilise and educate, or by leveraging investment in social projects off the back of the event; and,
- A legacy can make the event and associated public investment relevant to individuals and communities.

The above benefits are examples for an international sport event, but are equally valid for a national or regional sport event.

Whose responsibility is it?

Along with the right to host a sport event there is a responsibility to deliver the event in a way that maximises its positive impact. However, no LOC is an island, and it needs to work with a large circle of stakeholders and partners to deliver the event itself. The same is true for delivering the legacy; whilst the LOC is often well placed to inspire, convene and mobilise a community, it is rarely in a position to implement social legacy programmes directly, and certainly not in isolation.

Legacy benefits will be shared, so the responsibility must also be shared. For example, for a football development legacy, the LOC has a crucial coordinating role to play but can only deliver with the buy-in and contribution of the various bodies that are already operating in the football development space (see case study below). Furthermore, the LOC will not exist beyond the event, but partner organisations will remain. Sharing the legacy vision and delivery responsibility with such partners from the beginning increases their sense of ownership and likelihood of sustained impact even after the LOC has been wound down.

Case study: Shared benefits, shared responsibility – legacy planning by England 2018

In developing their football development legacy plans, the team bidding to host the FIFA World Cup™ in England in 2018 or 2022 worked with The English FA, the Premier League, the Football League, the Football Foundation, Sport England, the Department for Culture, Media and Sport (national government), the English Federation of Disability Sport and other key agencies at a national level, and local authorities, County Football Associations, professional clubs and community organisations in each Candidate Host City. This enabled the development of a shared vision for a three-tiered legacy plan (local, national and global), with jointly-owned, long-term plans and targets which significantly increases the likelihood of successful delivery. The domestic plans were in line with the existing National Game Strategy, which is a four-year strategic plan to improve grassroots football nationwide, developed as a result of a consultation with over 30,000 people at all levels of the game. The global plans were in line with the priorities of FIFA, the world governing body of football and owner of the rights to the FIFA World Cup™.

The same is true for a legacy plan which is more focused on using the event to tackle key social issues. A major event is not a panacea for fixing all social problems, although it can have a key role to play. Generating excitement among large audiences that are often in multiple territories, major events have the potential to be a catalyst for change by offering a powerful platform for communication, which can have a galvanising effect on others.

It is vital that the bid team (and the subsequent LOC) outline its own legacy vision, and articulates the legacy it intends to deliver at the earliest possible opportunity in order to channel collective energy towards a specific goal. If not, it is inevitable that the event will be judged by other people's view of what the legacy should look like. However, neither the bid team nor the LOC will have as good an understanding of the real social issues that need tackling as the agencies working on those issues on a daily basis in a community. Therefore, it is advisable to consult with a trusted group of key social stakeholders early on, to identify the key issues and the areas where the event could have the greatest positive impact.

It is also important to identify where the LOC will have control or influence (and where it won't), and understand the likely tangibility of impact. This will help determine how the LOC can set itself up to work best with partners and other stakeholders to maximise legacy benefits, without taking its eye off the ball for delivering the event itself.

The **Major event legacy planning: LOC influence vs. impact tangibility matrix** (Figure 1) has been developed as a tool to help sport event bidders and LOCs to:

- Identify priority areas of legacy and where to focus time, energy and resources for maximum positive impact;
- Identify key partners and wider stakeholders, and demonstrate where they can contribute;
- Communicate clearly about the LOC's responsibility;
- Set realistic targets where impact is most tangible;
- Develop appropriate monitoring and evaluation mechanisms; and,
- Shape legacy progress reporting.

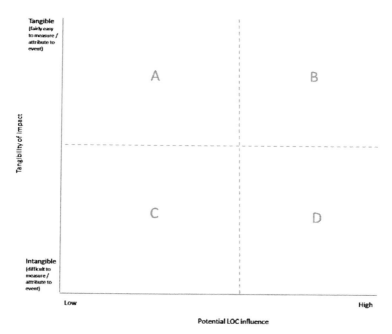

Fig 1: Major event legacy planning: LOC influence vs impact tangibility matrix

Matrix Section	Potential LOC Influence	Tangibility of Impact	Considerations for the LOC for legacy elements falling in this section of the matrix
A	LOW	HIGH	Influence may be low, as a separate body has main responsibility for this legacy element, or it happens because of the event rather than anything specific that the LOC does. However, the impact is likely to be fairly tangible, which allows demonstration of results and offers positive communications opportunities. The LOC must decide whether it is worth committing specific time and resources when it will likely happen anyway, or is the responsibility of another body (e.g., lasting increase in spectator numbers).
B	HIGH	HIGH	The LOC potentially has a strong influence on the success of this element of legacy, and the results are likely to be tangible. This is a logical area for the LOC to focus their efforts, which allows demonstration of results and offers positive communications opportunities (e.g., physical legacy of improved sporting infrastructure).
C	LOW	LOW	The LOC does not have a strong influence over this area of legacy work. Influence is difficult to measure, so it is unlikely that it is an area where the LOC should focus. Rather, if the LOC focuses on delivering a spectacular, safe event on time and within budget, these impacts are likely to be by-products of that anyway (e.g., an increase in national pride).
D	HIGH	LOW	Although the LOC can potentially have significant influence in this area, it may be difficult to measure and/or difficult to attribute specifically to the event. The decision for the LOC to focus time and resources in this area is therefore dependent on the LOC's legacy vision and attitude to CSR, which will determine how important this area is to the event. This area is becoming increasingly important in many major event legacy strategies due to the increased importance attributed to CSR by international sports governing bodies and major event rights holders. There is clearly a need for strengthened monitoring and evaluation tools to support this and tackle the challenges of tangibility and attribution of results to the event (e.g., sustained improvement in key social indicators).

Figure 2 provides an example of how the tool can be used to identify where the LOC has the greatest influence, and where the positive impact is likely to be most tangible, easy to measure and attributable to the event. The example is based on a hypothetical event and the legacy elements included are not an exhaustive list of possibilities. It should be noted that the building blocks of legacy would be positioned differently within the matrix for any given sport event depending on the nature and scale of that event. For example, if the national federation of a given sport is directly responsible for organising the event and the LOC sits within its structure, it is likely to have a greater influence over 'increased participation in relevant sport' than if the LOC is a separate body.

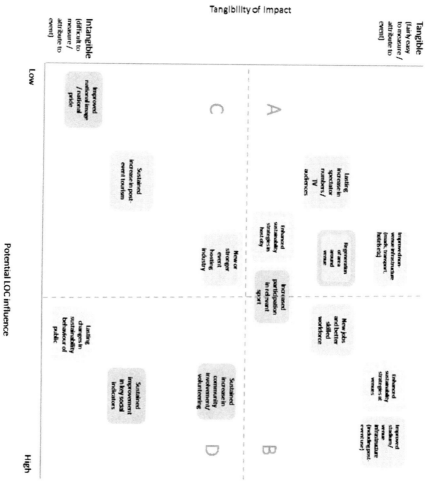

Fig 2: Major event legacy planning: LOC influence vs impact tangibility matrix
(completed for a hypothetical sport event)

Figure 2 demonstrates that several elements of legacy overlap (e.g., re-generation of the area around a new facility can have multiple impacts, primarily economic and social but also environmental and physical). While this chapter focuses on social elements, there is value in considering the event's legacy impacts in a holistic way to take in all areas of overlap.

What do you want to accomplish and where will you focus your attention and resources?

Using the tool in Figure 1, the bid team or LOC can determine where to fo-cus attention and resources. A useful way to prioritise is to split the legacy vision into several tiers, which each require different levels of commitment, access to LOC assets and resources, as show in Figure 3 below.

Priority	LOC relevance and responsibility	Social legacy example
Tier 1: Primary legacy	Activities are strongly linked to central legacy commitments of the bid/LOC. LOC contributes resources directly and provides a fully branded association to the event	The UEFA Women's Euro 2005 tournament in the North West of England committed to using the tournament to increase girls' participation in football in the local area. The English FA [who was responsible for organising the tournament] directly contributed cash and human resources to fully branded promotional activities in schools and the local community, resulting in a 20%+ increase in the number of girls' teams[1], which have all been sustained
Tier 2: Secondary legacy	Activities are inspired or galvanised by the event and loosely linked to legacy commitments of the bid/LOC, but are developed independently by stakeholders. LOC endorses and supports where possible, but unlikely to provide direct resource	When London bid to host the Olympic and Paralympic Games in 2012, it promised to "inspire young people all around the world to participate in sport and improve their lives as a result". This has been its primary focus through fully branded programmes such as International Inspiration[2]. However, London 2012 has also introduced an innovative tool to recognise outstanding non-commercial projects and events inspired by the event. The 'Inspire Mark'[3] is part of the London 2012 brand and family but does not contain the Olympic Rings. It provides a degree of tangibility and association for community organisations and events, and allows the Games to be 'felt' across the country, with minimal involvement of the LOC.
Tier 3: Bi-product legacy	Happens organically, with little LOC influence or control, although a spectacular event can contribute to achieving it	An unplanned, unmeasured but clearly visible positive impact of the 2006 FIFA World Cup™ in Germany was the increase in national pride, and in visitors' impressions of German nationals and their hospitality[4]. The LOC provided the environment to make it possible [welcoming Fan Fest areas, friendly policing etc], but many other factors contributed, including the attitude of the German people and visitors, the weather, team results etc.

Figure 3: Tiers of legacy priority

Figure 3 Citations
1. UEFA 2005 Women's Euro Tournament Review
2. London 2012 International Inspiration: Website accessed 20 May 2010: http://www.london2012.com/internationalinspiration
3. London 2012 Inspire Programme: Website accessed 20 May 2010: http://www.london2012.com/about-us/our-brand/inspire-pro-gramme.php
4. Referenced extensively in media coverage, for example http://blogs.guardian.co.uk/worldcup06/2006/06/30/germany_revels_in_explo-sion_of.html and experienced by the author

Once priorities have been identified and agreed, it is crucial to develop a realistic plan and resource it appropriately. Some aspects of the plan may be funded externally by existing or new key partners, or through the lever-aging of the event to attract new investment. Indeed, the generation of a sustainable new source of funding for grassroots sport or relevant social pro-grammes off the back of the competition can be a legacy in itself. However, whatever the ambition and scale, success is unlikely without the identifica-tion of sources of initial funding to develop and coordinate the plans.

How do you develop a sustainable social legacy strategy?

Each sport event, regardless of size, represents an opportunity to com-municate with an interested audience, demonstrate positive behaviour and leave a positive impact on the community, whether locally, nationally or internationally. Every event is an opportunity to harness the power of sport to effect positive social change, preferably in a way which fits with national/local priorities and builds on existing work and knowledge. In some cases, increasing grassroots sport participation in itself can have con-siderable social benefits, including improved health, reduced crime and stronger scitizenship[1]. In other cases there will be opportunities to use sport as a tool to tackle social issues in a more direct way[2].

It is beyond the scope of this chapter to detail how to go about develop-ing a specific sustainable social legacy strategy targeting a given social issue, although in summary it can be valuable to follow a staged process as shown in Figure 4 below.

---

[1] Right to Play (an international NGO) published *Harnessing the Power of Sport for Development and Peace: Recommendations to Governments* in 2008, which presents con-solidated up-to-date evidence of sport's effectiveness as a tool in tackling key social issues. Available online at: www.sportanddev.org/newsnviews/search.cfm?uNew-sID=234 (accessed 20 May 2010).

[2] See www.beyondsport.org for examples of the burgeoning number of projects using sport to tackle social issues all over the world.

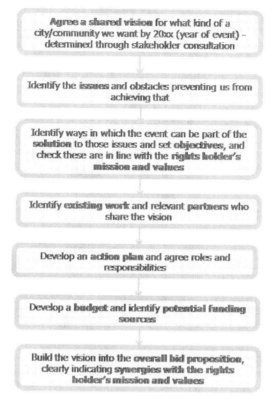

Figure 4: Example of staged progress for developing a sustainable social legacy
strategy at the event bidding stage

When identifying the issues, it is crucial to consult stakeholders and other experts and consider local priorities as laid out in existing local authority strategies, as it is likely these have been determined by an extensive needs analysis and on-the-ground understanding of the most pressing social challenges. Clearly linking local priorities can also help justify and secure government support.

It is vital that the sport event legacy vision and its supporting objectives can be communicated in a way which shows they complement or support the mission and objectives of the rights holder. Once the legacy strategy has been developed, it needs to be built into the LOC's communications and marketing plan, included in sustainability reporting and championed as an intrinsic part of the 'personality' of the event.

Is it possible to have multiple social legacy strands for one event?

For the largest of major sports events it can be complex but ultimately helpful to have multiple social legacy strands which appeal to different audiences. Clearly this then requires a vision, plan, budget and communications strategy for each strand. For example, the London 2012 international vision, as described by Lord Sebastian Coe to the International Olympic Committee (IOC) in 2005, is "to reach young people all around the world. To connect them with the inspirational power of the Games. So they are inspired to choose sport".[3] This was appealing to the IOC, who then awarded London the right to host the 2012 Olympic and Paralympic Games. However, for the local community around the newly constructed London 2012 Olympic Stadium, the regeneration of East London is a much more appealing aspect of the social legacy of the event. Similarly, the London 2012 Inspire programme strategy referred to in Figure 3 spreads the appeal of the London 2012 Olympic and Paralympic Games to the rest of the UK, which helps spread the benefits and justify significant central government investment in preparing for the event.

Conclusion

A sustainable legacy should be woven into the heart of any serious event bid. This can strengthen the technical bid itself, help secure vital support from a variety of stakeholders and ultimately deliver an event with multiple social benefits that makes the organisers, the rights holders, the stakeholders and the country proud. Event legacies can have multiple components over which the LOC has varying degrees of influence. Some of the impacts of legacy elements will be more tangible than others and more easily attributed to the event. The bid team (and/or LOC) must be clear from the start about its legacy priorities, which social issues it will tackle, how it will do this and who it will work with to make this happen.

Regardless of the sport involved or the scope and scale of the competition, any major sport event can deliver a meaningful and sustainable social legacy and has a responsibility to do so. However, this requires forward planning and extensive stakeholder engagement and consultation in order to develop a shared vision and commitment, and the sharing of responsibilities. Ultimately, this will give the event its best chance of delivering a legacy of shared benefits and lasting positive change, created through and catalysed by the bidding for, planning and hosting of that event.

Note: All Figures © Beth Nicholls 2010

3.Lord Sebastian Coe's presentation on behalf of the London 2012 bid team to the International Olympic Committee, Singapore 6th July 2005.

Chapter 24

Can Sports and the Sustainable Business Movement Learn from Each Other?

Andrew Winston

Introduction

I don't think it would surprise anyone to point out that sports are a business (and I suppose business is sport). The sporting world serves literally billions of customers and runs extensive operations around the world. While some big, high-profile events like the Olympic Games and the FIFA World Cup™ are individual events, most sports are part of ongoing enterprises. In the United States alone, every year sports teams stage thousands of college football games, 267 National Football League (NFL) games, 2,430 Major League Baseball (MLB) games, over 1,500 sanctioned NASCAR races, and more...the list is vast.

Major sports events are opportunities for profit and require complex organizations to execute. But they also produce prodigious environmental and social impacts, both good (enjoyment, community development, and encouraging healthy, athletic lifestyles) and bad (resource and water use, carbon emissions, and waste). Just one NFL game produces tons of waste, requires tens of thousands of kilowatt-hours of electricity, and uses hundreds of thousands of gallons of water.

The scale of the negative impacts of sports events has not gone unnoticed. Leagues, municipalities, sponsors, and fans are raising red flags. Teams and sports events are now feeling the same pressures that corporations feel to follow a sustainable path.

My perspective on this topic stems mostly from my work with companies to help them profit from environmental thinking. But I've also served as the Special Sustainability Advisor to United States Soccer on its bid for the 2018 and 2022 FIFA World Cup™. In preparing these bids I have thought a lot about the overlap between the two worlds of sports and business. In this chapter I want to highlight the forces coming to bear on companies, which are making sustainability an unavoidable strategic issue for any organization. I'll also review some of the key steps companies are taking to prepare themselves for our new environmentally-sensitive world.

The sporting world can learn something from what business is doing to deal with environmental pressures and profit from them. But business is also increasingly engaging with sports on these issues as well, especially vendors and sponsors that want to use sports events as platforms for their sustainability work. The two worlds, never that separate to begin with, are beginning to merge their green (environmental) and social missions.

The pressures driving sustainable thinking in business

In the business world, a core, stubborn misperception about sustainability remains. Executives often believe that going green is just an expense, or that it is mainly about compliance with the law, philanthropy, or public relations. But nothing could be further from the truth.

Of course sustainability is often "the right thing to do," but leading companies are going down a sustainable path because they are correctly reading the situation, understanding the drivers, and pursuing both profit and competitive advantage. What are these drivers? The sustainability pressures on business fall into three broad categories: natural world pressures, tectonic shifts in how the world works, and new questions from diverse stakeholders.

First, the pressures on business directly related to nature include changes in our climate, water shortages, the loss of biodiversity (the wealth of species we rely on), and even the unknown effects of man-made chemicals and toxics on natural systems, on us, and on our children. All of these issues, and more, create direct challenges to business as usual.

Second, business is feeling significant shifts in how society works. These pressures include globalization, the rise of technology-driven transparency (a new openness and questions about what is in every product and where it came from), and the increase in affluence around the world. Hundreds of millions of new middle class consumers in India, China, and elsewhere are demanding more goods and services every day. This unprecedented growth is good news for businesses and sports leagues looking for new customers.

But it also creates relentless demand on natural resources and fundamentally rising prices for every input that goes into our economy – think oil, copper, steel, wheat, and so on.

Third, all organizations are fielding tougher and tougher questions from a range of stakeholders, including employees, consumers, and business customers. For sporting events, the business customer is the all-important sponsor; companies that attach their names to sports are increasingly using big events to experiment with new sustainable products and technologies, and reach consumers with a green message.

During the 2010 Winter Olympic Games in Vancouver, Coca-Cola publicly set aggressive goals for its event operations, on waste (zero) and energy (carbon-neutral). It also used the Olympic Games platform to show off its new PlantBottle™ partially made from plant-based material. At golf's Phoenix Open in 2010, which attracted 500,000 fans, Waste Management acted as both sponsor and vendor, using the opportunity to test out new products such as reverse vending machines that give consumers points for returning empty bottles and solar-powered garbage cans that compact themselves (which saves fuel by reducing trips to pick up trash). Just a few months later, Waste Management, working with PepsiCo, rolled out the reverse vending machines across the United States.

Taking into consideration natural forces, tectonic shifts, and stakeholder pressures, it is no longer about whether businesses should opt to pursue environmental and social goals. Sustainability is no longer optional for our species. We will be fundamentally changing how we live, work, eat, and play. This verdict, that you have no other alternative, would be dire if it were not for the core reality that sustainability creates tremendous value; it represents a fundamentally better, more profitable way to operate any business or organization. Companies that go down the green path cut costs dramatically, reduce risk, create new products and revenues, and build brand value and loyalty from customers and employees alike. Those that ignore all of the massive pressures driving this movement will lose market share and struggle to survive. So in the end, the real pressure driving the corporate sustainability movement is profit; it is just good business. It makes overwhelming sense to use resources wisely, to please customers, consumers, and employees, and to innovate.

So how do companies get started and create sustainable value? In my books on environmental strategy (*Green to Gold* and *Green Recovery*), I lay out some core elements, which also apply to sports and sports events. Let's look at those now.

Key steps in developing and executing a sustainability strategy

Sustainability is a holistic pursuit that affects every aspect of an organization's operations; it requires simultaneous action on many fronts. The first step is gathering solid information and data about your business and its environmental and social impacts – only then will you know where the risks and opportunities lie.

Get Smart: Understand your sustainability footprint

Organizations need to gather information on two levels. First, conduct a qualitative assessment to understand, broadly, what the big impacts are and how your operations touch on significant sustainability issues. This exercise can help identify the largest risks and the greatest opportunities for change. Think through the total operations of the organization and how they affect, or are affected by, environmental and social issues. For a sporting event, the important areas may be energy and climate, water use, waste, and a host of social issues around community involvement, health and wellness, and even traffic and quality of life around venues.

It can also be very helpful to map out your biggest stakeholders – fans, communities, municipalities, players, vendors, sponsors, and so on. How do sustainability pressures affect them and what do they care about? For example, what if the event city is facing water shortages? How will that impact how the event is staged?

After these more strategic discussions, organizations need hard data to make tougher choices about where to spend scarce resources and time. The old saying that "what gets measured gets managed" remains true. You can't reduce your impacts and costs if you don't know what they are. So start with measuring or estimating the direct operational footprint of the total operations of a team, or of an event, even if it is just an estimate for a bid process. The boundaries on what is a "direct" footprint are a bit fluid, but for energy alone, include at least the following: all energy used at facilities either directly or through the electric grid, all fuel used to transport players and event executives, and the energy or emissions associated with fan travel to the venues. Just estimating those numbers will be eye-opening.

During the bid-writing process for U.S. Soccer's FIFA World Cup™ Bid, the team asked all the finalist venues (mostly American football stadiums) to provide their best data on the energy, water, and waste used at a sold out game, as well as their estimates on what percentage of fans arrive via different modes of transportation. Using an average of all of the venues, we estimated the total carbon footprint of operating the 64-match event. This kind of knowledge and data helps organizations focus their efforts on the biggest bang for the buck.

Having good data is more than just a reporting exercise – it can drive behavior. On a tactical level, measuring carbon, for example, will provide a good proxy for energy expense (which you should measure separately). But strategically, in a carbon-constrained world, managers can use carbon metrics as a management tool as well. Imagine setting a target on total energy use or emissions and providing allocations for all vendors, architects, building managers, and so on. Future events will need to manage carbon very carefully, in part to satisfy social demands for responsible use of resources, but also to manage risk and keep costs down.

The qualitative and quantitative data gathered so far only applies to the direct operational footprint. But for most organizations, much larger impacts lie "upstream" with suppliers or "downstream" with customers. This realization, that environmental impacts are outside of an organization's direct control, is a critical element of a modern sustainability strategy. And it's why leading organizations are now looking far outside their own "four walls" to consider their sustainability impacts up and down their value chains.

Think Value Chain: Build standards for supply chain and vendors

When a major consumer products company conducted an analysis of energy use and carbon emissions along the full value chain of its products, the results were fairly surprising. Only two to three percent of total carbon emissions come from the company's own manufacturing operations. For some of its products, the biggest impacts stem from the supplier operations, but for some other categories, such as laundry detergent, the energy use is concentrated in the "use phase" with consumers (washing clothes uses a lot of energy).

Over the last few years, the focus of sustainability strategy has moved toward a larger, systemic view of how companies affect the world. Walmart executives, for example, have realized that no matter how large its direct operations might be (and it is the largest corporation ever), the environmental and social footprint of its 100,000 suppliers is vastly larger. So the company has been pressuring its partners to slash fossil fuel use, redesign packaging, create modified versions of products (such as condensed laundry detergent), and even develop entirely new offerings. Walmart is changing the way its suppliers do business permanently.

Walmart's not alone. IBM, Kaiser Permanente, Procter & Gamble, and Pepsi, just to name a few, are setting much higher standards for suppliers, and value chains in every industry sector are changing. Companies are being "asked" by their biggest customers to measure, report on, and reduce their environmental impacts. On the social front, competitors often act together to set stricter standards on labor practices, pay, and worker rights around the world. All of these initiatives are lowering risk to business and lowering costs for suppliers and buyers alike.

Sports teams and events can also find value in their supply chains. Think of all the energy, water, and material needed to provide the food, merchandise, and equipment that go into a large scale event. Teams and leagues have a large influence over their vendors and can change practices permanently. The London Organizing Committee for the Olympic and Paralympic

Games (LOCOG), for example, have created a Sustainable Sourcing Code[1] with strict requirements.

But before asking suppliers to improve their performance, sports organizations need to walk the talk and get lean in their own operations.

Get Lean: Find ways to save money and resources

Given the relentless pressure on resources, the "normal" cost of doing business will continue to rise. Only the organizations that get lean and figure out a way to do business using drastically less stuff will thrive. Luckily, the opportunities to cut back on energy, water, and natural resources are vast. As much as industry has focused on lean principles, most companies find that they haven't paid attention to some large areas of operations that are ripe for cost-cutting. The savings opportunities go beyond the proverbial "low-hanging fruit" – they are what energy guru Amory Lovins calls "the fruit on the ground."

Companies are finding ways to cut back and save money very quickly in some key operational areas such as facilities (heating, cooling, lighting), distribution and fleet, IT systems, and waste. Industrial giants 3M and DuPont, for example, have cut literally billions out of their cost structures through eco-efficiency over the past 20 years. Many organizations are finding head-slappingly obvious ways (in retrospect) to save. Intercontinental Hotel Group, the world's largest hotel chain, changed 250,000 light bulbs and saved $1.2 million a year in energy costs – a four-month payback. Conway shipping slowed down its trucks a bit to reduce fuel costs by $10 million. Yahoo, Google, and Microsoft built data centers in cold climates and now just vent the hot air accumulating in the buildings instead of turning on expensive air conditioning units. They're saving millions, and the list of ways to get lean goes on and on.

Many sports teams and stadiums are now incorporating eco-efficiency into their operations as well. To take just one example, the NFL's Philadelphia Eagles has become one of the real green leaders in U.S. sports. In recent years the team has cut energy use 42 percent through aggressive building management systems and conservation, and slashed water use 53 percent with one-half-gallon per flush toilets and new water management approaches. Some Eagles executives admit that initially, they had been skeptical of green initiatives. But after saving so much money on energy, they became committed to the cause.

This reaction provides a good lesson for all organizations. Pursuing eco efficiency creates a number of benefits, including of course saving money and providing capital for larger green innovations and investments. But driv-

---

1.LOCOG Sustainable Sourcing Code, Second Edition, (December 2009). Available online at: http://www.london2012.com/documents/locog-publications/sustainable-sourcing-code.pdf (accessed 1 October 2010).

ing engagement through proof of success is another powerful reason to get lean.

Get Engaged: Bring employees, fans, and even athletes into the mission

Even with the large, measurable impacts of sporting events, they pale in comparison to the footprint of the everyday lives of hundreds of millions of people who watch sporting events. Or consider the impacts that all the suppliers and vendors of sports venues and events create in their operations. Arguably the most significant role events can play in the global quest for sustainability is to help the people so emotionally connected to sports to think differently about their lives. The opportunity is vast.

The FIFA World Cup™, for example, hosts millions of fans in the event stadiums, but literally billions watch or follow the action. The opportunity to engage fans in something larger than the game itself can build increased loyalty to teams and leagues, which is good for business, but really provides an opportunity to drive large-scale change across the world. While fans are captivated by sports, they can learn how the team, the venue, or a sponsor is handling sustainability challenges. They can find out about saving energy and reducing water use and waste. They can explore health and wellness issues and think more about social equity. Sports can use side events at games, messages from athletes, or game giveaways to drive a new kind of education and engagement. While the success stories of this kind of engagement are few, it remains a new and promising path to change.

In addition, most of the biggest events now include programs that donate money to development or sustainability causes, or establish new organizations with social missions. LOCOG created a charitable foundation that launched the program International Inspiration. The purpose of the organization is to enrich the lives of 12 million kids – of all abilities – in 20 countries through the power and joy of sport and play. The organization works with local communities and coaches to reach children with few resources and little chance to participate in group sports.

In the U.S. Soccer bid we included a program that would provide funds to water projects in the developing world. Fans would be included in the process, buying special cups at matches or donating directly. Many events, including the NFL's Super Bowl, now include projects closer to home, such as tree-planting events around main venues. All of these ideas try to leave a lasting legacy on the local community or the world.

Think Big: Set aspirational goals and seek heretical innovation

The sustainability challenges we face as a species are clearly very large. And while getting lean and getting smart are critical underpinnings of sustainability strategy and value creation, they won't be nearly enough. The world needs large-scale, disruptive change. In my book *Green Recovery* I suggest a new kind of creativity that I call heretical innovation. This kind of thinking requires asking very tough questions that challenge the fundamental nature of a business.

A few companies have started to ask completely new questions. Tennant, a mid-sized company that makes cleaning equipment, developed a new floor-cleaning machine that uses only tap water. The new technology avoids the use of legally hazardous chemicals, reduces the cost of ownership, and eliminates the need to train people how to handle those chemicals. And it works. The company asked a completely different question: Can we clean the floor without chemicals? Or consider how Boeing, major airlines such as Virgin Atlantic, and even the U.S. Navy are testing the use of biofuels in their planes. They've all asked whether we can fly without fossil fuels.

Leading companies are also setting big, aspirational goals that they often have no idea how to meet. Walmart says it wants to use 100% renewable energy at some point. Sony declared a goal of a zero environmental footprint by 2050. Many major manufacturers and retailers have set a goal of "zero waste to landfill" and companies such as Subaru, GM, and Tesco have hit the target in many facilities much faster than expected.

Sporting event organizers and sports teams need to set these kinds of goals to be competitive in a bid process, or to work well with local communities. The U.S. Soccer FIFA World Cup™ bid set the goal of zero fossil fuels in operations, zero waste, and net zero water use. Does any organization in the world know exactly how to deliver on multiple "zero" goals yet? Not really, but the technologies and processes are in development all over the business world.

In closing...

Sports engage people like nothing else besides family and religion (and it's a close race). All organizations and businesses can learn about building passionate customers from the sports world. And sports can learn from industry's experience pursuing sustainability. Companies such as Wal-Mart, GE, Nike, IBM, Pepsi, Tesco, 3M, Subaru and many others are taking action in their own operations, in their supply chains, and with their customers.

Sporting organizations, teams, and leagues can do so much to raise the bar and spread the word. They can walk the talk and reduce impacts in their own operations, setting aggressive goals to dramatically reduce use of energy, water, and materials. They can work in conjunction with their vendor partners to permanently change the supply chain for food, merchandise, and other major inputs to reduce impacts upstream.

Finally, sports can engage billions of fans to go down the sustainable path, saving money, living healthier, improving their lives, and helping to build a more sustainable world.

Chapter 25

The Sporting Stage

Delivering Sustainable Venues and Infrastructure

Kirsten Henson

Introduction

This chapter examines a range of delivery mechanisms and processes that can be utilised to integrate sustainability into the design and construction of large sporting venues and associated infrastructure. Case studies are presented, as well as examples from three key sporting events: Vancouver 2010 Olympic and Paralympic Winter Games (Vancouver 2010), 2010 FIFA World Cup South Africa™ (South Africa 2010), and the London 2012 Olympic and Paralympic Games (London 2012).

The first section details the adoption of environmental and sustainability criteria by two key sporting organisations: the International Olympic Committee (IOC) and International Football Association (FIFA). The next sections detail delivery strategies and engagement processes for responding to and delivering against the sustainability aspirations of these large sporting organisations. The discussion on delivery strategies utilises publicly available documentation on Vancouver 2010, South Africa 2010 and London 2012, while the engagement processes largely draw on the author's professional experience in delivering sustainability in large, complex construction projects. The chapter closes with a discussion on repeating the successes and avoidance of pitfalls associated with the integration of sustainability into construction of large sporting projects.

The predominant focus of the chapter is on delivering resource efficiency (or environmental sustainability) in large, complex sporting venue and infrastructure construction from a client's perspective. It is not unreasonable to assume that the principles discussed can be adapted and applied to address a broader range of sustainability requirements and suitably scaled for smaller projects.

Setting the Scene for Sustainability in Sport

Over the past two decades, the IOC and FIFA have increasingly recognised the impact of major sporting events on their local environment and community. The need to consider sustainability in the planning, design and construction of associated new sporting venues and infrastructure is developing at a rapid pace within these leading organisations.

A number of amendments to the Olympic Charter associated with protection of the environment followed the Centennial Olympic Congress in 1994. At this Congress, the Olympic Movement declared the Environment to be the third dimension of Olympism, alongside Sport and Culture. The IOC's new Mission #13 would be: "to encourage and support a responsible concern for environmental issues, to promote sustainable development in sport and to require that the Olympic Games are held accordingly" (IOC, 2010). The IOC firmly and publicly declared the environment as a key factor for any future Olympic Games, and subsequently established a Sport and Environment Commission and a formal collaboration with the United Nations Environment Programme (UNEP).

Following Germany's successful hosting of the 2006 FIFA World Cup™, FIFA demonstrated its support for sustainability by adding a Green Goal chapter in its manual *Football Stadiums: Technical Recommendation and Requirements*. The principal goals of the programme are: the reduction in the consumption of potable water, the avoidance and/or reduction of waste, the creation of more energy efficient systems and an increase in the use of public transport to FIFA events (FIFA, 2007).

Delivering Sustainable Sporting Events and Infrastructure

Setting a High-Level Strategy

The focus for any sporting infrastructure constructed for a specific event must be the long-term benefits of that infrastructure and the integration of the offering into existing community networks. A single, large international sporting event like the World Cup or Olympic Games may drive a temporary influx of financial capital, and bring with it a significant direct and indirect increase in consumption of natural resources. However, this is not reflective of the longer term operational impacts of venues and infrastructure. Figure 1 provides an indicative assessment of resource consumption during the construction, operation and redevelopment of areas selected for hosting sporting events. The time-based assessment interprets carbon footprint figures published for London 2012[1]. Due to the demonstrated imbalance of resource consumption, it could be argued that a single large sporting event must be considered an anomaly in the long term regeneration and resource consumption of an area – an anomaly that requires a different, but complimentary, sustainable approach than typical long term regeneration projects.

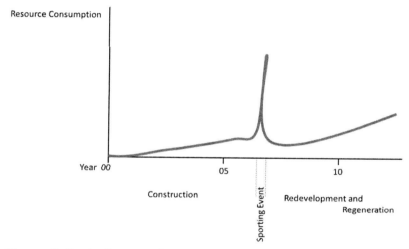

Figure 1: Indicative Resource Consumption in the Construction, Operation and Legacy phases of a Major Sporting Event

The implementation of such a sustainability strategy is evident with London 2012, whereby permanent sporting venues are being constructed only where a comprehensive and coherent legacy use can be established, and the associated supporting infrastructure network is scalable to suit legacy re-

---

1.*The London* 2012 *Carbon Footprint Study – Methodology and Reference Footprint* (March 2010) allocates 1889kt CO2e to Olympic Delivery Authority (ODA) activities (predominantly pre-Games construction of venues and infrastructure) and only 399kt CO2e to LOCOG activities (predominantly overlay construction). However 1159kt CO2e is allocated as 'shared' and 'associated' CO2 emissions, essentially spectator travel, use of facilities and consumption of perishables at Olympic venues. Although the ODA is responsible for a larger carbon footprint in total, this occurs over a four year construction timeframe. LOCOG's carbon footprint, including shared and associated emissions, occurs over approximately a year with an intense focus on the period of the Olympic and Paralympic Games. If these carbon emissions are considered against the timeframe in which they occur and are assumed representative of total resource consumption, Figure 1 is demonstrably a fair indicative representation of resource consumption.

quirements[2,3]. In addition, the two main organisations preparing for London 2012, the Olympic Delivery Authority (ODA) and the London Organising Committee of the Olympic and Paralympic Games (LOCOG), have complimentary sustainability strategies[4]. The ODA's focus is on balancing the embodied impacts of construction with the long term operational impacts of the permanent sporting venues, as well as the physical integration of the London 2012 Olympic Park into the wider community. Delivery of a Combined Cooling, Heating and Power Energy Centre (CCHP) and distribution system, construction of large areas of complex, biodiverse habitat, a Park-wide non-potable water network, investment in materials to improve the operational energy efficiency of venues and the upgrading of public transport infrastructure all have clear long-term benefits for the community, and it is argued these benefits warrant the initial public investment and consumption of natural resources.

Reference to LOCOG's Sustainable Sourcing Code would indicate they are rightly more concerned with minimising the embodied impacts of the additional construction required to deliver a successful sporting event. The strategy therefore seeks to maximise the use of existing hired components, eliminate all but essential material use, and promote design and procurement methods that minimise the generation of waste during temporary construction and at the end of the facilities short Olympic life. Technologies that deliver resource efficiency in operation are only promoted by LOCOG where there is no significant additional capital cost or embodied resource consumption; auto-off, low flow rate water fixtures and fittings and A-rated white goods are a good example. Promotion of extensive energy reduction, potable water consumption reduction and other initiatives that have a longer-term resource and capital pay-back period are in general, avoided. The exception being LOCOG's commitment to meeting 20% of the London 2012 Olympic Park electricity demands during the event from new, local renewable energy sources.

---

2. The only London 2012 sporting venue that has an uncertain future at the time of writing is the Olympic Stadium - designed as an 80,000-seat stadium that can be deconstructed to 25,000 seats, a scale that was deemed more suitable to an Athletics legacy during the planning stages..

3. Of the 30 bridges constructed at the London 2012 Olympic Park, a number are temporary, and will be either entirely deconstructed after the event or will have a temporary element that can be removed in legacy to deliver bridges that are more suited in scale to a city park than an international sporting arena.

4. It is important to differentiate between the role of the ODA and LOCOG. The ODA, together with their Delivery Partner, is the public body responsible developing and building the new venues and infrastructure for London 2012 and their legacy use, as well as delivering the necessary transport infrastructure and services to support the delivery the London 2012 event and legacy development. LOCOG is responsible for preparing and staging the London 2012 event. LOCOG is responsible for fundraising to host the event and will let most of the contracts for services to deliver the event.

Setting a Clear Vision and Targets

Sustainability has a number of different interpretations, with priorities and opportunities being location and scale dependent. Therefore, it is critical that any organisation responsible for delivering sporting venues present a cohesive and considered vision for *sustainability*, developed in conjunction with affected communities, key stakeholders and industry specialists. If this vision is not subsequently supported by decisive and measurable targets, progress is impossible to monitor and decision-making will lack a critical criteria for evaluation.

A common theme across South Africa 2010, London 2012 and Vancouver 2010 event bids is a clear vision for sustainability ingrained in the local context of sport and the host cities. After securing the 'host nation' title some hosts endeavoured to clarify early qualitative sustainability objectives through defining a measurable set of Key Performance Indicators (KPIs). In a number of circumstances, elements of the vision were further strengthened through planning conditions and integration into government policy objectives[5].

It is not clear if resource efficiency and sustainable development were key factors in South Africa 2010's winning bid, as the award was made prior to FIFA publishing its Green Goal requirements. However, the Host City Agreement signed by FIFA and the South African Host Cities after the award of the World Cup to South Africa committed South Africa to adherence to sustainability principles and promotion of environmental responsibility in organising and hosting the 2010 tournament. Review of the FIFA 2010 and South Africa 2010 Host City websites suggests that only Cape Town developed the vision and targets required to deliver on this high level vision. Cape Town produced a comprehensive Green Goal Action Plan that encapsulates greening and raising awareness of environmental and social issues pertinent to hosting the 2010 event (Green Goal 2010, 2008). The Green Goal Action Plan clearly states quantifiable deliverables for each of the defined priority themes, identifies specific targets where benchmarks are available, sets timescales for delivery and allocates budgets and resources to each priority theme. The Host City of Durban launched a Greening Durban 2010 Programme[6]; while it does identify some positive initiatives,

---

5. A number of the London 2012 targets were reinforced through the Planning Authority's decision to translate them into Section 106 requirement associated with the planning application. A Section 106 requirement allows a local Planning Authority to enter into a legal agreement with a landowner to ensure that matters that are deemed necessary to make the planning acceptable are addressed. See http://www.idea.gov.uk/idk/core/page.do?pageId-71631 (accessed August 2010). In South Africa, the Business Plan for the Environmental Protection work stream of the South Africa 2010 World Cup aligned the event greening programme with the City of Cape Town's Integrated Metropolitan Environmental Policy and Provincial Government of the Western Cape Growth and Development Strategy.

6. Greening Durban 2010 website accessed online September 2010 at: http://2010.adapt-it.co.za:9000/Pages/GreeningDurban2010.aspx

it does not offer the same clarity on targets, benchmarks and funding as the Cape Town Green Goal Action Plan[7].

In its bid to host the 2010 Olympic and Paralympic Winter Games, the Vancouver bid team set itself the vision of creating "sustainable legacies", and committed to building and using facilities with minimal environmental impact (Vancouver 2010, 2003). The bid also contained a strong focus on engagement and regeneration of First Nation Communities, an Aborigine group that has historically suffered land losses and disempowerment as a consequence of North America's development. After successfully bidding for the 2010 Games, the Vancouver Organising Committee for the 2010 Olympic and Paralympic Winter Games (VANOC) related its bid book commitments through six corporate-wide sustainability objectives[8], which were further supported by a sustainability scorecard comprising a list of 28 quantitative and qualitative performance measures designed to monitor, measure and evaluate sustainability performance. As the Torino 2006 Olympic and Paralympic Winter Games is credited with having raised the environmental bar for hosting the event, Vancouver 2010 is regarded as the first to firmly integrate sustainability into its mission and goals.

London 2012 identified the regeneration of East London and the event legacy as key bid themes. The London 2012 bid team partnered with NGOs BioRegional and WWF-UK to develop the *One Planet Olympics* sustainability framework that set out London 2012's plans to construct the most sustainable Olympic and Paralympic Games event to date using the ten One Planet Living principles (London 2012, 2005). This vision was then further refined through the London 2012 Sustainability Policy which narrowed the ten One Planet Living Principles into five themes, and the ODA's Sustainable Development Strategy (SDS) in January 2007, which set out objectives under 12 themes[9]. The SDS formed part of the original planning application for the London 2012 Olympic Park. It sets out a number of 'SMART'

---

7. Green Goal Action Plans for the remaining host cities were provided on request from the Department of Environmental Affairs in South Africa; however, the fact that the Action Plans are not easily accessible to the public raises concerns over accountability.

8. Vancouver 2010's six sustainability objectives are: accountability, environmental stewardship and impact reduction, social inclusion and responsibility, aboriginal participation and collaboration, economic benefits and sport for sustainable living.

9. The five London 2012 themes are: Climate Change, Waste, Biodiversity and Ecology, Inclusion and Healthy Living. The London 2012 Sustainability Policy is available online at http://www.london2012.com/documents/locog-publications/london-2012-sustainability-policy.pdf (accessed 30 October 2010). The ODA's SDS details 12 objectives: carbon, water, waste, materials, biodiversity and ecology, land, water, air and noise, supporting communities, transport and mobility, access, employment and skills, health and well-being, and inclusion. The SDS is available online at http://www.london2012.com/publications/sustainable-development-strategy-full-version.php (accessed 30 October 2010).

targets[10] as well as several less well defined aspirations. Industry specialist such as the Waste and Resources Action Programme (WRAP) and various consulting engineers were utilised to construct realistic yet challenging targets, considering current industry best practice and forthcoming advances in sustainable technologies, as it was acknowledged that suitable benchmarks did not exist for target setting. The lesser defined targets in the SDS were refined throughout the planning and design process to provide clarity for monitoring. For example, the original SDS aspiration of "enhancing the ecological value of the Park through the integration of habitat creation and landscape design" (ODA, 2007) was later quantified in the ODA's Biodiversity Action Plan as the provision of 45 hectares of new habitat which will eventually mature to meet a quality standard of Grade 1 Sites of Borough Importance for nature conservation[11].

Accountability and Reporting

Vancouver 2010 swiftly translated their six sustainability objectives into a Sustainability Management and Reporting System, enabling them to action their sustainability goals and track and measure performance (VANOC, 2007). Annual sustainability reports published from 2005 through 2009 detailed the processes for, and the progress of, defining and delivering the sustainability agenda[12]. The publication of annual comprehensive sustainability reporting allowed the public and the IOC to analyse progress, and hold VANOC accountable for delivering the sustainability vision.

At the time of writing this chapter, London 2012's progress on sustainability objectives is not as transparent or accessible as that of Vancouver 2010, even though London 2012 committed to reporting on progress and despite numerous sustainability reports being available on the London 2012 website[13]. The lack of clarity is largely due to confused document naming systems and separate reports for the London 2012 five overarching sustainability themes and the ODA's twelve SDS sustainability themes. The available documents give both qualitative and quantitative progress updates supported by case studies, but year on year progress is not obviously discernable

---

10. The acronym 'SMART' has a number of slightly different variations; the ODA's SDS defines SMART as: Specific, Measurable, Agreed Upon, Realistic and Time-based.

11. Grade 1 Site of Borough Importance for nature conservation is defined as having a special interest for flora and fauna in addition to having considerable wildlife value. The London 2012 Biodiversity Action Plan is available online at http://www.london2012.com/documents/oda-publications/olympic-park-biodiversity-action-plan.pdf (accessed 30 October 2010).

12. Available for download at: http://www.vancouver2010.com/more-2010-information/sustainability/reports-and-resources/sustainability-report/ (accessed August 2010)

13. London 2012: http://www.london2012.com/making-it-happen/sustainability/index.php (accessed August 2010)

and there is significant repetition between the London 2012 and ODA documentation.

However, London 2012's bid created the vision for an independent assurance body, the Commission for a Sustainable London 2012 (CSL)[14]. It is perhaps through this audit and review process that London 2012 are able to better demonstrate accountability to the public and the London 2012 Olympic Board rather than the internally-produced progress documents, although one must query the level of technical detail and insight a third party can obtain through an audit process.

FIFA have significant progress to make in terms of accountability and reporting. There are no comprehensive progress reports available detailing South Africa 2010's progress against the sustainability objectives; this is not surprising, as a comprehensive vision and supporting targets were never developed for the South Africa 2010 programme. Cape Town, however, detailed progress against their comprehensive Green Goal strategy in a 2009 publication[15]; this progress report usefully identifies achievements, outstanding funding requirements, lessons learned and next steps. Assuming Cape Town produce a final status report, they should be commended in demonstrating how subsequent World Cup Host Cities should manage the sustainability agenda.

A well-defined client vision supported by measurable targets, comprehensive and transparent reporting and clear lines of accountability are obviously critical in enabling the delivery of a sustainable sporting event and legacy. But how can designers, architects and engineers be engaged and empowered, and decision-makers inspired and educated to innovate and successfully change the norm?

Sporting Venue and Event Infrastructure Design and Development

The following sections consider each stage of the construction process from establishing a client team through to contractor start on site. Each section details strategies for integrating sustainability into the delivery of sporting event infrastructure.

Developing a Team Structure

There are two clear options for creating a team structure for delivery of sustainability across a programme. The benefits and shortcomings of the

---

14. Commission for Sustainable London 2012 reports are available at www.cslondon.org.

15. Green Goal Progress Report Cape Town, September 2009 (accessed online September 2010) http://www.capetown.gov.za/en/GreenGoal/Documents/GREEN%20GOAL%20PROGRESS%20REPORT_EMAIL.pdf

options presented herein should be evaluated on a programme[16] specific basis.

It is important to remember that people cannot be experts in everything; the same is true for the technical aspects of sustainability. A good sustainability specialist will have a broad understanding of the concepts behind all aspects of sustainability, with detailed technical knowledge of one or two key areas such as energy, waste and material management or community engagement. It is therefore essential that any team structure for delivering sustainability accounts for the level and range of expertise of team members. The team structures presented herein assume a programme is large enough to warrant a client team of sustainability specialists. On smaller programmes it is likely that the budget will support only a single sustainability resource, with specialist consultants engaged on an ad hoc basis to support the review of technical detail.

The first proposed team structure involves developing a dedicated sustainability team around a functional matrix structure. Each team member is responsible for a technical lead (such as energy, water, waste, materials, or biodiversity) as well as operating as a single point of contact, or project champion, for one or more projects associated with the programme (Figure 2). This structure supports the development of 'T-shaped' professionals[17], deemed by Oskam (2009) as essential for creativity and innovation, as well as promoting clear channels of communication to individual project teams. A single resource may provide the project champion role for a number of projects, depending on scale and complexity of the individual projects.

---

16. The term *programme* is used throughout the chapter to infer a collection of numerous individual projects delivered under a single client for a large sporting event. The term *project* is used in reference to the design and construction of an individual sporting arena or infrastructure element.

17. A T-shaped professional is defined as one with in depth knowledge in one discipline but with an ability to converse in a wide range of subject matter.

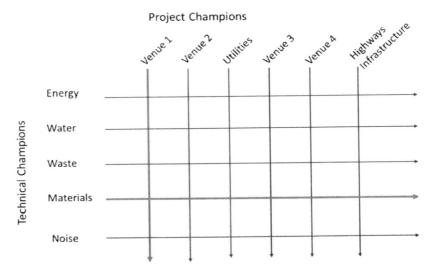

Figure 2: Team Structure supporting the development of 'T-shaped' professionals

An alternative structure for a sustainability team would be the entrenchment of a single sustainability specialist in each of the project teams, rather than having a dedicated stand-alone sustainability team. This structure, while requiring additional sustainability resources, does have the advantage of reinforcing the notion that sustainability is not an 'add-on', but rather is an integral part of project delivery. In addition, a sustainability specialist sitting alongside a project team has the advantage of more easily staying abreast of progress and decisions made.

A dedicated sustainability team environment will, however, aide significant learning and idea exchange between team members, and support networks within the team are indispensable in facing the challenge of integrating sustainability into a large sporting programme. Although it is not impossible to achieve sufficient morale within a disparate team, it would require management of a calibre rarely experienced.

Critically, both team structures enable sustainability specialists to develop strong working relationships within their allocated project teams, and provide projects with a single port of call for technical support rather than having to deal directly with an array of specialists. Therefore, the decision as to which team structure to adopt is likely to depend on the resource available and the overall programme structure.

Design Team Engagement

A team of high quality sustainability professionals has numerous strategies at their disposal to engage with project teams, including design guidance, workshops, formal client design reviews, personal communication, reporting systems and audits.

Design guides can be a useful reference tools for design teams. They allow the client to communicate information on specific targets, provide details on assessment tools and methodologies for demonstrating compliance, and identify reporting requirements. Large, complex programmes may find that a single guide for each technical subject area is more manageable than a single comprehensive design guide covering all sustainability requirements. The intention of a design guide is to detail a process to identify opportunities and monitor progress, not to provide *the* answer to sustainable design. Ideas for successful delivery of sustainability targets can be communicated through the design guides and supporting design team workshops, but innovation must come from the architects and engineers.

The identification of assessment tools, timeframes and formats for reporting are a particularly important aspect of the guides for programmes involving a number of design teams, and allow the client to compare project performance and collate data for reporting on a programme-wide basis.

It may be useful to set reporting requirements against each design stage, as this promotes sustainability as an integral part of the design process and ensures accurate recording of all decisions made during the design process that impact on sustainability, whether positive or negative. In setting out reporting requirements at recognised design stages, sustainability can be incorporated into a formal client design review process.

The engagement of a contractor during the final detailed design stages and specification is invaluable in adapting the design to deliver material efficiencies and introducing new, alternative products or construction methods with sustainability benefits[18]. The benefit is, of course, reliant on the contractor being fully engaged with project sustainability requirements, which is discussed later in this chapter. Formal client design reviews may be unmanageable at specification due to the sheer volume of information produced; subsequently engagement with contractors and promotion of a level of self-assurance is likely to be a more time-efficient delivery strategy.

Tender Stage and Contract Award

Involving the sustainability team at the project tender stage in the selection of tender question(s) and the subsequent review and evaluation of answer(s) supplied at tender return will ensure questions are pertinent and responses demonstrate the required level of contractor awareness and capabilities. Tender evaluation and award should follow a balanced scorecard approach, with sustainability evaluated and weighted alongside more conventional

---

18. The contractor for a project which the author acted as client sustainability representative invited alternative bids for a blockwork package. Tenderers were made aware of sustainability requirements and were invited to challenge the current design detail. An alternative bid was received replacing the windposts in the blockwork design with an innovative Y-beam system. The project realised a saving of 1632 liner metres of steel windposts with a resultant cost saving of over £40,000 equivalent to 6.5% of the work package value.

contract award criteria such as quality, commercial and financial. Provision of feedback to each tenderer on their tender submission is essential for any client wanting to improve the quality of subsequent submissions, and supply chain understanding of sustainability requirements.

Contractor Engagement

Generic programme and project specific sustainability requirements must be explicitly included in all contracts. Do not assume however, that if sustainability requirements are in the contract that they have been understood by the contractor and will be achieved. What recourse does a client have if after project completion it becomes apparent a sustainability requirement has not been delivered? Financial compensation or retrofit at the contractor's expense may be options, but there is no possibility for a project team to retrofit transport of materials to site by sustainable means once the project has been completed; the opportunity will have been missed and the social and environmental impacts realised. Installed water fixtures and fittings with flow rates that do not meet requirements for reduced water demands can be replaced, but at what environmental cost? Do the operational savings in water consumption warrant the waste generated and embodied impacts associated with manufacture and installation of new compliant taps?

It is essential to run sustainability workshops with successful contractors prior to their commencing work, as it is often the case that those involved in the preparation of the successful tender are not part of the site project team. Site teams will rarely be aware of the sustainability requirements outlined in the tender and subsequent contract documentation. The workshops are therefore essential for reiterating sustainability requirements and discussing project specifics with the contractors.

Many contractors will struggle with the practicalities of delivering against stated high level sustainability objectives, such as using 20% recycled content by value for project materials. This is predominantly due to a lack of understanding around opportunities, as well as the conventional procurement and construction approach focusing on individual work packages rather than high level objectives.

Promoting and supporting the development of work package based assessments should prove fruitful, whereby sustainability requirements and opportunities associated with each work package are clearly stated, whether it be minimum U-value, maximum flow rates, minimum recycled content or responsible sourcing requirements. This interpretation of high-level sustainability requirements into small packaged solutions, aligned with existing processes used by contractors, allows individuals within the contractor team to quickly take ownership of the sustainability elements associated with their work package, translate them into sub-contractor tender packages, knowledgeably discuss opportunities and invite innovation from the supply chain, and monitor delivery through construction.

This level of self-assurance among contractors is particularly important if formal client design reviews are not undertaken, relying instead on the contractors to ensure technical product information and specifications meet the requirements of their contracts.

To promote supply chain engagement and communication of sustainability requirements among sub-contractors, principal contractors should be encouraged to engage their supply chain in regular Sustainability Leadership Groups with the aim of sharing best-practice and garnering increased levels of support and engagement from sub-contractors. Reward and recognition schemes, both contractor and client led, are important initiatives for continued profile-raising of environment and sustainability among site operatives.

Contractor self-assurance needs to be supported by monthly data submissions to the client sustainability team to allow progress to be monitored and ensure the risk of missing sustainability targets is identified early enough for mitigation strategies to be initiated. There are a number of systems available for data collection, although large programmes may benefit from the development of a dedicated on-line KPI reporting tool. A well-designed KPI data collection system can remove an element of subjectivity from sustainability reporting, by instead objectively analysing data provided directly by the contractors. In reality, monthly reporting is likely to combine two approaches, utilising both collated data and an indicative progress assessment by the client project champion.

Monthly reporting and contractor self-assurance should be reinforced by regular client site inspections and detailed sustainability audits[19]. The purpose of the audit is to undertake a detailed review of contractors' systems and data to provide reassurance that projects are on track for achieving sustainability requirements and are able to produce a body of evidence to support sustainability claims. It is beneficial if client/contractor relationships are such that audits are seen as a learning and engagement process by the contractors, providing them with an opportunity to improve their systems and acquire knowledge on innovative solutions implemented by other projects on the site, rather than a regulatory role. This approach is reliant on the client sustainability team forming a supportive relationship with contractors, as opposed to a more conventional contractor/client relationship. This realignment of the client/contractor relationship is critical for delivering sustainability cost-effectively.

For a complex construction programme, it is reasonable to expect that within the first year of the majority of contracts starting on site, the client sustainability team will be able to operate predominantly in an assurance function, reviewing monthly reporting data for accuracy and raising issues to senior management. Throughout construction the sustainability team should, however, continue to be utilised as a support network for design

19. A suggested timeframe for large programmes is fortnightly site inspections supported by six-monthly audits, although this can be adapted depending on the contract timeframe and available sustainability resources.

teams and contractors wanting to further challenge the boundaries of conventional construction. For this to happen, the team needs to ensure a reputation for excellence in innovation and problem solving is developed and maintained.

Repeating successes and avoiding pitfalls

The first year of a programme will, without a doubt, be a challenge for any client sustainability team, to gain recognition and status on the programme both within the client body itself and subsequently within project design and contract teams. It is safe to assume that the main drivers for any construction programme in its early stages will be cost and programme. As costs stabilise and key milestones are achieved there may be a discernable shift in management focus towards other priority themes such as sustainability, equality and inclusion. The strong focus on programme cost is not necessarily a negative for achieving sustainability objectives; cost effectiveness is, after all, a key sustainability driver. A focus on cost will help veer a programme away from 'bling' sustainability solutions – the add-ons that provide little true value towards innovation and sustainability. Rather, it may keep the focus on true sustainability solutions that use fewer resources to do more – initiatives that can be delivered at no extra, or marginal, cost.

With each new contract award the process should become easier as more and more people shift their way of thinking and engage with sustainability. The job of the sustainability specialist becomes one of innovation rather than advocacy[20].

A sustainability team may be challenged by the misconception in upper management that 'sustainability finishes at design' and 'environmental management is sustainability in construction'. This attitude is likely to stem from a management team that rarely engages with site works, or when they do, they focus on cost and programme rather than other aspects of procurement and construction. Another common misconception in industry is that if something is in the design, or it is in the contract, it will be delivered. Often the contract is not clearly understood by the contractor (or the client), so the hope of demonstrating clear delivery against the contract is minimal. Procurement is a forgotten and important stage of delivering sustainability; it is the process that connects the design with what happens

---

20. A personal example from a time-critical, large sporting programme involves the search for alternatives to asphalt for hard paving. Advocacy at the design stage had not been successful in finding alternative paving solutions. Some two years into the programme, the author of this chapter was able to research alternative paving options and instigate site trials. The trials, including vegetable based binders and local stone paving blocks capable of being transformed to soft landscaping with little waste, and lean paving solutions were recorded and widely communicated to project teams. Numerous interested parties were escorted around the trial area resulting in two of the solutions demonstrated being adopted for use as an alternative to conventional bitumen-based paving.

on the ground. If procurement and commercial teams do not have a thorough grasp of how each procurement package contributes to the project's sustainability agenda, the risk is run that elements will be altered through a value engineering process or opportunities will be missed by not inviting innovation from the supply chain.

These misunderstandings can lead to late engagement of sustainability in contract award which will subsequently result in standard construction and lack of innovation. A significant process of awareness-raising within the client body is necessary to garner support for engagement and retention of a sustainability team post contract award.

If a web-based reporting system is used to collate data it must be developed with regular input from the sustainability team and in a timely manner. A lack of regular review during development of any reporting tool will cause the functionality of the system to suffer, ultimately resulting in the collection of meaningless data. Late implementation will lead to incomplete data sets for many projects and frustrated contractors, who potentially having developed reporting systems to demonstrate contract compliance in lieu of a site-wide reporting tool struggle to align the two reporting systems.

Communication of the opportunities and successes, ranging from the nationally significant to minor improvements, is an important contribution to the sustainability agenda. Demonstration projects for sustainable technologies increase awareness and confidence within the marketplace, and the less discernable behavioural changes and personal anecdotes will hopefully be taken forward by individuals onto future projects.

While individual technical solutions may be translated to other projects, it is possible that replicating sustainability as defined and delivered by any one programme will not result in sustainable outcomes elsewhere. Some practical innovations may not be scalable or are location dependent. However, the *process* of delivering sustainability is a valuable one that can easily be replicated elsewhere to beneficial effect. The levels and range of engagement necessary, recognition of gaps in understanding and communication, and the role of review and audit are all important learning to be taken from successful large sporting programmes.

Conclusion

The sustainability systems and processes developed to establish a defined agenda and objectives, to provide clear guidance on implementation, and establish an auditable structure for monitoring and reporting must underlie the delivery of any ambitious sustainability strategy to avoid the risk of a project becoming a well-intentioned but ultimately unsustainable venture. However, processes alone will not guarantee attainment of set objectives. Critical to success is a strong client focus, early ownership of the sustainability agenda by design teams and contractors, the creation of partnerships between the client, design teams, contractors and the supply chain, and the provision of a network for delivering innovation. This will largely be achieved through advocacy and diplomacy, interdisciplinary workshops and the perseverance of a core sustainability team.

References

FIFA (ed) (2007). Football Stadiums: Technical Recommendations and Requirements (4th Edition). FIFA. Zurich. Accessed online August 2010. http://www.fifa.com/

Green Goal (2010, 2008). Green Goal Action Plan, 2010 FIFA World Cup, Host City Cape Town. Accessed online August 2010. http://www.capetown.gov.za/en/GreenGoal/Documents/2010_GREE- N_GOAL_ACTION_PLAN.pdf

International Olympic Committee, (2010). Olympic Charter, accessed online August 2010. http://www.olympic.org/Documents/Olympic%20Charter/Charter_en_2010.pdf

London (2012, 2005). London 2012 bid brochure *Towards a One Planet Olympics*. Accessed online August 2010. http://www.london20-12.com/documents/bid-publications/towards-a-one-planet-olympics.pdf

Olympic Delivery Authority, (2007). Sustainable Development Strategy. Accessed online July 2010. http://www.london2012.com/publications/sustainable-development-strategy-full-version.php

Oskam, I.F., (2009). Op wegnaarinnovatiekracht; technischinnoveren en ondernemen als systematischactiviteit, Amsterdam: HvA publicaties.

Vancouver (2010, 2003). Vancouver 2010 Bid Book Accessed online August 2010. http://www.vancouver2010.com/more-2010-information/about-vanoc/organizing-committee/bid-history/bid-book/bid-book_88094qM.html

VANOC, (2007). Vancouver 2010 Sustainability Report 2005-2006. Accessed online August 2010. http://www.vancouver2010.com/dl/00/12/12/sustainability-report-2005-06_66d-UT.pdf

Chapter 26
Motorcycling and the Environment

An Impossible Marriage?

Alex Goldenberg

Introduction

The Fédération Internationale de Motocyclisme (International Motorcycling Federation - hereafter FIM) created in 1904, is the governing body for motorcycle sport and the global advocate for  motorcycling, representing 101 national motorcycle federations that are divided into six regional continental unions across the world. The FIM runs 49 FIM World Championships and prizes in five different sporting disciplines taking place on circuits or off-road courses. They are also engaged in non-sporting activities – for example, tourism, gatherings and leisure, mobility, transport, road safety, public policy and of course the environment – and activities linked with sport, such as the technical, medical and judicial aspects.

Motorcycle sport is a major constituent of the international and national sporting calendars, attracting an increasing audience and producing significant economic effects. It is a sport which, like most other sports and human activities in general, has an impact on the environment. The FIM considers it to be of major importance to develop a coherent environmental policy, taking into account the legislative and regulatory requirements of each country.

FIM Environmental Commission

FIM athletes and organisers in the past were generally not very concerned about the environment and its protection when practising their favourite sport. Nowadays, being more conscious of the importance of environmental issues within our sport and of the necessity to develop a better understanding of it, the FIM created in 1992 a working group with the aim of dealing with all questions related to the protection of the environment within the motorcycling world and defining an FIM environmental policy. This working group subsequently became the FIM International Environment Commission (CIE) in 1998, and is composed of 15 members from various countries, elected over four year terms. During the sporting season, these members are nominated as Environmental Delegates at various FIM events. Their role is to observe and verify the application of the FIM Environmental Code, to inform the International Jury of any serious breaches of the Code, and to carry out an inspection of the track/course and its facilities. They must also assist and collaborate with the Environmental Steward nominated for the event and send a detailed report of the event to the CIE. These reports are then used by the CIE to improve its work and define the weak areas of each discipline regarding the environment.

In order to promote an environmentally friendly approach towards events and instruct National Federations (FMNs) about sustainable practices, the FIM organises every year various environmental seminars around the world. The aim of these seminars is for interested delegates to obtain an official FIM Environmental Steward's licence, which is then valid for three years. FIM Environmental Stewards are compulsory at each event organised under the FIM umbrella, and the costs are borne by the event organising federation (FMNR). During an event, the Environmental Steward must check the application and compliance of the FIM Environmental Code, and draw up a report addressed to the CIE by using the checklist of the discipline concerned. The Environmental Steward is also the key person to advise the organisers and reduce the environmental footprint of an event.

FIM Environmental Code

One of the main tools developed by the CIE is the FIM Environmental Code, which outlines environmental recommendations and obligations (including financial penalties) that all organisers, promoters, riders and teams must apply in order to be part of a FIM World Championship or Prize. This Code was created in 1995 and is updated every year by taking into account the experiences accumulated during the season and comments made from

FMNs, stakeholders and partners. It covers most of the environmental issues that can be encountered at motorcycling events; from the protection of the ground to the cleaning of motorcycles; from the actions taken by the organisers to the behaviour of the riders and teams. It also describes the duties of the FIM Environmental Delegate and Environmental Steward and includes environmental checklists for all the FIM disciplines.

Cooperation Between FIM and the United Nations Environmental Programme

In December 2006, the FIM President, Vito Ippolito, and the United Nations Environmental Programme (UNEP) Executive Director, Achim Steiner, signed a Memorandum of Understanding (MoU), with the objective to provide a framework of cooperation and support to reduce the environmental impact of motorcycle events. The collaboration between the FIM and UNEP was also established in order to promote and support the monitoring of environmental programmes in the preparation and staging of FIM events. This MoU was extended in 2008 after two successful years of cooperation between the FIM and UNEP. The exchange of information and expertise allowed the FIM to continue and improve its work towards the protection of the environment within the motorcycling world. FIM Delegates also attend conferences and forums on sustainability and sport, notably those organised by UNEP, in order to share and take advantage of experiences gained from other sports and major events.

FIM Environmental Initiatives

One of the most concrete actions brought about by the MoU between the FIM and UNEP is the celebration of World Environment Day (WED) on the 5th of June each year. Since 2007, the FIM has celebrated this important day by organising actions (planting trees, recycling campaigns, signing of an Environmental Charter by top riders) that involve event organisers, promoters, riders and FIM officials. The participation of our best riders, together with everyone involved in motorcycle events, is designed to show the determination of our sport in addressing environmental issues and to make our fans conscious through messages and pictures of their favourite stars.

The great visibility of these actions has served as a catalyst for actions by FMNs during the course of the year. By setting the example, the FIM has highlighted environmental issues linked to the sport, proposed a list of initiatives that can be easily carried out and instigate FMNs to spread the environmental message to their motorcycle clubs and members.

The FIM Environmental logo *RIDE GREEN* was created to head all environmental initiatives taken within the motorcycling world in order to unify all actions under the same "flag" and provide a better visibility. This registered brand is now widely recognised and ensures credibility to those who act in favour of respecting the environment and who strive to organise sustainable motorcycling events. FIM believe that it is of great importance to use the *RIDE GREEN* logo on all communication tools (website, magazine, newsletters, e-mails) that are used to display an environmental action or initiative, as this brand is now understood by both the public and the media.

In order to encourage a greater awareness of environmental concerns, the FIM created in 1997 an Environmental Award. This distinction is granted to individuals, FMN's, clubs, organisers, manufacturers or other associations that have made a significant contribution or have done something important to enhance environmental awareness in the field of motorcycling. In 2009, an independent jury composed of five members (one FIM Vice-President, the CIE President and three international environmental experts) was launched in order to choose the winning candidate.

FIM Alternative Energy Working Group

In 2007, the FIM Alternative Energy Working Group (AEWG) was created with the aim of making motorcycle racing greener by integrating the latest technological developments in the field of alternative energy in FIM competitions and preparing the future of motorcycling. The AEWG is composed of experts from different fields, coming from the motorcycle industry, the world of sport and energy research centres. The core activity of this group is to identify and help to promote projects involving alternative means of propulsion for motorcycles and to use the FIM network and tools to disseminate good practices.

The work on alternative energy is not restricted to electrical power, but for now it is electrical power that has seen the most rapid development in the sport. Other areas of particular interest include the use of biofuels, and in particular the latest developments using new sources of raw materials and new processes. Electric vehicles are not a new concept; however, the last one and a half years have shown a dramatic acceleration in the pace of development in this technology. The Powered Two Wheelers (PTW – motorcycles, scooters and mopeds) are now providing a very practical base for the development of this technology, especially as battery technology is still accompanied by restraints imposed by the weight of the battery pack itself, and the amount of autonomy that can be achieved between recharges. The rapid development of competition motorcycles used in different disciplines within the sport during the last year points the way to a new future. Autonomy has now improved to the point where the best technology makes an electric PTW practical for daily transport to and from work for the majority of citizens living and working in urban environments in Europe. It is interesting to note that consumers do not expect from a PTW the same autonomy as for a car. A usable range of 60 km is considered acceptable.

Promotion of Alternative Energy

In 2009, the FIM supported the TTXGP (the first zero carbon, clean emissions Grand Prix race) event held on the Isle of Man, Great Britain. The electrically powered motorcycles had to complete one lap (60 km) of the traditional course, which is exceptionally demanding, not just on the rider but also on the machinery, starting at sea level and reaching a high point of 619 metres above sea level. This was a real test of battery capacity. The race winning speed was almost identical to that of Ralph Bryans racing a prototype petrol motorcycle at the 1966 TT (Tourist Trophy). This result may not seem very exciting, but to the FIM team who were there to observe and support this event, it was clear that development will now be very fast. It is also clear from the companies interested in sponsoring the event that the consumer electronics industry will be heavily involved in future racing activities.

In December 2009, the first FIM Ride Green Eco Enduro took place, opening a new page of motorcycle history by registering only electric motorcycles in this discipline. This international competition supported by the FIM took place at the same time as the COP15, the United Nations Climate Change Conference in Copenhagen, Denmark. The concept of this event was to show the world that motor sports and riders can be environmentally responsible and are prepared to seek new ways and innovative solutions to reduce their impact on the world's climate. The first two stages were configured as a regular Enduro race, on different kinds of terrain, but on the last day the race became a Super Motard race on a small circuit, built for the occasion in a military area not far from downtown Copenhagen.

On 19 November 2009, the FIM officially announced the launch of the first electric motorcycle racing championship in the world: the FIM e-Power International Championship. The 2010 rounds of this championship will be held during the opening race of a few selected rounds of FIM's prestigious world championships, such as the MotoGP, Superbike and Endurance. The FIM is concerned about the future of motorcycle sport, and aims to gather together a number of teams in the motorcycling world to strengthen its efforts in promoting new and alternative energies. The FIM e-Power International Championship will provide an international platform for the development of electric motorcycles and the technology behind them, to test them in an exciting and challenging way. It aims at driving low-carbon technological innovation forward, to demonstrate that clean-emission transport technologies have matured and can be fun, fast and exciting.

With the aim of keeping the motorcycling world aware of important information regarding alternative energy and initiatives taken in this field, the FIM publishes a bi-monthly newsletter that is circulated to the entire FIM family, as well as to other partners involved in our championships and prizes. This newsletter covers various issues including the EU's position on alternative energy, reports on conferences and forums, as well as many other subjects that are linked with the sport and its future.

Environmental Impact of Motorcycling Events

Like other sporting disciplines or entertainment events, the main environmental impact of motorcycling competitions comes from the spectators. This is an area where the FIM does not have direct control, but recommendations and suggestions can always be given to those who attend our events. In collaboration with the organisers, the FIM promotes the use of public transport, recycling of waste and its collection, protection of the ground, management of parking facilities, the correct signing for spectator access, sound levels (protective measures against race noise affecting the neighbourhood and sound level of the public address system), as well as many other issues that can be improved to organise more environmentally-friendly motorcycling events.

Conclusion

Due to the application of stricter rules by national governments and authorities regarding the environment and the practice of motorcycling, the environmental and sustainable policies put into place by the FIM and its FMNs will allow the motorcycling world to establish rules and organisational standards that will complement the current laws and highlight the proactive behaviour of motorcyclists. As a motor sport, we are often criticised by those who think that motorcyclists pollute for their own pleasure of riding a motorcycle. The FIM aims to be the leader in changing bad habits and negative thinking about motorcycling and the environment, and to show the example by acting and promoting sustainable practices within our events. This could also improve the current image of motorcycling and facilitate discussions with local authorities for the organisation of events.

It is also important to raise the awareness of the public and fans about the importance of respecting the environment through actions and communications involving our top riders, who are listened to more than politicians or administrative bodies. The education of young riders is also a major duty for the FIM as the governing body for motorcycling. By organising sustainable events and by promoting the use of alternative energy from the beginning of an athlete's motorcycling career, we can orientate their way to act in a responsible manner, not only in favour of the protection of the environment but also for the benefit of the sport.

Chapter 27

2016, 2022, 2030, Go! Sustainability and Arabian Gulf Sporting Megaprojects

Graham Barnfield

"We headed for our seats passing a long table groaning with food and spectacular centrepieces, including an ice sculpture of an elaborate Middle Eastern teapot, tall and ornate ... A frozen teapot in the warm desert air: contradictions within contradictions".

(Rushing with Elder 2007: 210).

Introduction

So bewildered was journalist Josh Rushing at an Al Jazeera reception in 2006 that he mistook a replica coffee pot, based on a traditional dalla, for a teapot. Yet his struggle for metaphors expresses a common perception about the problem with Arabian Gulf states. To outside observers, the environmental consequences of the ongoing battle to keep cool and hydrated are cause for concern. Carving out a modern existence in inhospitable deserts – even taking account of hydrocarbon wealth and the coastal locations of the major conurbations – strikes commentators as difficult, if not foolhardy. British TV travel presenter Simon Reeve caught the mood when he used the Virgin Holidays Responsible Tourism Awards 2010 to declare "we can't continue with the madness that is happening in Dubai ... pretty much the benchmark for humanity's greatest environmental folly" (Scott, 2010).

Yet a growing population survives and sometimes thrives in such urban habitats, accompanied by increasing unease about the environmental consequences of cities such as Doha and Dubai. In terms of their carbon footprints and consumption of water and energy alone, these settlements can seem environmentally suspect. This theme is hardly novel; in the early 1990s, the United Arab Emirates' (UAE) water supply was presented as the basis for future conflict, precluding continued economic growth (Bulloch and Darwish: 150-154). Against this backdrop, the "luxury" of sports mega projects being added to the mix can make the locales responsible appear wilfully destructive.

The two mega projects under discussion in this chapter are the Aspire Zone in Doha and Dubai Sports City. Both projects will feature in future bidding to host world sporting events, such as Qatar's bid for the 2022 FIFA World Cup™. It is argued that, contrary to their portrayal in western media as evidence of environmental recklessness – the built environment equivalent of Manchester City FC's Abu Dhabi-backed wage bill – both schemes have embraced the rhetoric of sustainability. (Credit crunch permitting, resources allow oil-rich Qatar – home to estimated natural gas reserves of more than 900 trillion cubic feet (25 trillion cubic metres) – to prepare for such activity.) Given the high profile of these sporting events, it is likely that more attention will be directed to such endeavors from prospective host nations.

Qatar and the UAE can seem like unlikely sport hosts for a number of reasons. The searing heat and summer humidity create a difficult environment for athletes. It could also be argued that sports mega projects lack authentic domestic support, since three traditional sports remain popular with nationals in both Qatar and the UAE. Camel racing, falconry and certain types of equestrianism all perform a symbolic function in which sport and national identity are linked, informed by norms and codes that appear analogous in form to pre-modern chivalry. Since in their most basic form such activities make a minimal environmental impact, the rhetoric surrounding them often connects the particular activities to wise stewardship of natural resources (anthropocentric sustainability). Yet this situation is changing; all three sports are moving in directions which increase their reliance on the latest technologies or state-of-the-art facilities. The Aspire Zone promises to build a futuristic cameldrome; Abu Dhabi is working with the British Museum to create a world-class falconry museum; and Dubai has an equestrian themed residential district under construction, centered on the Meydan Racecourse.

The changing fortunes of traditional sports in the Arabian Gulf typify a wider transition taking place. Present-day hydrocarbon reserves and the imperative for economic diversification have prompted a change in the scope for and meaning of these activities, distancing them from their tribal origins. As recently as the 1970s, the nation states where these sports are practised were still taking shape; each still relies heavily on the labor and expertise of large immigrant populations, again posing questions of political legitimacy. Against this backdrop, falconry, equestrianism and camel racing acquire a role in the ongoing attempts to construct and shore up Emirati and Qatari national identities. Yet unwittingly, the regional nature of these sports – coexisting with far greater levels of both participation in cricket and of English Premier League football TV spectatorship – makes it difficult for countries in the Arabian Peninsula to excel on the world sporting stage as a whole. One motive for building sporting mega projects in the Gulf is that it represents an attempt to shift the dynamic of international sport more towards the region.

Assuaging environmental critics of proposals for sports mega projects is significant, when throughout international institutions environmentalism has become a core value. Scan almost any marketing materials from a UAE real estate master developer and a familiar picture emerges. Thus it is commonplace for golf courses to stress their eco-credentials from the outset. For instance, the Saadiyat Beach Golf Club – close to the proposed falconry museum in Abu Dhabi – promises "The ultimate championship beach course designed by Gary Player. Environmentally sensitive, this will be one of the Gulf's very first ocean-side courses". Official support for Arabian Gulf sport mega projects appears well-versed in the language of sustainability. In response, critics evaluate whether these developments are feasible in the longer term, without either consuming disproportionate amounts of energy and water or relying on indirect subsidy from, in effect, their respective national oil and gas industries.

Before we can establish whether a particular sporting development is sustainable, the different interpretations of the concept require careful consideration. The contested meaning of *sustainability* – leading to ideological divisions schematically represented below as falling into three broad camps – obliges us to choose our terminology wisely. Conflicting concepts of sustainability mean that the ideological definitions need to be grasped before they can be used to discern the success or dangers inherent in a particular project.

The first such school of thought is predicated on the application of the principles of sustainable development within advanced capitalist nations. Typically, this leads to institutions conducting their affairs on a sustainable basis, for instance by drawing energy supplies from renewable sources. Incorporating such practices often means framing them in terms of a broader worldview, which emphasises the present generation's responsibility for handing over a liveable planet to the next generation. On this basis it is an "anthropocentric approach to needs" (Richardson: 50).

Secondly, there are critics of the official doctrine and practices of sustainable development and sustainability. They point to the shortcomings of actual eco-projects and are sensitive to the possibility of "greenwashing", where sustainability is reduced to a public relations exercise. Moreover, they treat the concept as having become ritual incantation prior to advocating "an understanding of the environment as a market problem, not ...

an analysis of the market as an environmental problem" (Middleton and O'Keefe: 3). At the rhetorical level, certain "adjectives, or adjectival phrases, have become so embedded in their nouns as to render them almost nugatory ... For some theorists they are a pleonasm since development which is not sustainable is not development, for those who see most, if not all, development as exploitative it is an oxymoron; there can be none for whom the expression is not an ideological battlefield" (ibid: 4).

Thirdly, a minority of writers and commentators argue that accepting the idea of sustainability, and adopting sustainable policies, serves to limit human prosperity and mastery of the environment (e.g. Lewis et al, pp.47-50; Heartfield, pp.14-20; 70-77; Ben-Ami, *passim*). From within this tradition, Dubai receives qualified support as a place where "social and economic development frequently gives rise to expressions of confidence, civic pride and urban experimentation", while noting that "many of these new developments in non-Western countries are borrowing from the Western sustainability agenda in their apparent break with materialism" (Williams: 70). Sport mega projects in the Gulf combine large-scale infrastructural investment with (at least) a rhetorical commitment to sustainability; the implications of this balancing act are considered below.

The hydrocarbon wealth of Qatar and the UAE determines their basic relationship with the world economy. Within Anglophone polities, a narrative has emerged post-OPEC which blamed the alleged coercive capacities of Arab wealth for "holding us to ransom" in the West. In contrast, official materials published within the Gulf Cooperation Council (GCC) often present its members as developing countries (albeit anchored to the global community by substantial reserves of historical legitimacy). For instance, a UAE government-produced booklet on water cites Sheikh Zayed approvingly – "our fathers were able to survive because they recognised the need to conserve the environment" – in the build-up to both describing vast desalination programmes and the pending development of Abu Dhabi's carbon-neutral Masdar City (UAE National Media Council, n.d, *passim*).

In recent years, Qatar's formal national planning documentation has noted its present-day reliance on dwindling supplies of oil and natural gas, while simultaneously regarding this as a spur to an alternative form of modernization based on a diversified economy. Reading between the lines only slightly, Qatar's own government regards its nation as a developing country. The latest document, *Qatar National Vision 2030*, is organized around Four Pillars, each comprising a type of development – human, social, economic, environmental. The last of these is defined in terms of a balance between developmental need and protecting the environment. It is claimed that this can be achieved through a combination of legal reform, population education and urban planning.

Sport, meanwhile, is to be found within the human development pillar, where in the future Qatari youth and children will participate "in a wide variety of cultural and sports activities" (ibid: p.16). The *Vision* implies that an education programme of this nature is a logical precursor to a "healthy population, physically and mentally" (ibid: 17). This official sentiment about physical activity performing a holistic role in nation-building also animates much of the outreach work conducted by Aspire (e.g. the project Aspire Active, which encourages exercise, programs for youth, women, diabetics and other target groups).

Both Dubai and Qatar promote ambitious goals, including deadlines, of a time to come when they will sit at the top table of developed states. Speaking for the UAE, Sheikh Mohammed bin Rashid al-Maktoum, declared the aim of becoming "a top modern nation with high living standards in 11 years under its Vision 2021 plan". The previously cited *Qatar National Vision 2030* specifies a similar date, albeit nine years later. Each state is happy to include hosting one or more global sport events in this timeline, either by official accommodation to rumors of an Olympic bid (Dubai) or through central government initiatives, not least the current bidding for the 2022 FIFA World Cup™ in Doha. In parallel to extracting energy, Qatar has developed its own modernizing project, centred on the city of Doha – especially its waterfront "Cornice" district. This project includes a sports component, often identified using the brand-name Aspire. As a city, contemporary Doha attracts relatively little global publicity, negative or otherwise (in contrast to Dubai). Indeed, one could speculate that a single Emirate's high-profile city has attracted almost all attention from critics of 'unsustainable' development while similar projects elsewhere go largely un-remarked upon.

The Doha project now known as the Aspire Zone started life as a sport venue in 2003. Architecturally, it consists of two main locations: the Aspire Dome, an indoor stadium comprising over a dozen different playing fields, and, set up the following year, a purpose-built training and educational venue, the Aspire Academy for Sports Excellence, also known as the Aspire Academy. A 15,000-capacity arena was opened in 2005. Taken collectively, the various components of the Aspire Zone feed into a wider economic complex, summarized by the London *Times* as follows:

> "Sport has become a key marketing tool for Qatar, helping quench not only the thirst of the local population for sport but also in actively promoting itself as the Gulf's leading 'sport capital.' Some of the sports facilities Qatar boasts are The Khalifa Olympic City, Hamad International Complex for Water Sports, and Doha Golf club. The Aspire academy for sports excellence is one of the world's most advanced sporting institutions and the first of its kind in the Middle East. It was inaugurated in September 2004" (Hoare and Henderson: 49).

The authorities have several key goals which they hope to cohere through the ongoing development of sports infrastructure. One of these is sustainability, backed by assertions about aspects of the built environment in these locations. Another is the transformation of the local population, where physical activity and exercise are viewed as bringing holistic benefits to the nation as a whole. Provided official enthusiasm for Aspire can be sustained, its success will be measured primarily in terms of the Olympic medal table and other international sport triumphs. One suspects that an additional indicator of achievement would be in any impact on the problems of obesity, type II diabetes and other sources of morbidity among Qatari nationals. In both its official literature and its program focused on public health and participation, Aspire seeks accordance with the current national plan, in which (anthropocentric) sustainable development and Islamic values are treated as interchangeable.

One apparent similarity between Doha's Aspire Zone and Dubai Sports City is the transitory presence of sporting celebrities in both. A steady flow of public figures features prominently in the promotion and public relations for each entity, ranging from photo opportunities to fleeting 'site inspections' to semi-permanent employment. Such personalities tend to be high earners – their income contrasts starkly with that of laborers at work on the various venues – who act as authentic sporting ambassadors (e.g. Pele for talent-scouting program Aspire Africa). Others are paid for their coaching services (e.g. Australian cricketer Rod Marsh for Dubai Sports City), while others still act as brand ambassadors for real estate developers, with varying degrees of practical commitment. (A liminal space is occupied by the Dubai 'signature golf course', lent credibility by the involvement of one or more former champions in designing a masterplan.)

Since critics of globalization often treat celebrity culture as symptomatic of a wider problem, current and former athletes endorsing Arabian Gulf sporting megaprojects may provoke further negative reactions. Indeed, one problem with instinctive celebrity-baiting in the name of sustainability is that it fails to differentiate the different functions performed by professional athletes, past and present, in the region. Loathing celebrity and being fearful of ostentatious and unsustainable development coalesce, perhaps meeting in the lobby of what one columnist called the 'Albert Speer meets Britney Spears hotel' (Turner, 2009). In these terms, Doha fares rather better than the UAE, since Aspire's closest equivalent institution, Dubai Sports City, can seem riddled with sporting celebrities on the make.

Sports megaprojects in Dubai are provoking controversy and scepticism. Prior to the so-called credit crunch, Dubai's international profile owed much to three key drivers: airline Emirates, reports of innovative architecture in its real estate sector, and perceived cultural liberalism, at least when compared to the more conservative polities found in neighboring territories. Yet it faced the damaging counter-narrative of being seen as "the west on steroids", since it was almost inevitable that the pro-growth stance of the city-state would anger the advocates of "sustainable development". One author recently presented Dubai as a place "where the very concept, let alone the practice, of environmental sustainability is barely acknowledged" (Pugh-Thomas: 30). In concluding this essay, I seek to complicate this picture, by looking at how the development of Dubai's major sports megaproject, Dubai Sports City, has fully embraced the rhetoric of sustainability.

For one influential critic, Dubai Sports City and its partnerships with high profile brands such as Manchester United typifies the dash for growth (Davidson: 128). Other long-term residents sigh wearily when promised yet more ground-breaking developments; as each new hotel promises to be the tallest, most innovative or most beautiful, PR fatigue becomes rife.

Although bemusing to visitors and outside observers, recent Dubai place names have – at a subjective level – a distinctive function. This municipal process gives 'cities', typically business zones, very literal names in English to denote their designated economic activity (and sometimes the authorities' preferred type of resident). The functional naming of places such as Dubai Media City, Internet City, International Humanitarian City and Dubai International Endurance City are top-down creations. A major motive here is to attract foreign direct investment and established bespoke business premises, often in "free zones" characterized by "light-touch" regulation and low (to no) direct taxation. Legal changes permitting foreign leasehold ownership accelerated this process.

Government desires and inward investment strategy drives semantic convention, meaning that Dubai Sports City was conceived as a locale organized around the unifying theme of sport, driven by the interactions of the master developer and the ruling family planner. In fact, the nation-building outlook overarches the project. Dubailand, a theme park named to sound like a new nation, will – if itself ever completed – contain within it Dubai Sports City, sports being one of Dubailand's six themed zones. Each zone is intended to combine numerous resorts and attractions intended to enhance the Emirate's standing as a global tourist destination or a place to do business.

That said, Dubailand's relatively privileged position within the target-driven relationship between the ruling family and interlinking state and private enterprise has not protected it completely from the debt-driven crisis that emerged in 2008-2009. The technically sustainable sounding elements of Dubai Sports City – for instance, systems to irrigate The Els golf course using processed sewage or greywater from the nearby Victory Heights gated community – will be tested by the way that the project itself was conceived in boom times and is now caught in slump. Questions of economic viability throw issues of environmental sustainability into sharp relief. This problem is also amplified by a key difference between Aspire and Dubai Sports City: whereas the former stresses training for sports excellence alongside spectatorship, the latter tries to combine these values with real estate (residential sales and retail/office rental) as a pivotal feature of the development.

In conclusion, conventional wisdom today maintains that sport megaprojects in deserts paid for by fossil fuel production are simply not acceptable. The controversy is heightened by the way sport is, in effect, a luxury, at least in comparison to basic needs such as nutrition and shelter. Yet to deny sections of the Earth's population the opportunity to widen their opportunities to participate in and watch sports would be to maintain some of the monopolistic tendencies which the Chinese medal haul at the 2008 Olympic Games helped to undermine. Moreover, sticking with the blunt observation that Aspire and Dubai Sports City are inherently unsustainable represents a missed opportunity. It means wilfully ignoring the experiments in new techniques needed to cultivate, say, the cross-continental soil types found in Dubai's cricket training facilities, or the innovative irrigation networks used to maintain golf courses. It also means refusing to engage with the way sustainability has been integrated into the official values of Qatar and the UAE, making a holistic vision of a fit population part of the rhetoric of statehood. Dismissing these evolving, ruling ideas as public relations chatter constitutes an evasion; surely it is better to form an understanding, both of Gulf sport megaprojects and of the real trajectory of the societies that house them.

References

Ben-Ami, D. (2010). *Ferraris for All: In Defence of Economic Progress*, London, Policy Press.

Bulloch, J. and Adel Darwish, A. (1993). *Water Wars: Coming Conflicts in the Middle East*, London, Victor Gollancz.

Davidson, C. (2007). *Dubai: The Vulnerability of Success London*, London: C Hurst & Co.

General Secretariat for Development Planning. (2008). *Qatar National Vision 2030*, Doha, General Secretariat for Development Planning.

Heartfield, J. (2008). *Green Capitalism: Manufacturing Scarcity in an Age of Abundance*, London, Mute.

Hoare, S. and Henderson, N. (2009). Qatar: The Business of Sport. *Times Focus Reports*, 3 December, 2-3.

Middleton, N. and Phil O'Keefe (2001). *Redefining Sustainable Development*, London, Pluto.

Lewis, N. et al (2010). *Big Potatoes: The London Manifesto for Innovation*, London, Big Potatoes.

Pugh-Thomas, C. (2010). *Times Literary Supplement*, February 26, No.5578.

Richardson D. (1997). The Politics of Sustainable Development. In Baker, S. et al *The Politics of Sustainable Development* London, Routledge pp.43-50.

Rushing, J. with S. Elder (2007). *Mission Al Jazeera*, London, Palgrave Macmillan.

Scott, L (2010). Responsible tourism: A world of difference. *Metro* 23rd April, 2010. Online at http://www.metro.co.uk/travel/ 823073-respo- nsible-tourism-a-world-of-difference

Turner, J. (2009). 'Jordan and Dubai, parallel universes collide', *The Times*, 28 November.

UAE National Media Council (n.d.). *Water: The Source of Life*, Abu Dhabi, National Media Council.

Williams, A. (2008). *The Enemies of Progress: Dangers of Sustainability* (Societas) London: Imprint Academic.

Chapter 28

Sports, Social Capital and Public Space

Developing an Educational Legacy

Neil Herrington

Introduction

The increasing urbanisation of humanity makes it imperative to engage with the urban and what this means in terms of physical, mental and emotional wellbeing. As Girardet (1996) stated:

> "Cities must become socially, economically and ecologically sustainable, fulfilling basic human needs for shelter, subsistence and social cohesion. For this to work the active participation of people in shaping their urban environment is crucial".

(Girardet 1996 p.119)

This agency, this sense of care for the environment, is conditioned in childhood through direct interaction with the natural and built environment. Indeed, the education of this generation, perhaps more than any other, must take responsibility for developing this interaction. This chapter looks to ask how a sporting mega event might help us in developing this awareness? In doing this it considers the case of the 2002 Commonwealth Games held in Manchester, and offers up some possible legacy outcomes of the

Olympic and Paralympic Games that will be held in London in 2012 (2012 Games).

Thomas and Thompson (2004) produced a report based on the assumption that "[t]ackling children's quality of life issues and environmental sustainability together can improve quality of life for everyone now, as well as in the future". A number of recommendations flow from the report, including a call to forge new ways to facilitate environmental education through out-of-school learning and green school design. The fact that children in urbanised, low-income communities are most likely to become disconnected from the natural environment, impacting on environmental learning and on other aspects of wellbeing, led to the recommendation that children from disadvantaged backgrounds should be given more opportunities to access quality public space. In terms of public space there is also a need for better consideration to be given to children's needs in decision-making on the design of public space. However, this is no easy task. As Worpole (2003) points out: "the concept of public space has never been so popular, but never so poorly conceptualised or understood, especially in its use by children and young people".

The Commonwealth Games of 2002, held in Manchester, was used by that city as a planning tool. The evaluation report on the event produced by Ecotec (2004) states that a key motivation for hosting the Games was the event's ability to stimulate sustainable regeneration. This was framed in terms of:

- Improving skills, educational attainment and personal development;
- Developing skills and improving cohesion through participation in events and health improvement projects; and,
- Improving the competitiveness of small and medium enterprises.

A central plank for securing these legacies came in the form of the 2002 Economic and Social Programme for the North West. This aimed to ensure that disadvantaged communities throughout the North West would benefit from Manchester hosting the event.

The reports on aspects of the Manchester legacy point out that school attendance rates increased at both primary (by two percentage points) and secondary (4.4 percentage points) levels. Furthermore, a higher proportion of Year 11 leavers were seen to progress into higher and further education (an increase of 17.5 percentage points). It is also reported that resident satisfaction with the quality of local schools increased to 76.5%. Thus, there are indicators of an effect of the event on educational outcomes, even though this was through a somewhat *ad hoc* structure of engagement. Indeed, some workers on the 2002 Commonwealth Games felt that opportunities were missed in terms of building a more concrete legacy able to operate after the funding for the event tailed off.

An issue also arises when legacy, which isn't necessarily self-evident, is measured only a short time after the event. Longer term benefits may be missed; what won't be measured may drift from the plan, and planning is essential as legacy doesn't flow automatically. Whilst Hall (2004) feels that:

"...investment in accessible and affordable education, health and communications technology, along with a diversified job creation strategy is far more likely to have long term benefits for urban economic and social well being than investment in elite mega sports events and infrastructure". (p.68)

This view neglects the catalytic nature of the event, and the opportunity it affords for re-engineering at all levels of society.

The architect Rod Sheard (2005) strongly believes that a stadium can shape a town or city. Making claims that sport is becoming an internationally recognised social currency, he sees a judicious use of a stadium as "the most useful urban planning tool a city can possess" (Sheard 2005). Increasingly, stadia are not designed as stand alone buildings, rather they are being viewed as ways, in the words of Horne and Manzenreiter (2006), of facilitating synergies "between previously discrete activities such as shopping, dining out, entertainment and education, lead[ing] to de-differentiation" of these roles for public space. However, there will be costs associated with this de-differentiation. Policy makers need to be aware of "the social distribution of the supposed benefits of urban development initiatives...which social groups actually benefit, which are excluded, and what scope is there for contestation of these developments" (p8).

Drawing on the stories from a number of Olympic Games host cities, Muñoz (2006) claims that "Olympic urbanism has even transformed the urban profile of a city, having a strong impact on the post-Olympic evolution of the whole urban space through the intensive production of public spaces that are in fact used by different urban populations from all over the city..." (p181-182). This impact on urban planning and policy is globally important: the alteration of the physical and social landscape of cities being driven by investment in infrastructure, renovation and real estate. Policy has to struggle with the inherent tension within urban development – the complex issues around the size, shape, distribution and density of the city, along with the impact on social inclusion and the quality of life.

It is vital that we understand how urban living affects people and the environment. It is equally important that we use this understanding to develop an education that allows a proper engagement with the urban. Studying mega events such as the Olympic Games offers us a lens through which to explore such issues. This is a particularly powerful lens in terms of the 2012 Games, as it is occurring in London, a global mega city with the challenges and opportunities that this poses.

The 2012 Games is seen as being one of the key regeneration catalysts for an urban landscape in East London that is fragmented and constrained by busy roads and train lines, but with large amounts of space and water in the Lower Lea Valley. The event facilities will be situated within this area, which it is envisaged will be an open environment and will engage local communities. Landscape architect Jason Prior stated in an address to the Royal Society for the encouragement of Arts, Manufactures and Commerce (RSA) in London, that:

"Existing conditions on both sides of the Lea Valley reflect a geography of separation. When talking to the boroughs and the community groups, it became obvious that we should be growing inwards from the edges, not creating new communities in the middle. The project should be about repairing the rift in the city fabric and promoting the greater integration of community with what we can bring forward as an improved environment".

The trick will be to successfully utilise the resource of the Olympic Park for educational purposes; this is likely to depend upon the linkages that are formed between the communities that 'gather' around the Park. This will require collective investment in the development of social relationships. This is particularly challenging in an area where disconnection from place, through poor design, urban mobility and negative perception, is a contributory factor in the decline of required social capital.

What role could the Olympic Park play in increasing this social capital and how might schools and educationalists help in the facilitation of these links?

At the moment the point of engagement of a school with its community is not clear. A study carried out by the Joseph Rowntree Foundation (Crowther et al 2003) saw some eclectic if not incoherent practice in community engagement. This ranged from schools with a focus exclusively on improving the life chances of individual young people by raising their attainment, to schools likewise seeking to raise attainment, but feeling that they can only do so by involving families and the community in the development of a wider range of attributes in their students.

Within London, the engagement of schools with communities is hampered by the size and fragmentation of the education system allied to a good transport infrastructure. Thus, in London, 99.6% of secondary school pupils have three schools within 5km (which compares to a figure of 78% in the rest of the country) and pupils are therefore less likely to go to their nearest one; in fact only 25% do so (Burgess *et al* 2005). There is thus no automatic link into the local community through the student population.

How might the presence of sports stadia help to facilitate these links? One way in which sports stadia have been used to impact on school students is through the Department for Children, Schools and Families initiative called Playing for Success. This aims to establish out of school hours study support centres at football clubs and other sports' grounds. The centres use the environment and medium of football, rugby and other sports as motivational tools, and focus on raising literacy, numeracy and ICT standards amongst upper primary (9-11 year olds) and lower secondary (11-14) school students. In 2007 the UK's National Foundation for Educational Research (Sharp *et al* 2007) published a report on the longer term impact of the initiative.

Overall, the report showed that the impact of the intervention was mixed in terms of pupil attainment. However, it was found that "if pupils [did] benefit from their experience at PfS but they are not offered opportunities to demonstrate their learning once they leave, then there is a possibility of increased frustration and disaffection as a result (p64)." Thus, there is a need to ensure that this activity, designed to motivate learning, is built into the overall educational offer to each student. This last point resonates with the issues surrounding legacy. In one centre that is involved in this project it was acknowledged that:

> "...there is no formal tracking of the extent to which programme participants fare once their attendance stops. However, contact with the participants, or at least some of them, is maintained. There is a celebration event when a group completes their programme, both at the stadium and often within the school as well. Pupils are asked to act as mentors and as advocates for the programme, by speaking at assemblies. One participant from each cohort becomes a graduate. Graduates attend on Saturday mornings and develop new resources. From this group, individuals are elected to the Student Council. This body is responsible, amongst other things, for organising the celebration events (Playing for Success Centre Manager 1)".

These celebration events are part of an issue touched upon in the NFER report, but more strongly expressed during some of the interviews undertaken with Playing for Success staff. This was the way in which the centres facilitated interaction between parents/carers and teachers:

> "Parents and teachers do tend to mix; parents will talk to teachers and share experiences. Obviously parents don't feel as threatened in some ways when they come here purely for celebration of their child's achievement and they may not have had that opportunity before, so it's really a big thing for the whole family (Playing for Success Centre Manager 2)".

This could be taken as an indicator of the potential for similar initiatives to be hubs for the development of social capital. The development of social networks within the local community may be facilitated through engagement with the 2012 Games. Whilst the opportunity to engage does not equate with engagement, the potential exists for high profile events to lever engagement. This is more likely to be effective if it is allied to structures and curricula which give attention "to the mechanisms of trust and reciprocity within pedagogy [which] could enhance young people's understanding of the need for such engagement..." (McGonigal *et al* 2007 p.83). The key point is that we shouldn't expect this to happen automatically, but plan to ensure that the levers can be pulled when they become available.

These levers of engagement might include the symbols associated with the Games. It was certainly the perception of those involved in the Manchester Commonwealth Games that they were a great hook and pulled people into activities that they wouldn't normally be involved in. In this way, the mega-event can be thought of as an organising principle, bringing people to projects and programmes. Rather than being a stand alone entity, it might operate to develop programmes from what the area already has to offer. Within these programmes the emphasis could be on experiencing the urban environment, developing the tools to witness the developments taking place within an area, the impacts that people have on the environment and the cultural aspects of community and urban development that flow from the hosting of the event. Such programmes can be structured to enable a celebration of the area, developing a sense of pride in the area that pupils live (and where teachers work). Around these programmes for students there will also be a need to develop complementary professional development activities, building the capacity and capability of using the urban environment as a learning resource

Therefore, the focus shifts from the event to the area, mediated and pulled together by the activities and programme designed as a series of processes through which people interact with their environment, becoming more sensitive to and knowledgeable about their environment in such a way as to encourage work with others and empowerment to recognise their agency in environmental change. Such a programme would move away from traditional environmental/ecological work to a consideration of, for example, traffic issues and the social aspects of urban living.

References

Burgess, S., B. McConnell, C. Propper and D. Wilson (2005). The impact of school choice on sorting by ability and socioeconomic factors in English secondary education. In L. Woessmann and P. Peterson (eds),*Schools and the Equal Opportunity Problem*, The MIT Press, Cambridge Massachusetts.

Crowther, D. Cummings C, Dyson A and Millward A (2003). *Schools and Area Regeneration* Joseph Rowntree Foundation

Ecotec (2004). *An Evaluation of the Commonwealth Games Legacy Programme*

Girardet, H. (1996). *The Gaia Atlas of Cities. New Directions for Sustainable Urban Living*, Gaia Books

Hall (2004). Sports Tourism and Urban Regeneration in B Ritchie and D Adair (eds) *Sports Tourism Interrelationship, Impacts and Issues* Clevedon Channel View Pubs.

Horne, J. and W. Manzenreiter (2006). An Introduction to the Sociology of Sports Mega-events. In J. Horne and W. Manzenreiter (eds) *Sports Mega-Events: Social Scientific Analyses of a Global Phenomenon*, Blackwell.

McGonigal, J., R. Doherty, et al. (2007). Social Capital, Social Inclusion and Changing School Contexts: A Scottish Perspective. *British Journal of Educational Studies* 55(1): 77-94.

Muñoz, F. (2006). Olympic Urbanism and Olympic Villages: Planning Strategies in Olympic Host Cities, London 1908-London 2012. In J. Horne and W. Manzenreiter (eds) *Sports Mega-Events: Social Scientific Analyses of a Global Phenomenon*, Blackwell.

Sharp, C., Chamberlain, T., Morrison, J. and Filmer-Sankey, C. (2007). *Playing for Success: an Evaluation of its Long Term Impact* (DfES Research Report 844). London: DfES.

Thomas, G and Thompson, G (2004) *A Child's Place: Why Environment Matters to Children*. Demos/Green Alliance

Worpole K (2003). *No Particular Place to Go – children, young people and public space*, Birmingham: Groundwork UK

Part V

Towards Sustainability and Sport

Chapter 29
A Metasynthesis of Sustainability and Sport

Keith Gilbert and Jill Savery

Introduction

The aim in this chapter is to synthesize the findings of the various chapters herein in order to contribute to the theoretical development of the notion of *sustainability and sport*. As such, this metasynthesis[1] seeks to build on the previous comments regarding sustainability and sport, including the successes, challenges and advice for the way forward. This type of metasynthesis is "would not necessarily result in theory development, although it could do so. More likely, it lays an excellent foundation for concept and future theory development" (Schreiber et al, 1997, p. 315). The topics broached by the authors are too broad to allow a thorough exploration of sustainability for theory building or an explication approach. Therefore, a theory development metasynthesis will be undertaken which will involve reanalysis of the original material and the use of an imposed structure to organise findings. This analysis is vital for development of a literature base in the area of future sus-

---

1. See Thorne and colleagues (2004, p.1346) who note: "Metasynthesis is not a method designed to produce oversimplification; rather, it is one in which difference is retained and complexity enlightened." Also, Schreiber (1997, p. 315) who suggests three types of metasynthesis exist, including theory building, theory explication and theory development approaches.

tainability and sport research. We believe that this text includes novel ideas which we hope will lay the foundation for future research work in the area of sustainability and sport.

Benchmarking

When designing sustainability programs for large sporting events or sport organizations, it is important to review industry standards and best practices. Indeed, the issues of benchmarking run throughout Part II of this book, written mostly by individuals who are currently driving the sustainability agenda at the Olympic and Paralympic Games (Games). These authors are working on the front lines to find answers to the challenges of delivering sustainable Games, and we argue that it is a valuable exercise to learn from their best practice and reflections before making important decisions for future sport events.

The section on *'Organizations and Tools Promoting Sustainability and Sport'* begins with respect to UNEP and their environmental capacity building work with major sport organizations and events. UNEP engages in activity across the world at various levels, promoting environmental protection through sport and greening of events. In particular, UNEP provides independent environmental assessments of major sport events that analyze whether event organizers are actually succeeding in their task to host sustainable events. Sue Riddlestone targets examples of sustainability NGOs working with the organizers of the London 2012 Games. BioRegional played a leading role in the development of the sustainability strategy for the London 2012 Games bid (*Towards a One Planet Olympics*), which Riddlestone argues is now classed as a major sustainability benchmark document for the event. BioRegional now supports the event organizers in the achievement of the bid's sustainability strategy in terms of a benchmark in order that the 2012 Games lives up to the high standard set in London's bid to the International Olympic Committee (IOC), and one which other bidding cities might follow. Both UNEP and Bioregional support the notion of setting up the benchmarking processes for major sport events, for example in the areas such as construction, greenhouse gas emissions, and creating sustainable legacies throughout the process of the event development period and beyond.

Deborah Carlson and Paul Lingl from the David Suzuki Foundation have provided ideas regarding sustainability benchmarking for major sporting events. Indeed, they are adamant that it is important for NGOs to work collectively "with government, business and individuals" in reducing carbon emissions associated with major sporting events. They encouraged the organizers of the Vancouver 2010 Games to adopt the benchmark of carbon neutrality, which was explained in their report *'Meeting the Challenge: A Carbon Neutral 2010 Winter Games Discussion Paper'*. In doing so they hoped to encourage benchmark best practices in carbon management for event organizers and businesses. They developed the program of 'Play it Cool' which was linked specifically to elite athletes promoting the minimization and off-setting of carbon emissions. We feel that it is increasingly important for athletes to become involved in promoting sustainable practices in sport, and to promote the ideas which can benefit the benchmarking processes begun for the Vancouver 2010 Games and that continue for the London 2012 Games. Sustainable benchmarking of events is of course also an important tool for sport event sponsors, and Carlson and Lingl praised Coca-Cola and 30 other sponsors of the Vancouver 2010 Games who participated in programs designed to offset their Games-related greenhouse gas emissions.

In order to ensure that sustainability standards are being met, Carlson and Lingl go onto argue, along with other authors in this section, that one of the most essential tasks is to "develop further guidelines to increase accountability." One of the ways in which this can be developed and encouraged is to look more closely at the practices employed by the Commission for a Sustainable London 2012, "which provides assurance to the Olympic Board and the public that the London 2012 Olympic and Paralympic Games are meeting their sustainability commitments." This Commission could serve as a benchmark of best practice utilized for all future major events and major construction projects such as building sport venues.

There appears then to be a set of realistic and measurable benchmarks which have been passed down from successive major sport event organizers and NGOs to enable new major sport event bids, events and organizations to embed sustainability themes and actions, and for these to be supported by professionally trained experts and practitioners.

Instruments of Sustainability in the Sporting Context

There is no doubt that there have recently been projects put into place by the sports and events industries to develop sustainability tools. Fiona Pelham, for example, describes the "frameworks that support the event industry in developing their understanding of how to identify and manage negative impacts, and report on sustainability more broadly." Her work highlights the influence that the BS8901 standard and emerging GRI Event Organizers Sector Supplement has had and will continue to have on the events industry. Matt Dolf in his chapter highlighting tools for sustainability argues for the use of the Sustainable Sport and Event Toolkit (SSET) to guide event organizers and sport organizations "down the path of sustainability." These tools have been developed in order to support the event management and sport industries, and are based on industry guidelines. David Stubbs in a later chapter argues for these types of standardized tools to combat "the clutter of information, tools and guidance of varying quality and consistency," and that can promote a "common language that demystifies the complexities of the subject." Indeed, these new instruments are actually serving "as a catalyst for change." Dolf states: "One of the challenges that sport event organisers face when tackling sustainability is that it is such a broad and transversal topic," thus SSET and BS8901 provide "sports organizations the knowledge and means to incorporate sustainability into their business practices."

Mathew Philpott and Russell Seymour target the relationship between health and sports stadia, and the impact of sport and sports stadia on local communities. The relationship between sports stadia and the surrounding community is also discussed later by Neil Herrington. Philpott and Seymour argue: "one of the most significant developments in the sustainability field in the last five years has been the formation of the Healthy Stadia Network." Interestingly, this Network looks closely at the community health issues and opportunities which exist in and around existing stadia across Europe. They suggest that sports stadia, as iconic community and globally significant structures, can promote the overlapping areas of public health, community cohesion and environmental sustainability. They provide the following definition of *healthy stadia*: "healthy stadia are those which promote the health of visitors, fans, players and employees and the surrounding community." These objectives could be added to the tools used to promote sustainability and sport, and then perhaps we can move even further towards achieving healthier and more sustainable communities through sport.

The Effect of the Olympic Games and Paralympic Games on Fostering Sustainable Sporting Events and Legacies

The early work of the IOC and its Sport and Environment Commission appears to have contributed greatly to the foundation of the third pillar of the Olympic Movement, namely the *Environment*. However, Stubbs suggests that the emerging broader sustainability agenda has given the IOC "a renewed and coherent focus in its relations with society." Stubbs and other authors in this section suggest that: "Taken in isolation, the Games do not appear to be a sustainable activity" because "international travel, energy use, consumption, and waste happen as part of the Games event, just for a few weeks of sport." However, we agree with his and others' conclusion that the Games "if channelled effectively can be a driver for positive change." Indeed, as Stubbs continues: "today the emphasis has shifted and sustainability in its full sense is integral to effective Games organisations."

Because the area of sustainability is growing rapidly there is arguably a need for leadership from and consistency across the sports industry. Perhaps one innovative approach to fostering sustainability at and through the Games is to organize an international structure, promoted by the IOC, UNEP and/or others. Consequently, a global organization such as this could seek to ensure accountability and consistent standards for embedding sustainability into the Olympic Movement and even across other major sporting events and organizations. This type of body could support what Oben, Carlson and Lingl suggest as a pressing need in all sport events – namely mandatory environmental considerations and decisive action on the part of the IOC and Games organizing committees.

The City of Vancouver has had a long history of environmental activism and sustainable practices, and set out to harness the power of hosting the 2010 Games to foster its objective to become a 'Green Capital.' Joseph Weiler, Patrick Weiler, Ann Duffy and Iain MacRury all agree that the organizing committee (VANOC) "took sustainability seriously," and Vancouver's bid for the 2010 Games used the notion of sustainability as "a critical distinguishing feature of selling the City as a model urban centre to the outside world." Weiler and Weiler state that "the Vancouver bid document singled out the objectives of creating green buildings, improving solid and liquid waste management, addressing air quality and greenhouse gas management, and protecting the natural and cultural heritage of Vancouver and surrounding regions." Duffy agrees by stating that "sustainability was a VANOC bid commitment to the International Olympic Committee and it became its mandate," and refers particularly to the notion of creating "lasting legacies" through "an enduring ethos" of sustainability at VANOC. The VANOC brief placed a heavy emphasis on accountability; each of the sustainability performance goals of Sport for Sustainable Living, Aboriginal Participation, Social Inclusion and Responsibility, Environmental Stewardship and Impact Reduction, and Economic Benefits could arguably be subsumed under the auspices of the performance goal of Accountability. In the final section of her chapter Duffy discusses the success of the seven year sustainability program and the importance of setting the benchmark for success in the sustainable sporting arena.

The Weilers argue that the success of the City of Vancouver's Green Capital industrial development strategy can only be assessed in the long term. Similarly, the success of VANOC's ambitions to leave "lasting legacies, locally and globally" will take time to measure, as the strategies which were put into place throughout the seven year journey to host the 2010 Games are judged against new sets of criteria which spring up from other major sporting events. MacRury notes that "organisers can make a practical contribution to legacy" through the development of the Athletes Village. He notes that both VANOC and the London 2012 Games organizers have used the concepts of sustainability to promote legacy benefits of their respective Athletes Villages. Whether the City of Vancouver and VANOC achieve their sustainability ambitions is a long term proposition which can only be fully tested in the future.

The London 2012 Games' strategies, like VANOC's, clearly link sustainability to the notion of legacy (see the following section on sustainable legacies). London 2012's objective and mantra is to host "the first sustainable Games." This goal has also been utilized, as McCarthy and others discuss, to link the 2012 Games as a catalyst for the redevelopment of East London. To ensure that the 2012 Games lives up to its bid vision, the organizers and the government created an independent body – the Commission for a Sustainable London 2012 – to provide assurance over sustainability across the London 2012 programme. McCarthy discusses this at length and mentions the difficulties in the delivery of a program of sustainability in the difficult economic times faced by London 2012 organizers. Dan Epstein discusses the notion of *sustainable development* and states that "sustainable development has become a ubiquitous term in the regeneration and development sectors in the United Kingdom." He argues that London 2102 has "adopted the most comprehensive set of social, economic and environmental objectives and targets of any Olympic and Paralympic Games host city." He provides examples, however, of the challenges that the Olympic Delivery Authority has faced in meeting their sustainability targets. What remains to be seen is whether the implemented sustainability practices are actually sustained across the London 2012 Olympic Park site long after the 2012 Games have ended. Maxine Newlands' chapter presents a more critical view of the Games and their claims of sustainability. She states: "The problem is that any brand that makes sweeping declarations on the environment faces the challenge of either risking 'green fatigue' or accusations of misleading the public through greenwashing." She also raises important issues around the selection of corporate sponsors by the IOC and the Games organizing committees, and suggests that these relationships can call into question any intentions to host a sustainable event.

Sustainable Partnerships

Undoubtedly, in today's sports environment, working in a sustainable manner is becoming increasingly important in order to win contracts from the organisers of major global sporting competitions. Linking with sustainable practices and the notion of legacy appears vital. There are several global businesses who aim to be seen as leaders in sustainability, including large multi-national companies such as Coca-Cola, Puma, and Technogym. Indeed, it could be argued that many of these companies are leading on implementing sustainability practices across their businesses and are driving many of the innovations and ideas which are currently being employed by major sports organizers. Gaillard and Symonds, for example, present the case of Coca-Cola, reflecting on sustainability and sport. As "the longest continuous corporate partner of the Olympic Movement," they describe how Coca-Cola is leveraging its partnership to show how their maturing corporate sustainability objectives align with those of the Olympic Movement's, and aim to use their support of the Games to "showcase the best-in-class initiatives" that Coca-Cola has implemented in their business. Tony Majakas from Technogym states that the company is "driven by a clear vision and mission – based on innovation, design and sustainability." Technogym, who have been an Exclusive Olympic Supplier for seven Games, appreciates that the London 2012 organizers have embraced sustainability in their mission, as it aligns with Technogym's corporate objectives. Increasingly, sustainability appears to make good business sense and provides answers to technical questions regarding many of the issues which sports administrators and sporting event organizers deal with on a daily basis.

Beth Nicholls suggests it is critically important for an event bid committee to establish strong partnerships in order to influence the legacy of an event. She states: "it is crucial to work with stakeholders and a variety of industry experts from the bid stage." Nicholls further argues that "any major sport event can deliver a meaningful and sustainable social legacy and has a responsibility to do so." Partner organisations also need to plan for sustainable long term community benefits and not just supply a short-term 'sustainable hit' as a result of their event partnership. Andrew Winston points out that while major sporting events provide an opportunity for organizers and business partners to make a profit, they can also create "prodigious environmental and social impacts." He outlines three categories of sustainability pressures on businesses: "natural world pressures; tectonic shifts in how the world works; and new questions from diverse stakeholders," such as employees and customers. He suggests that the sports industry can learn from how businesses have overcome these pressures and have reduced their environmental and social impacts while remaining profitable.

Sport Organizations and Sustainability

There are a growing number of sport organizations, such as National Olympic Committees, National Governing Bodies, and International Federations, who are developing sustainability policies and sustainable management practices. The International Motorcycling Federation (FIM) is one such example. Alex Goldenberg describes the sport of motorcycling's efforts to combat negative environmental impacts. The FIM has established an International Environment Commission, an Environment Code, a cooperation agreement between the FIM and UNEP to promote environmental protection and awareness, and a variety of other environmental initiatives such as the promotion of alternative energy and electric motorcycling. The processes used by the FIM can be replicated by other sports organizations to reduce their environmental impact.

Sustainability and Legacy

There is little doubt that the notions of legacy and sustainability have developed a symbiotic relationship. Indeed, Girginov and Hills (2008, p. 2091) refer to the IOC's quest for legacy as a result of hosting a Games in the following manner:

> ".....the concept of 'legacy', which together with the concept of 'sustainable sports development', has become an essential part of the IOC and the Organising [sic] Committee of the Olympic Games (OCOG) vocabulary. As a result, the IOC, among other things, amended the Olympic Charter to include a particular reference to the creation of positive legacies from the Games and the promotion of sports for all in the host country."

As Beth Nicholls points out in her chapter, it is important for sport event organizers to define what they mean by *legacy* so that they can judge themselves and be judged by others as to whether it has been achieved post event. She provides a definition of the *sustainable legacy* of a sport event as: "the lasting, positive change created through and catalysed [sic] by the bidding for, planning and hosting of a sport event." This change can be social, economic or environmental, and many sport event organizers have pledged a combination of all three, such as VANOC and London 2012.

The chapter by Pappous highlights the difficulties of sustaining a legacy promise of "thousands more individuals across the United Kingdom becoming more physically active," which was a pledge by the London 2012 organizers. For example, at the beginning he asks an important question: "Does hosting sport mega events such as the Games contribute to sustainable economic and social development, making them worthwhile government investments?" MacAloon (2008, p.2065-6) sees the importance of such programs and argues that "in the name of legacy, every sport is now claiming the right to have a substantial venue and sports programming left behind after the Games are concluded." It is perhaps an incredibly difficult task to leave a sustainable sport development legacy as a result of hosting a sports event; if programs are implemented, they need to be sustainable in design and long term in orientation. As Pappous comments when referring to the Athens 2004 Games, "data indicates that the sport participation increase between 2003 and 2004 was only temporary, with no long-lasting effect on the overall sport participation of the host country." According to the data Pappous presents, the Athens 2004 Games did not result in a sustainable legacy of sport development in Greece. Pappous, in his final statements, discusses whether the London 2012 organizers can achieve their ambition to turn the UK into a more active nation, or whether the results will have the same temporary effect as reported in Greece.

Herrington offers some sustainable event legacy outcomes which, if adopted, could "improve the quality of life for everyone now as well as in the future." He describes the importance of an educational legacy, and details how the 2002 Commonwealth Games in Manchester were used by the city as a "planning tool" to "stimulate sustainable regeneration." He suggests that one unique opportunity afforded to those involved in hosting major sport events is that they can uniquely draw people together, and thus "the mega-event can be thought of as an organising principle, bringing people to projects and programmes."

Delivery of Sustainability and Sport

Kirsten Henson's chapter provides an important discussion and clear guidance for the delivery of a sustainability strategy, using the specific example of sport venue construction, and highlighting the critical importance of establishing the correct *process* structures. She suggests, as do others mentioned above, that: "It is critical that any organisation responsible for delivering sporting venues present a cohesive and considered vision for *sustainability*, developed in conjunction with affected communities, key stakeholders and industry specialists." She goes on to discuss the significance of setting a clear vision, establishing achievable targets, establishing accountability, and structures for monitoring and reporting. In doing so Henson highlights and compares case studies from the Vancouver 2010 Games, the London 2012 Games, and the South Africa 2010 FIFA World Cup™, suggesting that London 2012 Games organizers and South Africa 2010 need to make significant progress in providing clear reporting against sustainability commitments.

Reis and DaCosta present the case for why progress on embedding the holistic concept of sustainability in sport has been hindered, citing the IOC's focus on environmental considerations in particular. They argue that the concept of *sustainability* has become complex, and put forth the ideas of Holden, Mackenzie and VanWynsberghe (2008) who argue that the term sustainability "derives from frustratingly ambiguous, perilous, contradictory and/or eminently co-optable concept [that is sustainability] that damages more than it provides." However, they suggest that the Vancouver 2010 Games were a "turning point" because the organizers set out to host the event according to the holistic concept of *sustainability* (social, economic and environmental considerations). They continue by arguing that regardless of the ambiguities present around the notion of *sustainability*, the sports industry has evolved to the point where sports event bidders must include it as a premise of their bid strategy.

Accarino recounts the process of developing an Olympic and Paralympic Games environmental strategy for the Chicago 2016 bid. He highlights the importance of engaging with stakeholders early in the process of developing a bid strategy, as does Nicholls, and also developing a clear vision, also suggested by Henson.

Jill Savery's chapter suggests, along with others, that: "Sporting mega events have the potential to be primary forces that drive sustainable development and catalyze lasting change in a host city, host nation, and worldwide." As such, she argues that sport event organizers can use their reach to foster pro-environmental behavior, and that no major sport event to date has effectively engaged with the sport event audience (including spectators, the media, athletes or local communities) in this regard. Carlson and Lingl, Winston and others also mention the opportunities afforded by sport and sport events to promote change. While acknowledging the challenging nature of influencing behavior, Savery offers a framework that can be used to begin this important endeavor.

Another emerging sustainability issue that is pertinent to sport is climate change. As discussed in Carlson and Lingl's chapter, Julius de Heer and Denis Bochatay argue that robust and consistent carbon accounting, emissions reduction and compensation strategies should be a priority when defining a bid and delivering a major event. They remind us that: "Scientists are clear that we must reduce GHG emissions quickly in order to avoid dangerous climate changes; *later* will be *too late* to act ..." Their insightful Polar Bear Rules outline priority considerations for accounting, mitigating and compensating for event greenhouse gas emissions. We need "new, ambitious and creative energy-efficient solutions to reduce emissions at the source."

Graham Barnfield's chapter presents a discussion of the sports mega projects in Doha (Aspire Zone) and Dubai (Dubai Sports City), stating that: "In terms of their carbon footprints and consumption of water and energy alone, these settlements can seem environmentally suspect." Barnfield provides examples of how these maga sports projects are using the "language of sustainability." He details a variety of viewpoints about the meaning of *sustainability* and how it might appropriately fit within the context of the Arabian Gulf and sport, allowing local people the opportunity "to participate in and watch sports," innovate new environmental technologies, and encourage a "fit population."

In an earlier chapter, Chernushenko suggests that with regard to delivering more sustainable events, we currently have a situation where "the level of ambition and the detail of plans have risen steadily, but delivery has often fallen well short of stated intention." He believes, and the other chapters herein might suggest, that there is "no excuse" for not delivering on sustainability commitments outlined in sport event bids, which should include reducing and compensating for greenhouse gas emissions. In this manner Chernushenko puts the strong point across that "It is a time for leaders and a time for vision," and that "A healthy transition can begin today. Otherwise demonstrable negligence starts tomorrow." There appears to be a wealth of enthusiastic and talented individuals working across the world in the sustainability and sport field, and it is time for everyone to make "bold steps, not defensive actions" and lead the sports world into prioritizing sustainable practices.

Conclusive Statements

In this book we have negotiated with the support of our friends and colleagues a multiplicity of subject matter and arguments, questions and anxieties connected with the research and practice surrounding the broad and burgeoning area of sustainability and sport. This has been synthesised and articulated to some extent in the metasynthesis above. We realise that there are several areas which we were unable to expand on due to issues of chapter length and the myriad of ideas and innovations associated with the subject matter. It is important to note that we began by attempting to understand and describe the varied aspects of sustainability in the sporting arena. While doing this we have, however, been able to add to the scarce literature in this area and to include many of the important practitioners and academics working in sustainability and sport. Indeed, we remain adamant that this text is only the beginning of the highly relevant literature subject matter in the sphere of sustainability and sport. We were pleased and grateful that so many experts were able to translate their practice and research for others to learn from and incorporate into their work. After this exercise we feel that one role for the practitioner and academic alike remains to produce documents and test ideas that challenge us to continue to move from the disconnected context of sustainability and sport towards connectedness for the professionals working in the area.

Finally, we argue that this shift could open a plethora of research and practical ideas and allow the voices of the individuals working in the area of sustainability and sport to be further heard in the current milieu of programs, plans and developments in the sports industry. Perhaps more important is our ability to open the fissures in sustainability research to move the issues into the mainstream within universities and sustainability and sport discourse. It is perhaps fitting then that we complete this text with the words of Julius de Heer and Denis Bochatay, where they note that "major events must show the way in their own interest, and cannot be inconsistent in their environmental action plan. With that goal in mind, the ever-growing audience of major sport events and sport stars represents a wonderful springboard that cannot be missed by international federations, event organizers and sport sponsors." We agree with these statements and add that without embedding sustainability into the sporting culture there can be no truly successful sporting events at any level. In actuality, as society becomes more technocratic, environmentally aware and sustainability oriented, it is not one person who will change the discipline for the better, but importantly the future of sustainability and sport is in all of our hands.

References

Girginov, V. And L. Hills (2008). A Sustainable Sports Legacy: Creating a Link between the London Olympics and Sports Participation. *International Journal of the History of Sport*, Vol. 25, No. 14. pp. 2091-2116.

Holden, M; Mackenzie, J. & R. VanWynberghe (2008). Vancouver's promise of the world's first sustainable Olympic Games. *Environment & Planning C: Government and Policy*, Vol.26, pp 882-905.

MacAloon, J.J. (2008). 'Legacy' as a Managerial/Magical Discourse in Contemporary Olympic Affairs, *International Journal of the History of Sport*, Vol. 25, No. 14.

Schrieber, R; Crooks, D. & N. Stern (2007). Qualitative Meta – analysis, In J.M.Morse (2nd Eds) *Research Methods for Nursing and Health Sciences*, Prentice Hall, N.S.W. Frenches Forest.

Thorne, S; Jenson. K; Kearney, L; Noblit, G; & M. Sandelowski (2004). Qualitative metasynthesis: reflections on methodological orientation and ideological agenda; Qualitative Health Research; Vol. 14, no. 10 pp 1342-1365.

CPSIA information can be obtained at www.ICGtesting.com
Printed in the USA
LVOW101455190612

286817LV00004B/48/P